COMPARATIVE PSYCHOTHERAPY

COMPARATIVE PSYCHOTHERAPY

An Experimental Analysis

ADOLPH O. DI LORETO

With critiques by Albert Ellis, Alan Goldstein and Joseph Wolpe, and Angelo V. Boy

Routledge
Taylor & Francis Group
LONDON AND NEW YORK

First published 1971 by Transaction Publishers

2 Park Square, Milton Park, Abingdon, Oxonfordshire OX14 4RN
711 Third Avenue, New York, NY 10017

Routledge is an imprint of the Taylor & Francis Group, an informa business

First issued in hardback 2017

Library of Congress Catalog Number: 2006045660

Library of Congress Cataloging-in-Publication Data

Di Loreto, Adolph O., 1941-
Comparative psychotherapy : an experimental analysis / Adolph O. Di Loreto ; with critiques by Albert Ellis...[et al.].
p. cm.—(Modern applications of psychology)
Includes bibliographical references.
ISBN 0-202-30852-9 (pbk. : alk. paper)
1. Psychotherapy—Evaluation. I. Title.

RC480D48 2006
616.89'14—dc22 2006045660

ISBN 13: 978-0-202-30852-4 (pbk)
ISBN 13: 978-1-138-52091-2 (hbk)

Contents

to my wife Margaret

Preface

In the past decade, counseling and psychotherapy have undergone drastic and significant changes; at the same time, however, the evaluation of these processes has remained psychology's main practical and theoretical problem. In this book, a number of contingencies, such as the process-outcome dichotomy, the criterion problem, and client and therapist variables are examined, and a unified, multivariate-comparative model is proposed in an attempt to incorporate and/or circumvent these real and imagined enigmas.

I believe that, although "schools" of counseling and psychotherapy were the inevitable consequence of theories based on tenacity, faith, and intuition, they have continued to exist largely because the bulk of contemporary research is of a process and treatment no-treatment nature, and thus addresses itself to meaningless questions. These approaches not only yield very little useful information—they also tend to maintain and perpetuate school distinctions by allowing therapists to transfer their loyalties and affections from a set of highly esoteric rituals to a highly selective body of "empirical findings" without ever once taking a closer look at their underlying personal convictions or whether these commitments are justified in terms of either the available evidence or the competing approaches. It is this pseudo-scientific base that makes these schools currently so implacable and unyielding.

In order to overcome this predicament, research in counseling and psychotherapy must move in two directions. First, we must move from research that emphasizes process to research that emphasizes outcome, but includes relevant process measures of client-therapist interactions as well as measures of sequential change in the target behaviors under study, so as to aid in our understanding of why we got the results we did. Second, movement must occur from outcome studies that emphasize the use of a treatment no-treatment model to studies that emphasize research based on a multivariate-comparative model.

With the inclusion of both process and outcome measures, in conjunction with assessment on relevant input variables, we can begin to ask the more appropriate question: "What form of treatment, administered by whom, is most effective for this particular client with that specific problem, and under what set of circumstances?" Not until we begin to employ research designs that address themselves to this question will we be able to circumscribe the limits of applicability of various techniques and demonstrate their efficacy in these delimited contexts—or, put another way, rid ourselves of the myths of which Kiesler (1966) speaks.

A review of the published literature reveals no studies dealing directly with the relationship between relative treatment outcome and personality type in clients with a specific, homogeneous problem. Consequently, the case studies and research presented in the first two chapters of this volume, which deal independently with these variables, served as the basis for the research hypotheses that were developed and tested in this study. These hypotheses are:

1. With regard to the extroverts, the order of effectiveness of these three techniques in reducing interpersonal anxiety will be (from most to least effective): Client-Centered, Rational-Emotive, and Systematic Desensitization treatment.

2. With regard to the extroverts, the order of effectiveness of these three techniques in reducing "general anxiety" will be (from most to least effective): Client-Centered, Rational-Emotive, and Systematic Desensitization treatment.
3. With regard to the introverts, the order of effectiveness of these three techniques in reducing interpersonal anxiety will be (from most to least effective): Systematic Desensitization, Rational-Emotive, and Client-Centered treatment.
4. With regard to the introverts, the order of effectiveness of these three techniques in reducing "general anxiety" will be (from most to least effective): Systematic Desensitization, Rational-Emotive, and Client-Centered treatment.
5. Each of the treatment conditions will produce significantly greater reduction in interpersonal anxiety than either of the control conditions.
6. Each of the treatment conditions will produce a significantly greater reduction in "general anxiety" than either of the control conditions.
7. The no-treatment (placebo) control condition will produce a significantly greater reduction in interpersonal anxiety than the no-contact control condition.
8. The no-treatment (placebo) control condition will produce a significantly greater reduction in "general anxiety" than the no-contact control condition.

The results of the present study confirmed hypotheses five through eight. All treated *S*s had a lower post-test and follow-up anxiety level than any of the control *S*s. In addition, the no-treatment (placebo) controls had a lower post-test and follow-up level of anxiety than the no-contact controls. However, the placebo benefits were limited almost exclusively to introverts. Hypotheses one through four were only partially supported. While both the CC and RT treatments exhibited significant introvert-extrovert differences in the predicted direction, the SD treatment was equally as effective with both introverts and extroverts. It was hypothesized that the former results were due to the differential effects of the RT and CC approaches in eliciting self-exploration in introverts and extroverts, respectively. The latter findings were attributed to the differential effects of group SD with introverts.

Acknowledgments

So many people were involved, directly and indirectly, in the successful completion of this research project that it is almost impossible to mention them all individually. To those many university officials, secretaries, and other staff members, I wish to express my deepest appreciation for their time and the use of their buildings, offices, and equipment.

In addition, I extend special thanks to the raters who participated in the present study: Paul Mierlie, Holly Boyd, Cheryl Osborne, Jim Buigenthal, Fred Murray, and Bob Riener. I would also like to thank the therapists who worked with these students and gave unstintingly of their time and effort: Drs. James Barrick, Roger Bauer, James Crowley, Frederick Hill, Donald Jabury, and James Lowe.

Furthermore, I would like to extend my deepest thanks to Drs. Gregory Miller, Robert Craig, Dozier Thornton, and John Jordon. Without the innumerable hours they spent with me in organization and preparation, this research would never have materialized. Special appreciation is extended to Dr. Gregory A. Miller for his patient and accepting attitude throughout the conduct of this entire project.

Finally, I am particularly grateful to the Department of Vocational Rehabilitation and to the Department of Health, Education, and Welfare, whose funds partially supported the research on which this monograph is based.

· 1 ·

Introduction

Interest in the investigation of counseling and psychotherapy has both a history and evolution. It is unfortunate, however, that this common and long-standing concern in the constructive change of behavior and personality has fractionated rather than unified the interested parties. As Rogers (1963) has pointed out,

> our differences as therapists do not lie simply in attaching different labels to the same phenomenon. The difference runs deeper. An experience which is seen by one therapist as healing, growth-promoting, helpful, is seen by another as none of these things. And the experience which to the second therapist is seen as possessing these qualities is not so perceived by the first. We differ at the most basic level of our personal experience.
>
> Some people may feel that though we differ regarding specific incidents, . . . nevertheless in our goals and in our general directions there is much agreement and unity. I think not. To me it seems that therapists are equally divergent in these realms [p. 7].

One can best grasp the reasons for this current state of affairs by a more intense look at the evolution of psychotherapy research.

• *Historical Perspective*

The era prior to the experimental investigation of psychotherapy can best be characterized as "academic tribalism."

The various schools of psychotherapy which existed consisted of more or less loosely organized theoretical formulations based on biased and unsystematic observations which could not be controlled and thus repeated in any reliable manner. Consequently, adherence to any of these theoretical views was based on faith, conviction, and personal satisfaction; and loyalties were maintained and perpetuated by identification with a particular set of esoteric rituals (Bandura & Walters, 1963). Blocker (1967) seems to have captured the essence of this evolutionary process when he states:

> Much of the history of change in counseling and psychotherapeutic theory and practice contains elements which closely parallel those which tend to dominate the evolution of religious movements and political ideologies. In both cases a movement tends to be originated by a messianic figure, characterized by a kind of *élan vital,* who translates a deeply moving personal experience into universalistic terms. This leader quickly attracts a group of worshipful disciples who immediately begin to generalize the precepts promulgated by the master into the most widely applicable terms. [p. 4]

With little more than faith and the sheer force of opinion to back their untested propositions and doctrinaire assertions, it is not surprising that these so-called coteries or "schools" existed as factions, often diametrically opposed to one another in terms of their aims, methods, and goals (Arbuckle, 1967; Bandura & Walters, 1963; Rogers, 1963). However, they exhibited such a faith and hope in the efficacy of their respective techniques that failures in practice engendered only a minimum of what Festinger (1957) has termed "cognitive dissonance."

Both Phillips (1956) and Blocher (1967) have shown how a number of convenient expressions arose to buttress and thus justify the already well developed and deeply held personal convictions of these "schools": for example, "the client is unmotivated," "he lacks ego-strength," "he doesn't have enough working-anxiety," etc. "The convenience of this type of thinking . . . for counselors who readily lose a third to a half of their clients prematurely, is, of course, obvious" (Blocher 1967, p. 14).

The net effect of these newly-coined rationalizations was to effectively screen out any negative feedback by automatically attributing untoward consequences to defects in the client (Ellis, 1962). When coupled with the enormous resistance to extinction generated by relatively few "successes" delivered on an aperiodic schedule, these factors served only to reduce any dissonance which may have resulted from failures in practice and thus eliminate any reason for change or modification in techniques.

Finally, dissonance between "schools" was further avoided by limited contacts between members of the dissonant factions. Even when they did interact, the violent polemics which resulted often generated more heat than light. According to Hoskisson (1965): "they . . . get together and wrangle and defame each other and have a wonderful time, . . . much of specialized scientific publication seems to consist in mutual condemnation of each other's work" (p. 29).

With the introduction of scientific methods into this formerly sacrosanct domain, it was hoped that a common core of empirical knowledge would replace the theories based on tenacity, faith, and intuition (Campbell & Stanley, 1963). This laudable but peremptory wave of optimism soon envanesced, however, when the predicted rapprochement somehow never really materialized.

Current status of the problem

In a summary of the overall impact of the past 25 years of research in counseling and psychotherapy, Shlien (1966) has pointed out that, "Continued subscription [to an existing school of psychotherapy] is based upon personal conviction, investment, and observation rather than upon general evidence" (p. 125). In a similar vein, Eysenck's (1952)[1] first review of the outcome literature concluded with, "The figures fail to support the hypothesis that [existing forms of] psychotherapy facilitates recovery from neurotic disorders" (p. 323). His more recent reviews (Eysenck, 1955, 1960, 1961, 1965), as well as those of others (Baily, 1956; Bandura, 1964; Levitt, 1957), have led to essentially the same conclusions.[2]

The factors contributing to this current state of skepticism regarding psychotherapy are many and varied. As seen earlier, for a number of years this predicament was due to a lack of empirical research. However, as a number of authors have pointed out, the more recent causes stem from the fact that the existing empirical evidence is derived from such poorly organized and controlled research that the findings could be used to support almost anything, and thus, nothing (Blocher, 1967; Edwards & Cronbach, 1952; Kiesler, 1966; Paul, 1967; Sprinthall, 1967). In spite of this, researchers and practitioners alike have *not* tried to maintain a respectful tentativeness commensurate with their real ignorance of the problem. Rather, there is a tendency among partisans of each of the various positions to apply one standard of adequacy to inherently poor research when that research supports their theoretical position and an entirely different standard to the same type research when it is contrary to their position (Hunt, 1956).

As Goldstein et al. (1966) have pointed out, it is not uncommon for clinically minded researchers to disqualify and

1. For an explanation of these findings in terms of the therapist variable, see Truax & Carkhuff (1967). For an explanation in terms of pre-treatment individual differences in clients, see Blocher (1967) and Sprinthall (1967). For a general critique of the validity of Eysenck's interpretations, see Kiesler (1966).
2. Cross (1964) surveyed the literature since Eysenck's 1952 review and found nine studies which used control groups. However, he felt they were so deficient in other respects that the findings still could not be interpreted unambiguously. More recent reviews (Dittman, 1966; Patterson, 1966) have led to essentially the same conclusions.

reject unfavorable results by pointing to methodological and control problems and then to cite at the same time favorably identical studies which support the position they advocate. More specifically, Bandura & Walters (1963) have shown how psychoanalysts frequently reject on the basis of inadequate translation negative findings when the research is based on a translation of psychoanalytic theory into learning terms. Yet the same psychoanalysts embrace positive findings with such enthusiasm that the purely psychic dividends which result unite to compel and further seduce their continued belief and increased entrenchment in psychoanalytic theory. What is the result? The era of "academic tribalism" still remains.

Schools of psychotherapy still exist with little more reliable, empirical foundations than before (Breger & McGaugh, 1965; London, 1964; Rogers, 1963). New schools continue to emerge here and there (Berne, 1961; Ellis, 1962; Eysenck, 1959, 1960, 1965; Salter, 1961; Stamphl, 1967; Wolpe, 1958) again as factions radically opposed to the traditional ways of psychotherapy. Freshly minted ideas and glimmerings of understanding become so quickly encapsulated into the dogma of a "school" or coterie that they are seldom subjected to the scrutiny and "natural selection" of experimentation (Blocher, 1967; Breger & McGaugh, 1965; Dittmann, 1966). In fact, every effort is often made to protect and guard what each deems desirable, should it be "mistakenly confused" with the facts of research, for "nonconfirmation of a cherished hypothesis is acutely painful" (Campbell & Stanley, 1963, p. 3).

Similarly, as before, these new schools maintain their autonomy and thus avoid any potential cognitive dissonance simply by building new jargons, creating new journals in which to publish their esoteric jargons (Behavior Research and Therapy, Voices, etc.), and generally divorcing themselves from the rest of the field. Successes by one school are either impugned as palliative, attributed to factors the critic's school deems relevant, or blatantly disreputed (Rogers, 1963; Strupp, 1962; Wolpe, 1963; Wolpe & Lazarus, 1966). Finally, as earlier, "Extremists on . . . [all] sides have not hesitated [in their expenditure of polemic words and ink] to discredit each other, even though well-controlled comparative studies are nonexistent" (Paul, 1966, p. 1).

Although collapse into a shapeless solipsism and feckless relativism, which are the death of science, is not eminent or pressing, this joint-catharsis-against-a-common-foe makes for little more than personal harmony and satisfaction within each faction; it contributes little in the way of constructive, cumulative knowledge (Campbell & Stanley, 1963). It is true that these precociously inspired theories often replace one another from time to time; however, since this displacement is typically not the result of well controlled, comparative research, the product rarely augments existing knowledge or serves as a sequel to what has gone before (Blocher, 1967). In short, it adds to the history of psychotherapy but *not* to its evolution.

The overall effect of this condition is forceably demonstrated in Colby's (1964) analysis of the current predicament in psychotherapy—"Chaos prevails" (p. 347). Similarly, Rogers's (1963) statement graphically portrays the net results of this current state of affairs—"The field of psychotherapy is a mess" (p. 8). Goldstein et al. (1966) feel that a "skein of confusion . . . represents our current level of understanding of the field of psychotherapy" (p. 10). Finally, London (1964) has conceded that "a detailed examination of the surfeit of schools and theories, of practices and practitioners that compete with each other conceptually and economically, shows vagaries which, taken all at once, make unclear what it is that psychotherapists do, or to whom, or why" (p. v).

Summary and prospective

As indicated above, a good portion of the confusion regarding psychotherapy is due to the fact that most existing schools of psychotherapy are based as much, if not more, on faith and dogma as on comparatively derived research findings. By worshiping their flimsy hypotheses into truths and then selecting "research" to bolster their already well developed personal convictions, these schools become implacable and categorically indestructable, that is, immune to dissonant empirical findings (Matarazzo, 1965). Evolution, if it can be called that, takes the form of "a fadish discard of old wisdom in favor of inferior novelties" (Campbell & Stanley, 1963, p. 2).

The foregoing analysis, although admittedly one-sided, is not intended to belie the importance of the immense problems and complexities which impede research in psychotherapy or allow, at best, for the most tenuous of controls (Rubinstein & Parloff, 1959; Shlien, 1968; Strupp & Luborski, 1962). Indeed, much of the defection from experimentation to essay writing may be based on this very fact. As intimated above, a substantial portion of these difficulties can be attributed to very real and formidable methodological and control problems (Frank, 1959; Paul, 1967) and to the lack of a universal model for research in counseling and psychotherapy (Kiesler, 1966; Paul, 1966).

• *Nature of the Problem*

If counseling and psychotherapy are ever to mature beyond the level of "an undefined technique applied to unspecified problems with an unpredictable outcome" (Raimy, 1950, p. 93), then experimenters must abandon research models which perpetuate distinctions between existing schools and adopt those models which seek to define their techniques, circumscribe their limits of applicability, and demonstrate their efficacy in these delimited contexts (Gendlin, 1967; Gilbert, 1952; Kiesler, 1966; Sanford, 1953). In spite of the formidable obstacles created by methodological and control problems, and in the face of admonitions to the contrary

(Hyman & Berger, 1965; Kiesler, 1966; Strupp, 1962), a number of investigators feel that there is an adequate paradigm for research in counseling and psychotherapy which follows the foregoing prescription (Blocher, 1967; Edwards & Cronbach, 1952; Frank, 1959; Paul, 1967; Sprinthall, 1967). Such a design would consider simultaneously the following: input variables; process variables; outcome variables; follow-up variables. Let us consider each of these areas separately.

Input variables

Input variables concern the ingredients that go into or make up the treatment process, that is, client variables and therapist variables. The former deals with the client's presenting problem or distressing behavior as well as with the more stable personal-social characteristics that constitute his life style. The physical-social environment or the client's life space completes this triad. Therapist variables incorporate primarily the techniques the therapist uses in treatment and the more stable personal-social characteristics that constitute his life style or personality.

CLIENT VARIABLES. In terms of research methodology, client variables can be reduced to the dual problem of sample selection and treatment focus. Borrowing his strategy from research on the effects of drugs, Frank (1959) has suggested a most promising approach to this problem. It involves the selection and description of clients in terms of what he calls "target behaviors." In other words, clients who are going to be used as *S*s for research are selected on the basis of common or similar distressing behaviors. The description or operational definition of this common presenting problem then becomes the dependent variable in the research design. Furthermore, with this approach the goal of treatment then becomes behavior change in a specified direction. The efficacy of this approach has been successfully demonstrated by Paul (1966) in his attempts to reduce interpersonal-performance anxiety in college freshmen.

According to Paul (1966), therapy research should "compare specific techniques in the treatment of an emotional problem that is delimited enough to allow rigorous experimental methodology, but significant enough to allow generalization from the findings and to have implications for further study in the broader field of counseling and psychotherapy" (p. 9). It is my belief that interpersonal anxiety is just such a problem.

Anxiety, generally, is a central explanatory concept in almost all contemporary theories of personality and is regarded as a principal causative agent for such diverse behavioral consequences as insomnia, immoral and sinful acts, instances of creative self-expression, debilitating psychological and psychosomatic symptoms, and idiosyncratic mannerisms of endless variety (Spielberger, 1966). It has been observed to have untoward consequences on motor behavior and coordination (Luria, 1932; Malmo, 1966), cognitive effectiveness (Saltz & Di Loreto, 1965; Spielberger, 1966), and physiological functioning (Grinker, 1966; Malmo & Shagass, 1949). Even more important, anxiety reduction is a cogent aspect of most, if not all, existing theories of psychopathology and is seen by most practitioners as a salient therapeutic goal.

Interpersonal anxiety, or anxiety that results from simple, routine interactions with other individuals, is particularly debilitating since it can disrupt normal, but required, daily routines, make otherwise healthy individuals unhappy and dissatisfied with themselves, and generally create discomforts that are unfortunate and otherwise avoidable. Consequently, the area of anxiety generally, and interpersonal anxiety in particular, seems fertile ground for research from both a theoretical and practical point of view.

In terms of a target focus for research, small interacting treatment groups provide a prototype stress situation for eliciting interpersonal anxiety, and thus they can be used as an *objective* criteria for assessing by means of behavioral ratings change in this target behavior from pre- to post-treatment.

The importance of this type of criteria has been exhorted by Strupp (1962): "if psychotherapy is effective, the benefits must be somehow demonstrable in the person's behavior" (p. 457). In addition, since interpersonal anxiety undoubtedly restricts interpersonal activity, a periodic sample of interpersonal contacts can also serve as an *external* criteria for assessing both progress during the course of treatment, and outcome. The importance of using behavioral criteria external to the treatment setting has been noted by a number of researchers (Luborsky & Strupp, 1962; Paul, 1967; Zax & Klein, 1960).

If one views the most important test of the effectiveness of a particular therapeutic treatment as involving first a change in the client's distressing *behaviors* and second a change in these behaviors *outside* of the treatment setting, then these two criteria, in conjunction with client self-reports, go a long way toward achieving these goals.

Even with selection on a homogeneous class of target behaviors, however, there is likely to be wide variation in the relatively stable personal-social characteristics of the client (Paul, 1967). However, if in addition to matching target behaviors, clients are further selected, described, and classified on the basis of these relatively stable life style characteristics, pre-treatment variability among clients can be reduced further. The importance of this type of research for purposes of assessing treatment effects *unambiguously* has been noted by many investigators (Blocher, 1967; Kiesler, 1966; Levinson, 1962; Paul, 1967; Sprinthall, 1967; Underwood, 1957). However, research of this nature is conspicuous by its absence.

Personality type, although an admittedly illusive and somewhat arbitrary choice in terms of the available empirical evidence on personal-social characteristics, looms as a salient prognostic construct in the minds of many experienced researchers and clinicians (Blocher, 1967; Gelder & Wolff, 1967; Kiesler, 1966; Lang et al., 1965; Lazarus, 1963; Sargent, 1961; Sprinthall, 1967). As Luborsky (1962) has noted, "Of all the influences which are thought to determine the change a patient can make through treatment, the patient's personality is most often thought to be predominant" (p. 123).

There are at least two reasons for this belief. First and foremost is the very real fact that the founders of nearly all existing forms of psychotherapy derived their theoretical formulations and based their techniques on observations of radically different types of clients (Kiesler, 1966). Second, the evidence which does exist, while not entirely satisfactory in terms of either scope or consistency, suggests that counseling and psychotherapy, as traditionally conceived, are processes which have restricted applicability for only selected subgroups of the population (Blocher, 1967). Considered together, these two factors suggest that perhaps different forms of treatment are needed for differing combinations of personality type and presenting problem (target behaviors).

There is a growing body of extant evidence which suggests that therapists do in fact behave quite differently with different types of clients (Dittmann, 1966; Matarazzo, 1965; Strupp, 1962). However, the relationship between this and treatment outcome is unclear. In one study (Truax & Carhuff, 1965), it was found that "therapist transparency" was positively related to self-exploration in both hospitalized neurotics and delinquent adolescents. However, whereas self-exploration was positively related to client improvement among the neurotic group it was inversely related to positive personality change in the delinquent population.

It is this author's belief that the dimension of introversion-extroversion has many attributes which warrant further interest and investigation. First, a number of investigators have identified these two continuous, bipolar qualities as accounting for the majority of variance on nearly all self-report personality questionnaires (Cattell, 1966; Eysenck, 1960; Guilford, 1959). Thus, we have here a major dimension of personality which is relatively easy to assess, has high empirical validity, and is relatively independent of any *one, idiosyncratic* operational definition. Personality attributes with such high construct validity are a rarity in this field and command further inquiry on that basis alone. Second, introverts and extroverts have been found to differ on a number of qualities which may be predictive of differential treatment outcome.

Extrapolating from Pavlov's (1957) findings, Eysenck (1961) and Wolpe (1958, 1966) hypothesized that individuals differ with regard to conditionability (the speed and firmness with which conditioned responses are built-up or learned) and autonomic activity (activity which affects the strength and intensity of a response once acquired). Eysenck (1961) further maintains that these qualities are related to the excitatory and inhibitory potential of an individual's central nervous system, and that the latter two factors can serve as a basis for classifying individuals along one of two dimensions—normal-neuroticism or introversion-extroversion.

Mowrer's (1966) concept of socialization further elaborates the relationship between nervous system functioning and the development of introvert-extrovert types. Since socialization is seen as dependent on conditioning, individuals with strong inhibitory potential and weak excitatory potential would be expected to form weak and unstable conditioned responses that extinguish easily. Such individuals would be weakly socialized. Those in whom the excitatory potential is strong and the inhibitory potential weak would be expected to form strong and stable conditioned responses that extinguish slowly. They would be strongly socialized. According to Eysenck (1961), "The former group would thus tend to develop introverted behavior traits . . . while the latter group would tend to develop extroverted behavior traits" (p. 27). If the foregoing analysis is correct, it would seem that a form of treatment based on counterconditioning would be more appropriate for introverts and one based on extinction more appropriate for extroverts.

Wolpin & Raines (1966) and Singer (1968) have suggested that introverts may have better visual imagery than extroverts, as they live in fantasy more and thus have more practice with visual imagery. Since he is cut off from his relationships with others (Hoskisson, 1965) an introvert's imaginary or fantasy life may, ostensibly at least, constitute reality for him. As Franks (1961) has implied, the introvert is a "thinking," "planning," or "ideational" type whereas the extrovert is a "doing" or "acting" type.

Wolpin & Raines (1966) and Eysenck & Rachman (1965) have also noted that introverts are more dependent, suggestible, and conforming. In fact, Wolpin & Raines (1966) have found that "scores on the *E* scale [of the Maudsley Personality Inventory] may predict more generally willingness to comply or conform" (p. 35). In addition, Eysenck & Rachman (1965) and Eysenck (1967) have suggested that introverts may prefer a more mechanical and impersonal form of treatment.

Consistent with Franks's (1961) description presented above, Eysenck & Rachman (1965) have characterized the extrovert as "sociable . . . needs to have people to talk to and does not like reading or studying by himself . . . he prefers to keep moving and doing things" (p. 19). He is "outgoing," "talkative," and "carefree" (p. 16). Experimental studies of introversion-extroversion (Eysenck & Rachman, 1965) indicate that extroverts, as compared to introverts, have a higher IQ-vocabulary ratio and higher sociability. Furthermore, unlike the introvert, the extrovert is cut off from himself and his feelings (Hoskisson, 1965) since, as Fenichel (1941) has pointed out, acting or doing often serves to circumvent awareness of one's feelings or motives.

All of these considerations, when taken together, suggest a form of treatment for introverts which is based on a counterconditioning model, is somewhat impersonal and mechanical in nature, and makes maximum use of the introvert's suggestibility, dependency, and conformity as well as his excellent visual imagery. By the same token, the aforementioned also suggests a form of treatment for the extroverts that is based on an extinction model, is predominantly verbal in nature, and requires involvement in an intimate and very personal group interaction that emphasizes looking at and focusing on one's "inner self" (i.e., thoughts, feelings, and fantasies).

In concluding this section on client variables, it appears that the selection, description, and classification of clients on the basis of pre-treatment individual differences provides a more adequate definition of the *S* sample, thus assuring both a greater replication of the sample across studies and a clearer focus for the assessment of outcome. In addition, utilization of a homogeneous problem area within personality type allows for more efficient assignment of *S*s and thus greater equivalence of treatment and control groups, since *S*s are classified along two dimensions simultaneously. All in all, it appears that the radical reduction in client pre-treatment variability permitted by these two operational distinctions undoubtedly will lead to more easily interpretable findings and more readily replicable results. Also, researchers should be able to better explain "inconsistent" or "contradictory" findings across studies.

THERAPIST VARIABLES. In discussing therapist variables, one is interested in both the therapist's approach (both his philosophical orientation to treatment and his therapeutic techniques) and the more stable personal-social characteristics which constitute his life style or personality.

There are at least three ways in which one can treat the therapist variable (the effects of his personality vs. the affects of his approach). The first approach, which exists predominantly in fantasy, involves using each therapist as his own control. The advocates of this approach (Paul, 1966, 1967) aver that by having each therapist administer each of the treatments, one can hold the personal-social attributes of the therapist constant across groups, reducing placebo effects which may masquerade as treatment.

Not only is this goal impossible to achieve, but the strategy on which it is based is internally inconsistent. Having therapists objectively indicate their degree of commitment to certain techniques, as Paul (1966) has done, for example, excludes by definition an equal commitment to alternative approaches. The therapist's personality already has entered into his choice and commitment. Once this is done, finding "therapists who are open-minded enough to learn to use contradictory methods without exhibiting attitudes that would greatly affect their approach" (Paul, 1966, p. 6) becomes an axiomatic impossibility.

Even if one were to grant the potential plausibility of the above approach, it does nothing to circumvent the original problem but rather creates a truly insoluable dilemma. If a therapist uses this approach and fails to achieve its supposed goal, then he is maximizing the *differential* influence of placebo effects in the direction of the techniques which he preferred originally. If one, in fact, succeeded in finding such "open-minded" therapists, they would most assuredly not be representative of other therapists of the same ilk. As Arbuckle (1967) has so appropriately pointed out, "Differences in counselors automatically become differences in counseling" (p. 224).

Perhaps the clearest statement regarding the inseparable nature of therapist and therapy variables has been offered by Frank (1959) who states:

> It is obvious that the therapist and therapy variables cannot be completely separated. It is unlikely that a therapist can conduct different types of treatment with precisely equal skill or that his attitudes towards them will be identical. Therefore, differences in results obtained by two forms of therapy conducted by the same therapist may be due to therapist rather than treatment variables, especially since the faith of a therapist in a form of treatment may account for much of its efficacy (7). In our psychotherapy study the psychiatists disliked minimal treatment. They gave it reluctantly and felt that they were shortchanging the patients. The patients remained just as long in this type of

treatment as in the other two, suggesting that they were not as lacking in confidence in it as the doctors. [p. 17]

An alternative and even more absurd approach is to attempt to get counselors to effectively role play confidence in techniques they regularly do not use or in which they do not believe (Snyder, 1962). This method, if effective, simply reintroduces any placebo effects in haphazard and uncontrollable amounts, mitigating the entire purpose of this circuitous approach. If ineffective, one has once again introduced placebo effects *systematically*. The real problem here, as above, is that one *never* really knows when and if one has or has not failed. In addition, in view of Rogers's (1963) and Frank's (1959) observations, it becomes difficult to imagine a Client-Centered therapist, for example, doing Rational Therapy or trying to role play confidence in such an approach, or vice versa! This is to say nothing of the inequity created by attempting to train three- to five-year veterans of Client-Centered therapy to do Rational Therapy in a week or less (Strupp, 1967, 1968).

Both of the above strategies lend an air of artificiality to the research treatments which is not present in the clinical treatment settings in which these techniques usually are administered. This latter fact serves only to reduce further the external validity or generality of the findings. Clearly, both of these approaches commit the error of misplaced precision.

A *partial* solution to the problem of therapist variables can be achieved by assuming, as Arbuckle (1967) does, that certain therapists choose certain techniques because they are certain kinds of people, that is, that the therapist's personality and his treatment techniques are integrally and inseparably linked. Then, by securing therapists who are committed to techniques which one wishes to compare, by having each administer the techniques they respectively deem effective, and by comparing what they say they do with what they actually do (by means of audio or video tape), one is in a much better position to assess treatment conditions as they are most often administered with little or no loss in scientific rigor. Contrary to the beliefs of some (Paul, 1966, 1967), there is no reason to assume that this approach produces any greater variability in the administration of the treatments than the aforementioned strategies.

Using the above approach, one finds that the more therapists there are representing any one treatment, the more the results can be attributed to the effects of the treatment approach *per se* and not to any one therapist or his unique personal-social makeup. This can be achieved either by replication within and across studies or, in larger facilities, by a sampling of therapists within a "school" or treatment approach. The latter is similar to sampling IQ, introversion, anxiety, etc., from a more general population. Viewed in this vein, the absurdity of using each therapist as his own control becomes even clearer, since it would be tantamount to having each *S* serve as both introvert and extrovert or both high and low anxious, etc., within the same study.

Another distinct advantage of the treatment approach proposed above is that one can check on whether or not the assumptions of this model are met, a notable disadvantage of the previously discussed strategies. In addition to comparing what therapists say they do with what they actually do by means of tape recordings, objective assessment of the therapist's personal-social characteristics can be made and similarities and differences noted. When client variables are spelled out in the manner described earlier, the data on therapist personal-social characteristics can be compared with the data on client personal-social characteristics, since, in many cases, assessment can be made by many of the same measuring devices. This is especially true of such personal-social characteristics as personality type, IQ, socio-economic status, age, sex, etc.

To the remaining dilatories, this does not mean that outcome results are simply a measure of therapist personal commitment. One can be committed strongly to walking to the moon, even though the efficacy of this technique (walking) can be proven virtually useless. This third approach attempts to hold personal commitment as constant as possible. Then, by using uniform outcome criteria for all treatment and control groups, the results can be interpreted as commitment to either effective or ineffective treatment, whatever the case may be.

It should be remembered that Paul's (1966) conclusions, strictly speaking, are relevant only to insight-oriented therapists practicing systematic desensitization; and, at last count, there don't seem to be too many of these individuals around.[3] This, of course, assumes that one accepts Paul's (1966) initial distinction between therapist personal-social characteristics and treatment techniques. If one discards this initial provision, then one is left with the conclusion that personal-social attributes are largely irrelevant to the issue of treatment techniques. The approach offered above, however, allows one to conclude that personal commitment is either too effective or ineffective counseling, whatever the results support.

In concluding this section on input variables, it becomes clear that selecting, describing, and classifying both clients and therapists on the basis of pre-treatment individual differences make for better controlled, more easily interpretable, and thus more legitimately generalizable research. The importance of defining clearly the variables within these two broad domains has been exhorted by Garfield & Affleck (1961) who maintain that the time to begin outcome studies is prior to intake. Similarly, Strupp (1962) has noted the potential value of this area when he states, "Research might make an important contribution by refining the selection of particular

3. Furthermore, no attempt was made to check on the nature or quality of the insight treatment *as it was administered* (Strupp, 1967). Consequently, his conclusions must be restricted to therapists who say they are insight oriented, and not to insight-oriented therapy *per se*.

patients for particular therapists and for particular therapeutic methods" (p. 471).

In this manner, one may begin to bury the myths which, according to Kiesler (1966), have retarded progress in both the research and practice of counseling and psychotherapy, namely, the assumption that clients, therapists, and treatments are homogeneous entities. In so doing, one will simultaneously give birth to the area of "individual differences" within the fields of counseling and psychotherapy, an area which gave to psychology, generally, some of its earliest and most important discoveries (Sprinthall, 1967).

Process and outcome variables

Process research, or the study of client-therapist interactions, owes its existence, reputation, and current fame to two historical events. The first of these has to do with the traditional role ascribed to insight and the second with the so-called criterion problem.

THE INSIGHT MODEL. Until relatively recently, it was felt that client self-exploration leading to insight was *the* modus operandi of successful treatment (Coons, 1957). Successful outcomes were believed to follow correct insight as surely as night followed day. Thus, the "natural" research focus was on the kinds of client-therapist interactions leading to "movement," "improvement," or "insight" during the course of treatment. Positive outcomes and generalization to "real life" settings could be expected to follow inevitably and thus need not be focused on directly. However, recent reviews of this area have demonstrated clearly that not only is this not the *only* way successful treatment comes about (Blocher, 1967; Matarazzo, 1965; Sprinthall, 1967), but that this entire model, in fact, may be in error (Hobbs, 1962; Paul, 1966; Szasz, 1961).

In view of the above, it seems clear that treating process rather than outcome as the end product and assessing the effectiveness of one or more treatment regimes by so-called process research is precarious business, to say the least. With the uncertainty of success following insight, it becomes immediately apparent that studies of the process of psychotherapy depend, for their validity, on the *assumption* that counseling and psychotherapy work (Frank, 1967; Greenhouse, 1964). However, in view of Eysenck's (1952, 1961, 1965) and Shlien's (1966) conclusions, the tenability of this assumption seems in grave doubt. If, as noted earlier, counseling and psychotherapy, as traditionally practiced, do work, they most certainly have restricted applicability for only a highly select subgroup of clients (Blocher, 1967; Sprinthall, 1967).

The problems of process research are even further exacerbated by the fact that the very nature of the research focus (i.e., client-therapist interaction) precludes the use of adequate control groups. Certainly, the use of a no-treatment control group does little or nothing to improve the design of process research. Similarly, the use of a placebo control provides for only the barest minimum beyond which the findings are uninterpretable. Utilizing a comparative approach, where a number of treatments are administered and thus a number of different types of client-therapist interactions are compared, does circumvent this problem somewhat. However, even with this approach, the absence of a control group makes it difficult to determine any cause-effect relationships. Finally, without at least outcome, if not both pre- and post-test measures, the results are of dubious value since one is, in effect, *assuming* at least a uniform and more often a positive outcome.

In regard to outcome, Goldstein et al. (1966) have offered very timely advice:

> Research efforts should be directed toward the study of outcome(s) of psychotherapy. . . . Only after we have been able to demonstrate that we can consistently produce a particular change in behavior as a result of a particular manipulation does

> it seem advisable to expend effort in studying the "process" involved in the manipulation. We suggest that research be done on the changing of behavior. [p. 10]

Similarly, Edgar (1966) has made what seems an empirically reasonable demand when he states that, " 'Good' counseling must be judged in relation to 'good' outcomes" (p. 1029).

THE CRITERION PROBLEM. A second and certainly not unrelated problem is the fact that interest in process variables has been a product of defection from interest in outcome. This "flight into process" (p. 127) as Zubin (1964) has termed it, was due largely to the so-called criterion problem. The problem of deciding what criteria to employ in evaluating outcomes owes much of its existence and is mute testimony to the fact that schools of psychotherapy still exist. In fact, the so-called criterion problem has virtually no operational definition outside the realm of "school" distinctions.[4]

It is interesting to note that although there are at least as many potential areas of focus in process as in outcome research, and thus as many, if not more, potential "criterion problems," process research has never been strapped with similar problems of definition. This, it is believed, is due to the fact that process research was initiated and is being conducted currently by predominantly one "school" of psychotherapy, namely, the Client-Centered group; and, since their beliefs about the nature of the therapeutic process are relatively homogeneous, at least more so than between schools, the "criterion problem" never openly appeared in this area. But it is most assuredly there and cannot be used either as an excuse for avoiding outcome research or as a criticism of it.

As both Frank (1959) and Paul (1966, 1967, 1967a) have demonstrated, the selection, description, and classifica-

4. Although Strupp (1963) would have us believe that this problem is due solely to our lack of a theory of "normal" behavior, it seems he is saying the same thing since each "school" has an implicit or explicit theory of normal behavior and they are often in severe conflict with one another as Rogers (1963) has indicated.

tion of clients on the basis of relatively homogeneous pre-treatment variables, as described earlier, goes a long way in circumventing the problem of criteria selection. By selecting clients on common target behaviors, for example, one can begin to separate the criteria of successful treatment from school affiliation and in so doing construct a model for research which is more sensitive to client individual differences and less sensitive to the theoretical predilections of individual therapists. With this approach, one is in a much better position to assess the effects of counseling and psychotherapy in light of the only laudable criteria—whether or not the client gets better (Battle et al., 1966; Betz, 1962; Hoppock, 1953; Rickard, 1965).

The above approach does not require the abandonment of process research but rather involves a recasting of both process and outcome research into a unified model. Instead of treating the client-therapist interaction as the goal or focus of research, process variables could be incorporated into outcome research in such a manner that they aid in the assessment and understanding of how change occurs, during the course of treatment, in the pre-selected behaviors one is attempting to modify. This approach calls for the fusion of outcome and process variables within a single model and involves measuring sequential outcomes, as the client moves toward the ultimate goal of reduction in target behaviors and the kinds of client-therapist interactions which *actually* occur during each treatment session (Strupp, 1968).

By employing process data to assess how far along the client has progressed toward or away from a predefined or expected goal, one is in a much better position to offer plausible explanations rather than wild speculations regarding the outcome results (Gelfand & Hartmann, 1968; Reyna, 1964). As Bandura (1968) has pointed out, "By confining analyses solely to outcomes, investigators could readily affirm all sorts of causal conditions with immunity" (p. 247). Finally, the sequential measurement of change in pre-selected target behaviors, both within and outside of the treatment setting, by either self-report or behavioral observation, will not only allow one to observe how behavioral change proceeds but will undoubtedly make future directional predictions more probable and research more controllable.

Bandura (1968) has captured the essential features of this paradigm when he states:

> In summary, one might reiterate the basic requirement that any study designed to elucidate change processes should include adequately measured outcomes that are systematically linked to their presumed controlling variables. When causal linkages are loose and ill-defined, spirited disputes flourish but little headway is made in delineating the conditions controlling behavioral changes and the mechanisms through which the effects are produced. [p. 249]

THE COMPARATIVE APPROACH. In addition to the aforementioned, there is a third and related problem which has hampered the evaluation of counseling and psychotherapy. This problem centers around the use of a research model that compares one treated group with one untreated or (no contact) control group. It seems of little or no value, in terms of adding to the general fund of knowledge concerning the efficacy of counseling and psychotherapy, to employ a simple treatment no-treatment model (Edwards & Cronbach, 1952; Paul, 1967). To demonstrate the effectiveness of a particular treatment by comparing it with no treatment at all, at least in psychotherapy research, is in effect stacking the cards in one's own favor (Bergin, 1963; Blocher, 1967; Kiesler, 1966). All forms of intervention, from faith healing to aspirin to psychoanalysis, will undoubtedly produce some desirable effects, as will simply the passage of time (Eysenck, 1952).

As the above implies, and as a number of researchers have noted (Blocher, 1967; Kiesler, 1966; Paul, 1967), the simple treatment no-treatment model asks a meaningless question, that is, "Does psychotherapy work?" Furthermore, in terms of research methodology, this paradigm provides for only the barest minimum beyond which the research findings become uninterpretable (Campbell & Stanley, 1963; Goldstein et al., 1966; Underwood, 1957). Finally, since all forms of intervention undoubtedly "work," this model, like the simple process model discussed earlier, serves only to perpetuate "school" distinctions by maximizing the occurrence of "positive" outcomes.

Research which purports to demonstrate the efficacy of a particular therapeutic approach must be based on a multivariate comparative model which either compares the outcomes of different techniques with the same problem and/or compares different problems with the same techniques, again on the basis of outcome and follow-up. Although an attention-placebo group may serve as an alternative treatment (Paul, 1967), considerably more information is gained by employing two or more "traditional" treatment approaches, in addition to a placebo and no-contact control group.

The comparative approach allows for the following: (a) a test of the relative effectiveness of each of the treatment techniques; (b) aids in pinpointing which approach(es) works best with which problem(s) and which type(s) of client; and (c) provision for the elimination of the maximum number of rival, yet plausible, explanations of the obtained results, which, of course, is the goal of empirical research (Campbell & Stanley, 1963). With regard to this latter asset, the comparative approach is potentially without equal. Moreover, it also has the potential of minimizing or even ultimately eliminating the "schools" approach, replacing it with a systematic eclectic approach founded on a common core of empirical knowledge derived from the commonalities and uniquenesses of each of the various competing approaches now in existence.

Grummon (1965) has captured the importance of this approach when he states that:

> If we are going to rest our case about the effectiveness of counseling on whether or not it promotes this or that desirable behavior, we must also consider whether some other procedure might not produce the result more economically and to an even greater degree. We need much more of this kind of information before we can make intelligent value judgements about the usefulness of particular kinds of counseling. [pp. 63–64]

Grummon's reasoning is especially important in an area such as counseling and psychotherapy where all approaches to treatment implicitly or explicitly claim to be effective with all problems. As London (1964) has pointed out:

> Now if this plentitude of treatments involved much variety of techniques to apply to different persons under different circumstances by different specialists, there would be no embarrassment of therapeutic riches here, just as there is not within the many specialties of medicine or law or engineering. But this is not the case, ... One hardly goes to a psychoanalyst to be cured of anxiety and a nondirective therapist to be treated for homosexuality, as he might to a cardiologist for one condition and a radiologist for another. Nor does the same doctor use Freudian therapy for psychogenic ulcers and Rogerian treatment for functional headaches, as a physician might use medicine for one ailment and surgery for another. [p. 30]

The decision to utilize these three particular treatment approaches was based on a number of considerations. First and foremost is the fact that all three of these treatment approaches have dealt with the problem of interpersonal anxiety theoretically (Bandura & Walters, 1963; Ellis, 1962; Grummon, 1965; Rogers, 1955; Wolpe, 1958), and each claims to have treated it successfully with the techniques they respectively advocate (Bartlett, 1949; Dymond 1954; Ellis, 1962; Grummon, 1965; Grummon & John, 1954; Lazarus, 1960, 1963; Lazarus & Rachman, 1957; Rogers, 1954; Truax & Carkhuff, 1967; Wolpe, 1958; Wolpe, Salter & Reyna, 1964).

Second, there is reason to believe that these three treatment approaches may be differentially effective with the dependent variable of interpersonal anxiety. For example, Desensitization has been found to be quite effective with similar target behaviors (Land et al., 1965; Lazarus, 1963, 1966; Paul, 1966, 1967a). Similarly, if Ellis's (1957, 1962) observations are correct, Rational-Emotive treatment may be superior to the more classical insight approaches such as Psychoanalytic and Client-Centered therapy. Although these approaches have never been compared in a single study, these preliminary observations suggest a tentative order of effectiveness as follows: Systematic Desensitization, a Rational-Emotive and Client-Centered treatment.

Furthermore, the characteristics of introverts and extroverts, presented earlier, may well make them differentially receptive to these three forms of treatment, thus producing different outcomes. For example, if the introvert was legitimately characterized as one who would profit most from a form of treatment based on counter-conditioning and one that makes maximum use of his suggestibility, dependency, conformity, and excellent visual imagery, then Desensitization is probably the most appropriate and Client-Centered the least appropriate form of treatment for him. Similarly, if the extrovert was legitimately characterized as one who would profit most from a form of treatment which is based on extinction but is predominantly verbal in nature and requires involvement in an intimate and personal group interaction which emphasizes self-exploration, then Client-Centered treatment seems the most appropriate and Desensitization the least appropriate form of treatment for him.

Finally, these three approaches represent radically different forms of therapy in terms of technique, treatment model, and level of organization addressed during treatment (affective, behavioral, cognitive). By maximizing the treatment differences, in this manner, one is in a much better position to control and check on the ongoing in-treatment procedures and thus make more definitive cause-effect conclusions, while capturing the essential features of most contemporary systems of psychotherapy currently in existence.

In summary, it is this author's view that although "schools" were the inevitable consequence of theories based on tenacity, faith, and intuition, they have continued to exist largely because the bulk of contemporary research is of a process and treatment no-treatment nature and thus addresses itself to meaningless questions. Not only do these approaches yield very little useful information, they also tend to maintain and perpetuate school distinctions by allowing therapists to transfer their loyalties and affections from a set of highly esoteric rituals to a highly selective body of "empirical findings" without ever once taking a closer look at their underlying personal convictions (Hunt, 1956) to see whether these commitments are justified in terms of either the available evidence or competing approaches. It is this pseudo-scientific base which makes these schools currently so implacable and unyielding.

In order to overcome this predicament, it is believed that research in counseling and psychotherapy must move in two directions. First, it must move from research which emphasizes process to research which emphasizes outcome, with the inclusion of relevant process measures of client-therapist interactions and measures of sequential changes in the target behaviors under study to enhance understanding of the final results. Second, movement must occur from outcome studies which emphasize the use of a treatment no-treatment model to studies which emphasize research based on a multivariate comparative model.

With the inclusion of both process and outcome measures, in conjunction with assessment on relevant input variables, one can begin to ask the more appropriate question, "What form of treatment, administered by whom, is most effective for this particular client with that specific problem and under what set of circumstances?" (Blocher, 1967; Paul, 1967). Not until one begins to employ research designs which address themselves to this question will one be able to circumscribe the limits of applicability of various techniques and demonstrate their efficacy in these delimited contexts and thus be rid of the myths of which Kiesler (1966) speaks.

Follow-up Variables

The need for follow-up data on clients receiving counseling and psychotherapy is of the utmost importance. In an area where placebo effects confound with and frequently masquerade as treatment, only the passage of time will reveal whether clients have truly changed or are simply placating their therapists by responding in a socially desirable manner. Although this problem is less severe when objective, behavioral criteria are employed, there are always immediate, short-term benefits which accrue from treatment but which never really become incorporated into the client's permanent behavioral repetoire.

The other side of this issue is equally as important; namely, that what is learned or acquired as a consequence of treatment takes time to become effectively assimilated and implemented into action. The period immediately following treatment is undoubtedly the most crucial in terms of which behaviors will be discarded and which incorporated into the client's way of life. Thus, without at least a brief follow-up period, treatment approaches may well get branded as either effective or ineffective on the basis of spurious information alone. This is to say nothing of the importance of checking on such currently controversial phenomenon as spontaneous remission, symptom substitution, or complete recitivism.

As Sargent (1960) has pointed out, however, "the importance of follow-up is equaled only by the magnitude of the methodological problems it presents" (p. 101). The most important of these problems is the very practical difficulty of sample maintenance and attrition (Paul, 1967). Since the rate of dropout seems to be directly related to the amount of time between post-testing and follow-up, and since dropout rates tend to be differential, selectively biasing the follow-up findings, tactical decisions favor the use of a short-term follow-up, since it improves the probability of total sample assessment. As Paul (1966, 1967a) has shown, when an *adequate design* with proper controls is evaluated by means of the same criteria, a six-week follow-up is as good as a two-year one.

Follow-up studies also suffer from "the uncontrollable nature of client experiences during the post-treatment period" (Paul, 1967, p. 333). This predicament may be eased somewhat by keeping the follow-up period brief and checking on such blatantly confounding factors as *S*s receiving additional treatment. Without some knowledge of whether or not *S*s receive additional post-therapy treatment, cause-effect statements may be invalidly drawn.

Thus, the need for follow-up studies is obvious. The practical problems which surround such an effort, however, favor the use of short-term follow-ups which employ identical criterion measures and make every effort to secure data on crucial client behaviors during this post-treatment period.

• *Statement of the Problem*

The present study was organized in an attempt to compare the outcome of three distinct forms of counseling with two distinct personality types in the treatment of a specific, homogeneous problem. More succinctly, it is the purpose of this study to compare the relative effectiveness of Systematic Desensitization, Rational-Emotive, and Client-Centered group psychotherapy in the reduction of interpersonal anxiety in introverts and extroverts.

· 2 ·

Method

• *Subjects*

The *S*s for this study were one hundred (58 female and 42 male) college freshmen and sophomores (mean and median ages of 18.8 and 19.3 years, respectively) from Michigan State University who volunteered to participate in this project because of high self-reported interpersonal anxiety and a desire for treatment. This sample was obtained from a larger population of six hundred students who were enrolled in one section of Introductory Psychology at MSU in the fall of 1967.

• *Instrumentation*

The main battery of scales administered to this sample was designed to assess: (a) client personality type (*Myers-Briggs Type Indicator,*[1] Myers, 1962); (b) the target behaviors of interpersonal anxiety (Interpersonal Anxiety Scales, Di Loreto; *S-R Inventory of Anxiousness,* Interpersonal Subsection,[2] Endler et al., 1962; Behavior Checklist of Interpersonal

1. Although the entire test was administered, only the introvert-extrovert subscale was employed.
2. Included here were the following items: "Job Interview," "Competitive Contest," "Going for Counseling," "Speech Before a Large Group," and "Meeting a New Date."

Anxiety, Di Loreto; Index of Interpersonal Activity, Di Loreto); and (c) the broader area of "general anxiety" (*S-R Inventory of Anxiousness,* Fear of the Unknown Subsection,[3] Endler et al., 1962; *Trait Anxiety Inventory,* Spielberger & Gorsuch, 1966). In addition, a number of miscellaneous scales were employed in an attempt to gauge the degree of client defensiveness (*Edwards Social Desirability Scale,* Edwards, 1957), the depth of client self-exploration (*Basic Scale of Depth of Self-Exploration,* Truax & Carkhuff, 1967), the quality of the client-therapist relationship (*Relationship Questionnaire,* Truax & Carkhuff, 1967), and the course of anxiety reduction during the client's treatment (*State Anxiety Inventory,* Spielberger & Gorsuch, 1966; Therapist Rating Sheet, Neuman, 1968).

Although a salient criterion for inclusions in this study was *S*'s verbal report of discomfort in interpersonal situations and an expressed desire for treatment, the operational definition of these constructs was based on the aforementioned psychometrically scored questionnaries, rating scales, and checklists. For the crucial dependent variable of interpersonal anxiety, both self-report and behavioral criteria were employed, as well as measures within and outside of the treatment setting.

Pre-treatment battery

The battery of scales administered prior to treatment included: The Interpersonal Anxiety Scales[4] (IPAS, forms A

3. Included here were the following items: "Final Course Examination," "Alone in the Woods at Night," "Sail Boat," and "Crawling on a Mountain Ledge."
4. Two forms of this one hundred item questionnaire, half of the items keyed "true" and half "false," were developed and independently validated by the author in a pilot study employing twenty *S*s (see Appendix C). The Peason product moment correlations were as follows: IPAS, forms A & B, r=.891; IPAS (combined score for form A & B) and $S\text{-}R_I$, r=.683; IPAS (combined) and $S\text{-}R_G$, r=.411; IPAS (combined) and ratings on a five-point scale of anxiousness, r=.619; $S\text{-}R_I$ and ratings on the

and B), the *S-R Inventory of Anxiousness* (Interpersonal, $S\text{-}R_I$, and Fear of the Unknown, $S\text{-}R_G$), the *Trait Anxiety Inventory* (TAI), the *State Anxiety Inventory* (SAI), the *Edwards Social Desirability Scale* (ESD), and the *Myers-Briggs Type Indicator* (MBTI). In addition, behavioral ratings of interpersonal anxiety were secured on each *S* by means of the Behavior Checklist of Interpersonal Anxiety (see Appendix A) at the time of the first treatment session. Finally, a Data Sheet (see Appendix B) requesting demographic information, time schedules, and motivation for treatment was also completed by each *S*.

In-treatment battery

The battery of scales administered at each treatment session included: the *State Anxiety Inventory* (SAI), completed by each *S* immediately before each session, the Index of Interpersonal Activity[5] (IIA), completed by each *S* during the course of each week and returned prior to each weekly session, and the Therapist Rating Sheet[6] (TRS), completed by each

---

same-five point scale, r=.584, $S\text{-}R_G$ and ratings on the same five-point scale, r=.475. Thus, the IPAS seem to have good alternate form reliability and are more valid when interpreted as a measure of interpersonal anxiety rather than "general anxiety."

5. This instrument, which I developed, lists five criteria, the combined presence or absence of which determines the nature and extent of each *S*'s interpersonal activity outside of the treatment setting (see Appendix D). Each *S* was asked to keep a daily record of the frequency of interpersonal contacts which conformed to these five criteria. Each *S* submitted his log weekly as he attended the treatment sessions and received a new one to be filled out daily, in the same manner, and returned at the next weekly meeting. The total score, derived by pooling the daily incidents of interpersonal contacts, thus served as as objective indicant of weekly changes in interpersonal activity outside of the treatment setting.
6. This instrument, developed by Neuman (1968), is a five-point scale ranging from low (1) to high (5) anxiousness (see Appendix E). Each therapist was asked to judge the degree of anxiety displayed by each *S* and circle the number (1 through 5) which best described each *S*'s anxiety level *during that session.* Each therapist rated each *S* for each of the nine sessions. The total score, derived by pooling the weekly scores across *S*s, served as an indication of weekly changes in anxiety level as viewed by the therapist.

counselor immediately following each treatment session. These instruments were employed to assess weekly changes in anxiety levels from the point of view of both the client (SAI) and the therapist (TRS), as well as weekly changes in the amount of interpersonal activity (IIA) on the part of each *S* outside of the treatment setting.

Post-treatment battery

The battery of scales administered subsequent to the completion of treatment was identical to the pre-treatment battery with the following exceptions. The Data Sheet (see Appendix B) was revised to obtain from each *S* information regarding any additional treatment received either prior to or during the project. In addition, only form A of the IPAS was used and the MBTI was not readministered at this time. Finally, the *Relationship Questionnaire* (RQ) was added as part of the post-test battery.

Follow-up battery

The battery of scales administered three months (thirteen weeks) following the completion of treatment was identical to the pre-treatment battery with two exceptions. Only form B of the IPAS was readministered at this time, and the Data Sheet was revised to secure from each *S* data on crucial client behaviors during the post-treatment period.

Procedure

One large section of an Introductory Psychology class, consisting of approximately six hundred students, was given an orientation lecture regarding the nature and purpose of the project at the time of their first class meeting of the term. Every effort was exerted to portray the project *not* as research but as "a program of help for students with interpersonal anxiety." At that time, the program was explained to them as follows:

More and more the university has come to realize that students who fail in college do so because of personal and social, not academic problems. In fact, there is a growing body of evidence which suggests that in many instances it is the more intelligent student who flunks out or drops out before graduation. Consequently, a number of universities around the country, MSU included, have begun to develop programs to deal with these personal and social problems.

Last year, when this program began, it was limited to students who were what we might call "test anxious." That is, they experienced so much anxiety either preparing for or taking course examinations that they were failing. We found that helping them learn to control their anxiety, which is a personal not an academic problem, enabled nearly all of them to improve their grades enough to return this fall. Again, we did not teach them how to study better or how to take tests, but rather we tried to teach them how to deal with their anxiety and other personal problems which prevented them from studying and taking tests more effectively. All of you here, I'm sure, have felt on a number of occasions that you could have done much better on a course examination had you been less anxious.

This year the program has been extended to include students who experience what we might call social or interpersonal anxiety. That is, students who become fearful or anxious when they have to meet new people, express themselves in a group, such as a class like this, or at a dorm meeting, or students who find themselves so anxious at a party they can't pick up a dish or glass because their hands tremble; or students who are afraid to shake hands with someone they've just met because their hands are all sweaty. If you find you can't eat before your speech class or before going to a party or meeting a new date because your stomach is so upset, or if you find your neck or face turning red when you have to speak up in a group or your heart beating so fast and your breathing so irregular you can hardly speak, then you are the kind of person who can profit from this project. If you experience any of these social fears or interpersonal anxieties, then I think we can help you, if you are interested.

Let me tell you a bit more about the program. The university has hired a number of counselors and is paying them each $200.00 to work with you. If you choose to participate in this project, you will be required to meet with a counselor for one

> hour each week for ten weeks. You will work in a small group; you, four other students and a counselor, for as I indicated, ten, one-hour meetings. They will be spread out over the entire term so you will have one, one-hour meeting a week for ten weeks.
>
> If you are interested, however, you will be obligated to commit yourself to ten one-hour meetings during this fall term. The meetings will probably be held in the early evening, but in any case, they will be arranged to fit your fall schedule. *Do not* volunteer for this program unless you are willing to come to *all ten meetings,* since you will not derive full benefit nor will this be fair to those who are investing their time, effort, and money in working with you.
>
> Thank you for your cooperation.

The students were then informed that those who wished to volunteer for the project would be required to fill out a number of questionnaires. They were given two optional dates when they could complete this pre-test battery. At the time of pre-testing, the program was further elaborated as follows:

> Some of you have inquired as to whether or not this is simply a research project, or what. As I tried to indicate in class, the main purpose of this program is to help students with interpersonal anxiety. We are asking you to fill out a number of questionnaires, it is true, so as to be able to evaluate the effectiveness of the overall program, and you may or may not want to call this research. However, the main purpose is not research, but to help you deal more effectively with your interpersonal problems. We know the techniques we are going to employ work, since they have been proven effective on other students just like yourself both here and at other universities.
>
> The idea is simply this, since you have learned to be anxious in the presence of others, the goal of this program is to help you learn not to be anxious in social or interpersonal situations. Just as you learn to be anxious you can unlearn it as well. We are going to help you learn not to be too anxious when faced with meeting new people, speaking up in a group or expressing what you really feel in the presence of others. Since you often have to do these things as a student, the net result is that you will be able to do them while remaining calm and relaxed.

Just to reiterate briefly, you will meet for one hour per week, probably in the evening, for ten weeks. You will meet in a small group with four other students and a counselor who is being paid to work with you.

Before you begin filling out the questionnaires you have just received, I want to just mention that we will try our best to accommodate all students who request help. However, our facilities, staff, and finances are somewhat limited and some of you may have to wait until a little later in the term to be assigned to a group.

Finally, as I stated in class, if you do volunteer for this program, you are committing yourself to ten sessions. Not nine or eight or seven, but ten. *Do not* volunteer if you are not going to attend all ten sessions. You must not miss *any* meetings, since you will not derive full benefit, nor will this be fair to those who are investing their time and considerable money to help you or to those students who were turned away because of limited facilities.

You will now fill out the questionnaires which have been passed out to you. You will be assigned to a group on the basis of the free time you have indicated on your class schedule. You will be notified by phone of the time and place of your first meeting.

Thank you for coming today.

Two hundred and seventeen students volunteered and took the pre-test battery. Those who obtained a preference score $\geqq 15$ on the MBTI (97 introverts and 79 extroverts) and a raw score of $\geqq 50$ on the IPAS (89 introverts and 60 extroverts) were then randomly assigned, within stratified blocks, to one of ten introvert and ten extrovert groups (total N = 100). Each of the twenty groups consisted of five *S*s. The modal composition of each group was two male and three females *S*. Each of the ten introvert and ten extrovert groups was then randomly assigned to one of the three treatment or two control groups and then to one of the counselors within treatments.

Once this was completed, each student was contacted by phone and notified of the time and place of the first meeting.

None of the students who volunteered and were selected refused to participate when contacted by phone. All students who were selected attended the first session.

At the time of the first session, each *S* was rated on the Behavior Checklist of Interpersonal Anxiety (see Appendix A). This instrument, developed by the author, lists approximately three dozen observable manifestations of anxiety, the presence or absence of which was recorded by two trained raters from behind a one-way mirror.[7] It was felt that since these students were meeting together for the first time as a group and since they had not seen prior to this time the counselor with whom they were to work, the first interview would constitute a prototype stress situation for eliciting interpersonal anxiety.

One advanced graduate student and one secretary were trained together for approximately ten hours by means of both live and video-tape recorded interviews in the detection and recording of behaviors indicative of anxiety, so that each rater had a common definition of desired responses. During the first interview, each rater observed the same *S* for ten 30-second intervals. A third person, employing a stopwatch, signaled the end of each 30-second interval at which time the raters moved, in a clockwise fashion, to the next *S* in the group. In this manner, each *S* in the group was rated for 30 seconds every two and one-half minutes for the first half hour of the first session. The total score, derived by pooling the total incidence of behavioral manifestations across raters, thus served as an objective behavioral indicant of interpersonal anxiety. The pre-treatment inter-rater reliability, thus computed, was .825.

After the ninth and final treatment session, the groups ($N = 80$) were reorganized so that no two *S*s were in the same group or had the same counselor at the time of post-testing as

7. There was no evidence to indicate that any of the *Ss* were aware of the raters presence either at the time of the pre-, post-, or follow-up evaluations.

they did during treatment (introverts and extroverts were not mixed). It was felt that this maneuver provided all the necessary ingredients of a new prototype stress situation for eliciting interpersonal anxiety (new counselor, new group), and that the new groupings were comparable in nature to the pre-treatment stress-condition.

All *S*s were informed of this pending maneuver at the ninth and final treatment session. They were told they would be notified by phone of the time of the final or post-test interview, and that it would consist of an "active group discussion" in which they would be asked to evaluate the program they had participated in for the last nine weeks. They were also told that the groups were being reorganized so that they would feel freer in evaluating the other *S*s in their group and their counselor, since neither would be present at this time. Two make-up groups were scheduled for those *S*s who missed the post-treatment evaluation sessions. One group consisted of six extroverts and the other of four introverts.

During the post-treatment evaluation sessions, each *S* was asked to respond to the following questions: "What kinds of things did you do in your group?" "What was your reaction to the other group members?" "How did you feel about the counselor who worked with you?" "How would you change the program now that you have gone through it yourself?"

The post-treatment evaluation interviews lasted approximately one hour each. The modal composition of each group at post-testing was two male and three female *S*s. During these active group discussions, ratings were secured from behind a one-way mirror by the same raters and in the same manner described earlier. The inter-rater reliability at post-testing was .889.[8]

8. With the exception of the *Relationship Questionnaire,* which was mailed to each *S* the day of their last treatment session and returned completed at the tenth or post-test session, all post-testing took place one week after the last treatment interview, immediately following the post-treatment evaluation interviews.

Three months (13 weeks) after the post-treatment evaluation interviews, each *S* was contacted by phone and asked to return for one last meeting. All *S*s were still in attendance at MSU at this time, and all agreed to return for this follow-up evaluation. However, it was necessary to schedule three make-up groups for those *S*s who missed the regularly scheduled follow-up interviews. One group consisted of five introverts and the remaining two groups of four extroverts each. The modal composition of each group at follow-up was three female and two male *S*s.

Once again the groups (N = 80) were reorganized so that no two *S*s were in the same group at follow-up as they were either during treatment or at post-testing. Once again, introverts and extroverts were not mixed. Because of the large number of *S*s involved, this second reorganization was possible with the exception of seven *S*s. It was felt that these newly constituted groups provided a reasonable facsimile of both the pre- and post-treatment stress-conditions for eliciting interpersonal anxiety.

At this follow-up evaluation, three *new* counselors asked each *S* in the newly constituted groups the following: "Now that some time has passed since your last group meeting, how do you feel about what you did in your group?" "Was it helpful, or not?" "What, if any, *specific* differences do you notice in yourself or in the way you think, feel or act?"

In order to avoid any "halo" effects, two new raters were employed in securing the follow-up ratings on the Behavior Checklist of Interpersonal Anxiety. However, in order to profit from their learning experience, and thus avoid a spurious reduction in inter-rater reliability, the author had the first two raters train the second rating team in the detection and recording of appropriate behaviors. The new raters, two advanced graduate students in counseling, were also trained for ten hours by means of both live and video-tape recordings so that they shared a common definition of the desired responses. The

Table 2.1 · *General experimental design and procedure*

Treatments	*First Class Meeting*	*Pre-treatment Battery*	*Assignment to Groups*
1. Systematic Desensitization N = 20	1. Brief explanation of the project as a program of help for students with interpersonal anxiety	1. Elaboration of program	1. Those *S*s with a preference ≧ 15 on the *Myers-Briggs Type Indicator* and a raw score ≧ than 50 o the Interpersonal Anxiety Scales (Forms A and B) were randomly assigned, within stra fied blocks, to groups of 5. Each group was then randomly assignec within blocks, to one of the 3 treatment or 2 control groups anc then to one of the counselors within treatment.
2. Client-Centered therapy N = 20	2. Students informed of time and place of pre-testing	2. Data Sheet	2. *S*s were then notified by phone of time and place of first meeting.
3. Rational-Emotive Psycho-Therapy N = 20		3. Interpersonal Anxiety Scales (Forms A and B)	
4. No-treatment (Placebo) Control N = 20		4. *S-R Inventory of Anxiousness*	
5. No-Contact Control N = 20		5. *Trait Anxiety Inventory*	
		6. *Edwards Social Desirability Scale*	
		7. *Myers-Briggs Type Indicator*	
		8. *State Anxiety Inventory*	
Total N = 100		N = 217	Final N = 100

inter-rater reliability for this new rating team, secured and computed in the manner described earlier, was .831.

Table 2.1 presents a summary of treatments and procedures used in assigning and evaluating the *S*s in this study.

• *Treatment Counselors*

Six advanced graduate students in the final stages of their doctoral program in Counseling and Clinical Psychology

First Treatment Session	*Treatment Sessions*	*Post-treatment Battery (10th session)*	*Follow-up Battery*
1. Ratings on Behavior Checklist of Interpersonal Anxiety	1. 9 one hr. sessions of systematic desensitization	1. Data Sheet	1. Data Sheet
2. Explanation of Interpersonal Anxiety	2. 9 one hr. sessions of Client-Centered Therapy	2. Interpersonal Anxiety Scales (Form A)	2. Interpersonal Anxiety Scales (Form B)
3. Explanation and rationale of treatment	3. 9 one hr. sessions of Rational-Emotive Psychotherapy	3. *S-R Inventory of Anxiousness*	3. *S-R Inventory of Anxiousness*
4. One hour discussion session with no-treatment (placebo) controls at which time future treatment was promised.	4. Approximately 9 hours of attention (*State Anxiety Inventory* and Index of Interpersonal Activity at each session)	4. *Trait Anxiety Inventory*	4. *Trait Anxiety Inventory*
		5. *Edwards Social Desirability Scale*	5. *Edwards Social Desirability Scale*
		6. *Relationship Questionnaire*	6. Ratings on Behavior Checklist of Interpersonal Anxiety by new raters
		7. *Index of Interpersonal Activity*	7. *Myers-Briggs Type Indicator*
		8. Ratings on Behavior Checklist of Interpersonal Anxiety	
		9. *State Anxiety Inventory*	
Classroom Attendance Only			

served as therapists in this study and were paid $200.00 each for their participation.[9] Each therapist had had supervised training in the techniques they respectively deemed effective prior to the onset of the project. In addition, each had had at least one year of practical experience with his respective tech-

9. Special acknowledgement and considerable gratitude is extended to the therapists who participated in this study and gave unstintingly of their time and effort—Drs. James Barrick, Roger Bauer, James Crowley, Frederick Hill, Donald Jabury, and James Lowe.

nique and indicated a personal commitment to the approach he was to represent.

Before working with any *S*s, each therapist completed self-ratings on the Therapist Personal Data Sheet and the Therapist Orientation Sheet (see Appendix F). These two questionnaires, developed by Sundland & Barker (1962) and modified by Paul (1966) and the author, consist of the following: a number of questions geared at assessing each therapist's experience level, school affiliation, and amount of personal analysis and/or psychotherapy; a series of five-point scales in

Table 2.2 · Experience level and general orientation of the six participating counselors

Therapist	*Code*	*Most Influential Authors*	*Closest School Affiliation*	*Experience Level*
1	C	Kell & Mueller Rogers Sullivan Truax & Carkhuff	Rogerian Sullivanian	2½ yrs.
2	c	Sullivan Kell & Mueller Whitaker Rogers	Sullivanian Rogerian	4 yrs.
3	B	Bandura & Walters Krasner & Ullman Wolpe Ellis	Behavioristic	2½ yrs.
4	b	Wolpe Ullman & Krasner Dollard & Miller Paul	Behavioristic	1½ yrs.
5	R	Ellis Berne Haley Phillips & Weiner	Rational-Emotive	4 yrs.
6	r	Ellis Haley Dollard & Miller Milton Erickson	Rational-Emotive	2 yrs.

25 areas of treatment orientation; 25 specific treatment techniques.

Table 2.2 presents the experience level and general treatment orientation of the six counselors employed in this study. As anticipated, three homogeneous groupings appear which are relatively independent of each other and which might be labeled Client-Centered (therapist one and two), Behavioistic (therapist three and four) and Rational-Emotive (therapist five and six) orientations. In addition, one therapist had completed 30 hours of personal therapy; two others had completed 50 hours; one had completed 75 hours; and one 90 hours of personal therapy. Only one therapist had never undergone either personal or didactic treatment.

Table 2.3 presents the more specific theoretical orientation of each therapist. As might be expected, the within "school" differences in specific theoretical orientation are substantially less than the between "school" differences. The CC[10] counselors differed from the RT counselors by responding at opposite ends of the continuum on 13 of the 25 areas covered: Nos. 1 and 2, activity—frequency and type; No. 7, relationship—therapist actions; Nos. 9 and 10, goals—source and formalization; No. 13, client personal growth; Nos. 14, 15, and 16, therapeutic gains—self-understanding, emotional understanding, and "symptom" reduction; No. 19, learning process in therapy; Nos. 23, 24, and 25, theory of motivation and curative aspects of therapist.

Not completely surprising is the fact that no *substantial* differences appear between the B counselors and those representative of RT. Only slight, and probably not significant, differences appear on 5 of the 25 areas covered: No. 5, relationship—structure; No. 13, client personal growth; No. 19, learning process in therapy; No. 21, therapeutically significant

10. The following notation will be employed in designating the title of each treatment approach: Client-Centered, CC; Behavioristic, B; Rational-Emotive, RT.

Table 2.3 • Specific theoretical orientation to treatment of the six participating counselors

Item	Pole						Pole
1. Activity-frequency:	Active (Talkative)	Br	Rb	c	C		Passive (Non-talkative)
2. Activity-type:	Directive		BbRr		Cc		Non-directive
3. Activity-structure:	Informal	c	CB	Rr	b		Formal
4. Relationship-tenor:	Personal (Involved)	Cc	Bb	Rr			Impersonal (Detached)
5. Relationship-structure:	Unstructured	CC	Rr	Bb			Structured
6. Relationship-atmosphere:	Permissive	Ccb	BRr				Non-permissive
7. Relationship-therapist actions:	Planned		BbRr		C	c	Spontaneous
8. Relationship-client dynamics:	Non-conceptualized		C		cBb	Rr	Conceptualized
9. Goals-source:	Therapist		BbRr		C	c	Client
10. Goals-formalization:	Planned (Formalized)	B	bRr		Cc		Unplained (Unformalized)
11. Therapist Comfort and Security:	Always Secure (Comfortable)		CcBRr	b			Never Secure (Uncomfortable)
12. Client Comfort and Security:	Never Secure (Uncomfortable)			Cc	BbRr		Always Secure (Comfortable)
13. Client Personal Growth:	Not Inherent	Bb	Rr		C	c	Inherent
14. Therapeutic Gains-self understanding (cognitive insight):	Important	rB	bR		c	C	Unimportant
15. Therapeutic Gains-emotional understanding (affective awareness)	Unimportant		Bbr	R		Cc	Important
16. Therapeutic Gains- "symptom" reduction:	Important	BbRr		c	C		Unimportant
17. Therapeutic Gains-self disclosure:	Unimportant	Br	Rb		Cc		Important
18. Therapeutic Gains-social adjustment:	Important	Bbrc	CR				Unimportant
19. Theapeutic Gains-confidence in effecting change:	Confident	CcR	rBb				Unconfident
20. Learning Process in Therapy:	Verbal-conceptual	Bb	Rr		C	c	Non-verbal -affective
21. Therapeutically Significant Topics:	Historical		C	cb	B	Rr	Current
22. Therapeutically Significant Topics:	Client-centered	C	cRr	Bb			Theory-centered

Table 2.3 • Continued

23. Therapeutically Significant Topics:						
Ego Functions		RrcBb	C			Superego, id
24. Theory of Motivation:						
Unconscious	C	c	Bb	Rr		Conscious
25. Curative Aspects of Therapist:						
Personality		Cc		BbRr		Training
26. Curative Aspects of Therapist:						
Relationship	c	C	R	Bbr		Techniques

Note: Therapists are coded by "school" as in Table 2.2.

topics; No. 23, theory of motivation. Thus, the specific theoretical orientation of the RT and B counselors is, by and large, similar and can best be characterized as an active-directive learning theory based form of treatment which stresses symptom reduction and self (cognitive) understanding and views the therapist's training and techniques as salient. In marked contrast is the specific treatment orientation of the CC counselors which can best be characterized as a passive, non-directive, phenomonologically based form of treatment which stresses emotional (affective) understanding and views the therapist's personality and the client-therapist relationship as salient. These two operational distinctions in specific treatment orientation parallel the "school" distinctions put forth by the advocates of these respective approaches (see Appendix G).

Table 2.4 presents the frequency with which 25 treatment techniques are employed by each therapist. As might be expected, the CC counselors rely predominantly on reflection and clarification, warmth and understanding, self-disclosure, and a close interpersonal relationship. In marked contrast are the RT and B counselors who although similar, are nontheless still somewhat different in the techniques they stress. Whereas the RT counselors tend to employ learning theory based treatment techniques, that is, direct confrontation, information and advice giving, positive attitude, and homework assignments involving the performance of feared acts, the B counselors tend to favor straightforward learning principles, that is, modeling, reinforcement, conditioning-counterconditioning, etc.

Table 2.4 • Frequency of use of specific techniques by each of the six participating therapists

Technique	*Use of Techniques*: *almost always*		*50/50*		*never*
Reflection and Clarification of Feelings:	Cc		B	Rb	r
Reflection and Clarification of Thinking:		Cc	RrB	b	
Reflection and Clarification of Content:	c	C	B	Rrb	
Reflection and Clarification of Behavior:		CB	Rcb	r	
Questioning of Feelings:		Cc	Rr	Bb	
Questioning of Thinking:	r	R	Bb	Cc	
Questioning of Content:		Br	Rcb	C	
Questioning of Behavior:	r	RB	Ccb		
Interpretation of Feelings:	Cc		B	Rrb	
Interpretation of Thinking:		Rr	Bb	Cc	
Interpretation of Content:		Cc	Rrb	B	
Interpretation of Behavior:		Rr	Ccb	B	
Direct Confrontation with Feelings:	r	R	cb	CB	
Direct Confrontation with Thinking:	Rr		B	Ccb	
Direct Confrontation with Content:	r	R	B	cb	c
Direct Confrontation with Behavior:	Rr		Bbc	C	
Suggestion (not hypnosis):	r	RB	b	c	C
Reassurance:		Rc	BbCr		
Information and Advice Giving:	Rr	b	B	c	C
Redirecting Questions Back to the Group:	Cc		R	Br	b
Attentive Listening:	RcCc	Bb			
Self-disclosure:	c	C		Rb	Br
Free Association:			cr	CB	Rb
Modeling Techniques:	bB		R	Cr	c
Positive Attitude-confidence:	r	R	Bb	Cc	
Warmth and Understanding:	Cc		Rb	rB	
Reinforcement (Approval-disapproval):	Bb		RC	cr	
Conditioning, Counter-Conditioning:	Bb		R	cr	C
Home Work Assignments:	R	r	B	cb	C
Others (Please Specify):					

Note: Therapist are coded by "school" as in Table 2.2.

Thus, with regard to treatment approaches, there are six therapists representing three "schools" who have two different specific treatment orientations and who employ three distinctly different kinds of treatment techniques. Since only techniques are relevant here, in the sense that they represent what the therapist "does" to the client (London, 1964), one may consider that, operationally, there are three distinct approaches to treatment represented here.

Prior to working with any *S*s, each therapist also completed a battery of self-report personality questionnaires (*Edwards Personal Preference Schedule,* Edwards, 1959; *Myers-Briggs Type Indicator,* Myers, 1962; *Interpersonal Checklist,* Leary, 1956). This procedure provided a normative description of the sample of therapists in terms of relatively stable personal-social characteristics. Table 2.5 presents the scores of each therapist on these various scales.

Quite unexpectedly, all six therapists seem to be more similar than different, indicating a fairly homogeneous distribution of personal-social characteristics, at least in terms of the operational distinctions offered here. On the EPPS, all therapists are more alike than different on 7 of the 15 "need" subscales (deference, order, autonomy, intraception, abasement, endurance, and heterosexuality). Similarly, on the MBTI, all therapists are more similar than different on two or the four subscales, preferring the intuitive mode to the sensing one and the perceiving mode to the judging one. Although the ICL reveals more heterogeneity than either of the other two scales, there is still a marked similarity on at least two of the four interpersonal modes of responding (dominance and submission).

The RT counselors scored differently than either the B or CC counselors by ranking high on the EPPS on achievement and dominance and low on affiliation, succorance, and nurturance and by scoring highest on the dominance and hate and lowest on the submission modes of the ICL. The RT and B counselors ranked about the same on the exhibition and

Table 2.5 • *Therapist self-ratings of personal-social characteristics on the Edwards Personal Preference Schedule, Myers-Briggs Type Indicator, and Interpersonal Checklist*[1]

Therapist	*Edwards Personal Preference Schedule (percentiles)*															
Code	*ach*	*def*	*ord*	*exh*	*aut*	*aff*	*int*	*suc*	*dom*	*aba*	*nur*	*chg*	*end*	*het*	*agg*	*con*
C	37	02	00	29	70	97	97	65	57	01	86	91	23	87	29	99
c	46	18	00	47	84	94	99	71	44	09	86	96	07	76	46	70
B	46	18	11	75	95	39	92	58	69	04	26	18	10	89	69	87
b	37	04	20	87	88	58	99	42	57	12	26	62	07	87	76	70
R	86	05	00	82	92	24	95	40	89	00	15	91	01	85	82	97
r	98	02	01	97	98	18	92	33	80	01	07	91	03	87	87	97

	Myers-Briggs Type Indicator (preference score)				*Interpersonal Checklist*			
Therapist Code	*introvert extrovert*	*sensing judging*	*thinking feeling*	*judging perceiving*	*dom*	*love*	*subm*	*hate*
C	E = 35	N = 29	F = 41	P = 31	14.7	18.5	8.3	8.1
c	E = 29	N = 11	F = 17	P = 45	18.5	15.4	6.9	14.0
B	I = 01	N = 41	T = 11	P = 41	16.8	13.0	11.4	19.2
b	E = 33	N = 37	T = 11	P = 41	19.2	10.0	12.8	15.0
R	E = 17	N = 27	T = 29	P = 23	26.2	10.2	7.6	25.6
r	I = 07	N = 33	T = 15	P = 51	19.4	10.2	6.8	18.1

1. See Appendix H for a graphic representation of these sources.

aggression scales of the EPPS, the introvert-extrovert and thinking modes of the MBTI, and the love and hate dimension of the ICL. The only areas in which the RT and CC counselors ranked uniquely similar were the need for change subscale of the EPPS and the submission mode of the ICL.

The CC counselors scored differently than either of the other two groups by ranking low on the exhibition and aggression, and high on the affiliation, succorance, and nurturance subscales of the EPPS, the extrovert and feeling modes of the MBTI, and the love and hate scales of the ICL. The CC and B counselors ranked similarly by scoring low only on the achievement scale of the EPPS.

Finally, the B counselors can be distinguished from either of the groups by ranking low on the change subscale and about "average" on the affiliation, succorance, dominance, and nurturance scales of the EPPS, as well as low on the submission mode of the ICL. It should be noted that while differences in personal-social characteristics between the CC and other counselors tend to be qualitative, differences between the RT and B counselors tend to be only quantitative.

Thus, in terms of relatively stable personal-social characteristics, there tends to be more similarity among the six counselors than their "school" affiliations would suggest. By and large they tend to be more autonomous, intraceptive, and heterosexually motivated than the general adult population and less enduring, deferent, orderly, and self-abasing. This is consistent with their reliance on intuitive and perceiving modes and their tendency to be somewhat dominant in interpersonal situations.

The differences that do appear tend to follow *somewhat* the differences noted earlier in specific treatment orientation, in that the six therapists tend to fall into two qualitatively distinct groups with the CC counselors in one group and the B and RT counselors in the other. The former group seems best described as gregarious, non-aggressive, and extremely extroverted. In addition, they not only like to be needed by others but need others themselves and prefer interpersonal relationships characterized by strong feelings and emotions. In marked contrast is the latter group which can best be characterized as exhibitionistic, aggressive, and markedly independent and non-conforming. They tend to rely more on themselves than others and prefer to relate interpersonally on a thinking, logical, or factual level.

• *Treatments*

The *S*s in this study were treated concurrently in groups of five. Each of the six therapists treated one introvert and one extrovert group. Each therapist understood that the goal of treatment was to be a reduction in interpersonal anxiety. Since not only the efficacy, but also the efficiency, of the various therapeutic approaches was considered crucial, treatment was limited to nine sessions of approximately one to one and a half hours each. Make-up sessions were not possible. Two therapists were used as representative of each approach and were told to behave as they normally would with clients of this nature. The only information given to each therapist was that the presenting problem was interpersonal anxiety, and that the groups were scheduled to meet for nine sessions.[11] Each therapist was also given a copy of the IPAS and $S\text{-}R_I$ with a ranked listing of the frequency with which each *S* endorsed a statement in the direction of "high anxiety."

The opening two and one-half minutes of *all* of the first interviews was spent in formal introduction and informal "getting acquainted." The next five minutes were spent explaining interpersonal anxiety. The explanations offered, partially pre-

11. By the second interview, the therapists began to notice a drastic difference in the introvert and extrovert groups they were treating. Although this difference was acknowledged, the specific nature of the difference was not revealed to them at this time.

pared prior to the first interview, were based on the theoretical orientation of each therapist (see Appendix G); thus, three distinct explanations were offered. The next five minutes were spent presenting a rationale for the course of treatment to be employed (see Appendix G). Finally, the actual treatment portion of the first interview, lasting approximately 50 minutes, began at this point and ended with an explanation of the construction and use of the Index of Interpersonal Activity.[12]

Rational-Emotive treatment

This treatment consisted of implementing the procedures put forth by Ellis (1962) and outlined in Appendix G. With this approach, the therapist attempts to reduce interpersonal anxiety by: (a) directly, and often forcefully, confronting the client with his irrational and maladaptive philosophies of life:[13] (b) showing him how his current perceptions and evaluations, and more importantly his emotional reactions to interpersonal situations, are based on these irrational ideas; and (c) teaching him that he can change his perceptions, evaluations, and thus his emotional reactions to interpersonal situations by adopting more rational philosophies of living. According to this approach, any sustained negative emotion is based on an irrational idea, and without this idea or philosophy the emotion could not endure over time. Thus, its removal and replacement with a more rational idea is the goal of treatment.

With group treatment, every effort is made to get the clients to challenge each other's irrational ideas. Weekly "homework" assignments, where clients are given tasks to per-

12. In the case of *S*s who missed subsequent sessions, the information for the IIA was secured by phone the same days as their regularly scheduled treatment session, and a new form was immediately mailed to the *S*s to be returned at the next meeting. In this manner, a one hundred percent return of the data was assured.
13. These irrational ideas, as well as their rational analogies, are presented in Chapter 3 of Ellis's (1962) book.

form which either successively approximate or actually duplicate the fear stimulus, are an integral part of this treatment approach.

Client-Centered treatment

This treatment consisted of implementing the procedures put forth by Rogers (1959), Sullivan (Perry & Garvel, 1953), and Truax and Carkhuff (1967) and outlined in Appendix G. With this approach, the therapist attempts to reduce interpersonal anxiety by encouraging the client to experience, in a psychologically safe relationship, the feeling or feelings which have hitherto been too threatening for him to experience freely (Rogers, 1963, p. 8). The therapist does his "encouraging" both by reflecting and clarifying the feelings and thoughts "behind" or implied in the client's current actions and verbalizations and by disclosing his own feelings in such situations. With group treatment, each client is encouraged to disclose his feelings to other members of the group and to work with each other in unraveling the thoughts and feelings of each group member.

Systematic Desensitization treatment

This treatment consisted of implementing the procedures put forth by Wolpe (1958) and outlined in Appendix G. With this approach, the therapist attempts to reduce interpersonal anxiety by training the client in deep muscle relaxation and then presenting verbally a series of stimulus scenes which the client while remaining relaxed is to visualize for 15 to 30 seconds. The scenes are constructed prior to the desensitization proper and consist of a graded series of situations which range from the least to the most anxiety producing. The object is to present the hierarchy of scenes in a controlled fashion, so that the client experiences little or no anxiety as he moves up the hierarchy to the most anxiety producing or target behavior. Relaxation is employed, since it is physiologically antagonistic to anxiety and thus automatically inhibits anxiety responses, assuming that the hierarchy is properly constructed and the client properly relaxed.

Group treatment, although quite similar in terms of desensitization proper, requires a slight modification, since a common hierarchy is employed and the therapist must be sure that all members are and remain relaxed before presenting the scenes to be visualized.

No-treatment (placebo) control

The twenty *S*s in this group attended the first, last, and follow-up sessions along with the other *S*s, so that behavior ratings of interpersonal anxiety could be secured. During the first group meeting, the author spent approximately 15 minutes with each *S* exploring the history and current status of his problem. In addition, roughly 50 minutes were spent discussing his educational plans, major areas of academic interest, and feelings about the change from high school to university life. Every effort was made to foster and maintain strong rapport with each client.

The remainder of the time was spent explaining that financial limitations made it necessary to start this and three other groups at the end of the term. However, every effort was made to insure each *S* that relief was forthcoming, and that as much help as possible would be given, on an informal basis, during the interim. Each *S* was informed of the University's concern for his welfare and was told that he would receive a questionnaire (*State Anxiety Inventory* and Index of Interpersonal Activity) in the mail each week which he should fill out and return, so that the university would know how he was doing.

Two weeks later, the author arranged to meet separately with each of the four groups for a two-hour luncheon. The topic of conversation was limited to their reactions to university life and any academic problems they might be experiencing. Any explanations offered were given from a learning theory frame of reference.

Approximately two weeks later, the week of mid-terms, the author again met with each group, this time for about four hours. The focus of the group meeting was their pending psychology mid-term examination. At this time the author answered any questions the group had pertaining to the content of the course and pending examination. The content of this session was, not surprisingly, predominantly that of a "study-skills" group.

Two weeks later, the author again arranged a two-hour luncheon for each of the four groups. The topic of discussion at this time was centered again around academic and educational matters. At all times concern, understanding, and tolerance were expressed in an attempt to maintain good rapport.

Finally, each of these four groups met with the other groups for both the post-treatment and follow-up evaluations. Altogether, the no-treatment (placebo) control groups received approximately eleven hours of attention each.

No-contact control group

The twenty *S*s assigned to this group met all the selection criteria but were never contacted and thus were unaware of their participation in the study. Although the pre-treatment battery was taken with the other *S*s, the post-test and follow-up batteries were secured by mail under the guise of a "random sampling" for test validation. The answer sheets were coded, so that *S*s were not required to either sign or address them.

• *Experimental Design and Statistical Analysis*

The basic experimental design for this study, which is graphically presented in Table 2.6, emerged as a three-way

Table 2.6 • *Experimental design*

Client Personality Type	*Treatments*								
	Client-Centered		*Rational-Emotive*		*Systematic Desensitization*		*No-Treatment (Placebo) Control*		*No-Contact Control*
	C_1	C_2	C_3	C_4	C_5	C_6	C_7	C_7	
Introvert									
Extrovert									

Note: C = counselor.

analysis of variance (5 × 2 × 2) with counselors nested within treatments. The unit of analysis employed in testing the main effects of personality type and treatment, as well as their interaction, was the individual scores for each *S*.

Since *S*s were assigned at random, after selection on pretest data, the most appropriate statistical procedure is the analysis of variance of the post-test and follow-up mean scores. This design allows for a test of the main effects of personality type, treatment effects, and their respective interactions. Individual comparisons were then made to locate the specific source of significant variance by means of Scheffe's method of post hoc comparisons (Hayes, 1963, Chapter 14). The unit of analysis employed in making the Scheffe post hoc comparisons was the individual scores for each *S*.

· 3 ·

Analysis of results

Consistent with the research model presented in Chapter 1, the data reported in this chapter will be concerned with input, process, outcome, and follow-up variables.* It was felt that this procedure would provide a better understanding of the type of client being treated, the course of treatment with this type of client, and the eventual outcome and lasting effects. As indicated previously, the overall importance of this approach is to provide a clearer, more focused understanding of the outcome and follow-up results.

• *Input Data*

The date presented in this section is concerned with establishing the construct validity of the various scales employed in selecting and evaluating the *S* sample and, more importantly, in defining the target behaviors and personal-social characteristics of the *S*s in the various treatment and control groups. With regard to the former, Table 3.1 presents the intercorrelations of the various scales that were employed in this study.

*All tables and figures for this chapter appear at the end of the chapter. Tables begin on p. 104; figures begin on p. 149.

These correlations were based on the entire (unselected) sample tested (N = 217).

The relatively high correlation between the IPAS (Forms A and B) and the S-R_I, coupled with their low intercorrelation with other scales, indicates they are measuring essentially the same construct. Content and factor analysis suggests this construct is best labeled "interpersonal anxiety" (Endler et al., 1962). High scores on these scales seem most descriptive of the timid, socially insecure individual who experiences fear in connection with most aspects of interpersonal interaction (Levitt, 1967).

The moderately high intercorrelation between the TAI and the S-R_G, in addition to their low correlation with other scales, suggests they are measures of a common construct somewhat different in nature from interpersonal anxiety. Content and factor analysis indicates that this construct is best labeled "general anxiety" (Endler et al., 1962; Spielberger & Gorsuch, 1966). High scores on this instrument appear most descriptive of the so-called generally or chronically anxious individual, that is, one who has the personality trait of anxiousness and who fears most unknown situations (Levitt, 1967).

Finally, the relatively low intercorrelation between the SAI and the various other scales employed is consistent with the author's (Spielberger & Gorsuch, 1966) intent in designing this instrument as a measure of fluctuations in the state of anxiety from a base line determined by the TAI. Its sensitivity to fluctuations in anxiety level was the primary reason for employing this scale as a process measure to assess weekly changes in anxiety level during the course of treatment. Thus, in view of these data, it seems reasonable to conclude that the various self-report questionnaires employed in this study are measures of two relatively independent constructs, namely, interpersonal and general anxiety.

Table 3.2 presents an analysis of variance of the pre-test data on the *S*s selected for treatment (N = 100). The unit of analysis for comparing the main effects of personality and treatment, as well as their interaction, was the individual scores for each *S*.

As indicated earlier, there appear to be consistent and radical pre-treatment differences between introverts and extroverts on most all of the instruments employed. Of the five scales used to assess the target behaviors of interpersonal and general anxiety (IPAS, A & B; S-R_I; TAI; S-R_G), all but one showed a significant difference. A glance at the means presented in Table 3.3 indicates that prior to treatment introverts tended to report higher levels of anxiety than extroverts. Thus, in addition to the hypothesized differences between introverts and extroverts presented in Chapter 1, these two groups appear to differ in actual anxiety level as well.

Furthermore, there appear to be reliable pretreatment differences between introverts and extroverts on behavior ratings of interpersonal anxiety and defensiveness. In this case, the means in Table 3.3 indicate that the extroverts scored higher than the introverts. Although at first blush this may seem contradictory, two possible explanations seem relevant.

First, one might hypothesize that since the extroverts are significantly more defensive, they would be expected to score lower on self-report questionnaires but not on behavior ratings secured by impartial, objective observers. Similarly, introvert-extrovert differences in behavior ratings could be explained by reference to the former group's tendency to "internalize" anxiety, producing increased psychophysiological changes and cognitive complaints, and the latter group's tendency to "externalize" anxiety, producing increased motoric and behavioral changes (Buss, 1962, 1966; Hamilton, 1959). This would lead to the conclusion that what is reflected here is a difference in defensiveness and *mode* of anxiety expression but not anxiety level *per se*. An alternative hypothesis would be that since extroverts are probably more animated to begin with, simply because they are extroverts, one would expect higher scores on *behavior* ratings for this group. This would lead to the conclusion that extroverts are, indeed, less anxious than introverts, as these self-report measures suggest.

There is some evidence to support both of the above views. The latter hypothesis seems consistent with the fact that the introverts scored significantly higher ($t = 3.47$, $p < .001$) on the Neuroticism Scale of the *Maudsley Personality Inventory* (Eysenck, 1962).[1] However, advocates of the former thesis could rebut with the disclaimer that this is simply another self-report questionnaire subject to the extrovert's defensiveness. In spite of the intuitive appeal of the "extroverts are healthier" hypothesis, this view fails to account for the fact that the extroverts did score *higher* on measures of defensiveness. By the same token, however, the former, more "dynamic" hypothesis, while explaining the obtained results well, certainly goes far beyond the data for its explanation and, in so doing, contradicts some extant evidence regarding extroversion and interpersonal anxiety (Eysenck, 1960, Eysenck & Rachman, 1965, Wienstein, 1968). Perhaps the results of this study, to be presented later, will shed further light on this issue.

Finally, a lack of significant personality main effects on the MBTI indicates no difference in the intensity of introversion and extroversion, that is, the introverts were no more introverted than the extroverts were extroverted. Similarly, none of the treatment main effects or the treatment by personality interactions were significant at pre-testing, indicating random assignment within the limits of chance expectations.

In conclusion, actuarial interpretation of these pre-test data indicates two distinct types of client. On the one hand, there is the group labeled introverts who report high anxiety and low defensiveness but do not exhibit a large number of overt behavioral manifestations of anxiety. On the other hand, there is the group labeled extroverts who report moderate lev-

1. This scale was administered by the instructor to the entire class at the time of the first class meeting but was not used as part of the regular test battery.

els of anxiety, high defensiveness, and exhibit a large number of overt behavioral manifestations usually thought to be indicative of anxiety.

This is a rather interesting finding in that it suggests that researchers who select *S*s on the basis of high self-reported anxiety are selecting predominantly introverts, whereas those who select *S*s who report only moderate levels of anxiety are selecting extroverts. The reverse holds true of *S*s selected on behavioral criteria. Perhaps this is one reason for the contradictory findings in this area (Frank, 1961; Levitt, 1967; Lorr et al., 1958; Spielberger, 1966; Sprinthall, 1967; Weinstein, 1968).

Since the (input) data on therapist personal-social characteristics were presented in detail in the previous chapter, they will not be elaborated on again here.

• *Process Data*

The data reported in this section are concerned with accounting for as much of the client's and therapist's behavior during the treatment period as possible. With regard to client variables, data on changes in target behaviors both within and outside of the treatment setting, level of self-exploration, and self-report observations on crucial client behaviors prior to, during, and following treatment are reported. With regard to therapist variables, data on in-treatment therapist behavior, level of therapeutic conditions offered, and changes in client target behaviors, as viewed by the therapist, are also reported.

Data on client variables

Table 3.4 presents the total amount of treatment received by *S*s in each of the treatment groups and the amount of attention given the no-treatment (placebo) control *S*s. Although the range is fairly substantial (roughly one hour), especially in view of the limited number of contact hours, the differences appear to be fairly evenly distributed, at least across treatments, if not counselors. When viewed in relation to the outcome results to be presented later, however, any biasing which may have resulted seems to favor the treatment groups who improved least receiving the most treatment. Thus, in and of itself, gross differences in treatment time did not appear to have a major influence on the treatment outcomes.

Table 3.5 presents the number of interviews missed by each *S* for the nine treatment sessions. Since make-up sessions were not possible, it was felt that this data might prove important in attempting to account for the outcome results obtained. Apparently, the distribution of missed sessions across treatments and counselors was relatively constant. Approximately one-third of the sample (31 *S*s) missed one treatment session. Only two *S*s missed two sessions and no *S*s missed three or more sessions. In no instance were there less than four group members present at any one meeting. Since the distribution of missed sessions was fairly uniform across treatments and counselors, this variable probably did not influence the outcome results systematically and thus can be ruled out as a viable explanatory hypothesis.

Table 3.6 presents the number of extra treatment sessions received by each *S* prior to, during, and following treatment. Since it was impossible to control additional treatment received by each *S*, it was felt that this data might prove to be a salient factor in understanding the treatment outcomes.

Prior to treatment, 12 *S*s, or roughly 10 percent of the sample, reported receiving a total of 69 treatment interviews of which 24 were for educational-vocational concerns (see items marked with an a) and 45 for personal-social concerns. Although the distribution of extra, pre-treatment interviews was far from uniform, in only two cases (counselor C's extroverts and counselor R's introverts) was the deviation severe.

During treatment, 13 *S*s, or again approximately 10 percent of the sample, reported receiving 33 additional treatment interviews, five of which were educational-vocational and 28 personal-social in nature. In only four cases was extra treatment received by the same *S* both prior to and during treatment (see items marked with a b). Although the distribution of extra in-treatment interviews was by no means uniform, again, only two radical departures appeared (counselor C's introverts and counselor r's extroverts). Fortunately, however, 10 of the 13 *S*s who received additional in-treatment interviews were the same *S*s who missed one or more of the regularly scheduled treatment sessions, vitiating somewhat the importance of these extra interviews.

Finally, eight *S*s, or again about 10 percent of the sample, reported receiving 13 additional treatment interviews during the follow-up period, all of which were for personal-social reasons. In only one instance was additional treatment received by the same *S* during both treatment and follow-up periods (see items marked with a b). No *S*s reported receiving extra treatment interviews both prior to and following the treatment period.

Because of the sporadic and uncontrollable nature of the additional treatment received, and since tactical decisions favor maintenance and assessment of the entire sample (Campbell & Stanley, 1963), this factor could not be ruled out completely as a potential explanation of the treatment outcomes. It should be noted, however, that when the data in Table 3.6 are compared with the outcome results in the next section, those *S*s who sought and received additional counseling both during and following treatment were, by and large, *S*s from groups which showed the least improvement. This is especially true of those *S*s who received additional treatment during the follow-up period.

Figure 3.1 presents the mean level of client intrapersonal or self-exploration for each treatment session and for each of the CC and RT counselor's introverts and extroverts. These data were obtained by taking four, five-minute samples—one near the beginning, two near the middle, and one near the end—of each tape-recorded interview for counselor's C, c, R, and r. Two undergraduate psychology majors, equipped only with the manual presented by Truax & Carkhuff (1967, pp. 194-208) and working independently of one another, rated each of the tape segments. The total score, derived by pooling the mean scores for each tape across raters, dividing by two, and rounding to the nearest half-number, thus served as an objective indicant of the level of client self-exploration for each group and each treatment session.[2] The interrater reliability, computed on the raw observations, was .813.

Since it was impossible to secure similar data on a comparable control group, the most convenient unit of comparison was the frequency of scores above and below the level three, the figure which the authors (Truax & Carkhuff, 1967) feel represents the minimum level of client self-exploration which is therapeutic.

Before examining more closely the impact of the various treatments on the level of client self-exploration, it should be noted that at least three common situational factors seem to have influenced all the remaining process data. At roughly the time of the third interview and during the week of the sixth interview, each *S* was preparing for mid-term and psychology course examinations, respectively. Finally, during the week of the post-test evaluations, each *S* was in the process of preparing for and taking final examinations. Thus, radical and con-

2. Mean score in this case represents the sum of the depth of self-exploration scores for one tape-recorded interview (four, five-minute samples) divided by the number of scores summed to equal that total. In other words, if the overall score obtained by one rater for one tape was 21.3 (raw observation) and eight ratings summed to equal this score, the mean would be 2.67. If the mean for the second rater for the same four, five-minute samples was 3.32, the total score would be the combined mean (5.99), divided by two (2.99), and rounded to the nearest half-number (3.00).

sistent changes at these points were probably more a function of situational factors rather than treatment effects.

Simple observation reveals that nearly all the CC interviews with extroverted *S*s and all the RT interviews with introverted *S*s were well beyond the minimum prescribed level, while only half of the CC interviews with introverts and half of the RT interviews with extroverts were beyond this minimal level. In addition, while there tends to be a marked similarity across counselors (within treatment) for the former two groups, there appears to be a marked dissimilarity between counselors (within treatment) for the latter two groups. That is, whereas CC counselor c's introverts and RT counselor R's extroverts seem to have achieved satisfactory, if only intermediate, levels of self-exploration, CC counselor C's introverts and RT counselor r's extroverts achieved only "average" levels, at best. This "interaction," as we shall see later, was probably due to changes in in-treatment behavior on the part of counselors c and R. As indicated above, however, an interview-by-interview comparison of both CC counselors' extroverted *S*s and both RT counselors' introverted *S*s reveals a marked similarity, with all four groups of *S*s achieving the greatest amount and depth of self-exploration.

Those portions of the SD interviews concerned with hierarchy construction were also rated as to level of client intrapersonal exploration. At no time during these periods did the depth of client self-exploration exceed the three level, thus ruling out this factor as a possible explanation of the SD outcome results.

Figure 3.2 presents a graphic representation of the mean changes in anxiety level throughout the course of therapy for treatment and no-treatment (placebo) control *S*s. The same interpretative restrictions presented earlier regarding the third, sixth, and post-test interviews are relevant here also.

As predicted, the C treatment approach seems to have produced the greatest amount of anxiety reduction with extroverted *S*s while the SD and RT treatment approaches resulted in the greatest amount of anxiety reduction with introverted *S*s. Similarly, as predicted, all forms of treatment appear to have been more effective in reducing anxiety than simple attention or the nonspecific, ancillary benefits derived from personal contact, interviewing, and expectation of future treatment and relief. These conclusions seem to hold regardless of whether the unit of analysis is mean change from pre- to post-testing or simply the ultimate post-test mean.

A closer examination of the individual counselor effects reveals a marked similarity between the various aforementioned counselors. The post-test means and mean pre-post change scores for the CC counselors' extroverts were 41 and 39 and 13 and 11, respectively. For the SD counselors' introverts the post-test means and mean pre-post changes were 36 and 35 and 18 and 18, respectively. The same scores for the RT counselors' introverts were 39 and 38 and 27 and 15, respectively.

With regard to the remaining groups, the extroverts receiving SD improved far beyond expectation, equaling the CC extroverts in both post-test mean scores (40 and 30) and mean pre-post anxiety reduction (12 and 10). As predicted, both the CC introverts and the RT extroverts seem to have improved least, with RT counselor R's extroverts (post-test mean, 42; mean pre-post change, 7) and CC counselor c's introverts (post-test mean, 45; mean pre-post change, 10) improving somewhat and RT counselor r's extroverts (post-test mean, 46; mean pre-post change, 2) and CC counselor C's introverts (post-test mean, 54; mean pre-post change, 2) showing even less anxiety reduction than the comparable no-treatment (placebo) control groups (post-test means and mean pre-post changes were 48 and 55, and 4 and 4 for the introverted *S*s and 44 and 48 and 4 and 4 for the extroverted *S*s, respectively). Finally, it appears that the placebo treatment exhibited a fairly uniform influence on both the introverted and extroverted no-treatment (placebo) control *S*s.

It is interesting to note that these latter "interaction" effects follow very closely the data reported earlier on level of client self-exploration. That is, counselor R's extroverts and counselor c's introverts engaged in more and deeper, if only intermediate, levels of self-exploration and showed more anxiety reduction than either counselor r's extroverts or counselor C's introverts. Similarly, both CC counselors' extroverted *S*s and both RT counselors' introverted *S*s explored the most and at the deepest levels, and that these four groups improved the most, SD treatments not included. These findings are consistent with the data reported by Carkhuff & Berenson (1967), Rogers et al. (1967), and Truax & Carkhuff (1967).

Level of client self-exploration does seem to be a predictor variable as far as process measures of anxiety reduction are concerned. *S*s who explore more and at deeper levels show greater amounts of anxiety reduction than those who explore little or at only intermediate levels. Those *S*s who explore the least show no greater improvement than those receiving simple attention or the so-called non-specific benefits derived from personal contact, interviewing, and expectation of future treatment and relief.

Finally, there appears to be a relationship between the in-treatment, self-reported anxiety level and the degree of client self-exploration during treatment. Whereas with the CC treatment approach the deepest levels of client self-exploration tended to occur in conjunction with low levels of client self-reported anxiety, just the opposite seems to hold for the RT treatment approach. The greatest levels of client self-exploration seemed to occur in the context of high levels of self-reported anxiety. This is not the complete story, however, since as seen earlier, the CC treatment approach produced the greatest amount of anxiety reduction with extroverts while the RT treatment approach produced the greatest amount of anxiety reduction with introverted *S*s. Thus, a more accurate statement of this relationship would be that the CC extroverts engaged in more frequent and deeper levels of self-exploration in conjunction with low levels of self-reported anxiety, whereas the RT introverts engaged in more frequent and deeper levels of self-exploration in conjunction with high levels of self-reported anxiety. As we shall see when examining therapist in-treatment behavior, the two *apparent* exceptions to this rule, counselor c's introverts and counselor R's extroverts, actually further substantiate this finding.

Although it is impossible to specify the direction of this cause-effect relationship, or whether it is due to treatment, therapist, or client variables, some speculation seems relevant here. Namely, that both Roger's notion of therapy as a "psychologically safe" relationship and Ellis's notion of therapy as a probing, challenging, and confronting one, are consistent with these findings.

Figure 3.3 presents each therapist's rating of weekly changes in mean anxiety level for each of the treatment groups only. The most outstanding feature of these data is the somewhat unexpected agreement between *S*'s self-reports (Figure 3.2) and therapist's ratings (Figure 3.3) regarding the course of anxiety reduction during treatment. A session-by-session examination of each graph reveals *no* marked discrepancies between the counselor's view of the *S*'s anxiety level and the *S*'s view of his own anxiety level. In fact, in most cases, the therapists were even able to detect changes in the *S*'s anxiety level which were due to situational influences other than the treatment (third and sixth interviews).

Once again, observation of these process data seem to suggest that the CC (post-test means, 2.0 and 2.0; mean pre-post changes, 2.0 and 1.7) and SD (post-test means, 2.0 and 1.7; mean pre-post changes, 2.0 and 1.3) treatment approaches were the most effective in reducing interpersonal anxiety with extroverted *S*s, while the RT (post-test means, 1.6 and 1.7; mean pre-post changes, 2.4 and 2.3) and SD (post-test means, 1.7 and 1.6; mean pre-post changes, 2.8 and 1.9) treatment approaches appeared most effective in reducing interpersonal anxiety with introverted *S*s. As in Figure 3.2, the differential effectiveness of SD with introverts and extroverts, while in the predicted direction, was small and probably not significant, especially in view of the large introvert-extrovert differences with the CC and RT approaches.

A closer examination of the individual counselor effects reveals a similar type of "interaction" as reported earlier. That is, CC counselor c's introverts (post-test mean, 2.7; mean pre-post change, 1.3) improved more than CC counselor C's introverts (post-test mean, 3.5; mean pre-post change, 0.6) and RT counselor R's extroverts (post-test mean, 2.7; mean pre-post change, 1.3) improved more than RT counselor r's extroverts (post-test mean, 3.2; mean pre-post change, 0.3). As before, the "interaction" between the SD counselors and *S* personality type appears minimal, if not non-existent.

From both the point of view of those receiving treatment and those administering it, the general consensus seems to favor the SD treatment approach over both the CC and RT approaches when *S* personality type is ignored. When *S* personality is considered, the CC and SD treatment regimes seem to be equally effective in producing the greatest amount of anxiety reduction in extroverted *S*s, while the RT and SD treatment approaches appear equally as effective in producing the greatest amount of anxiety reduction in introverted *S*s.

Finally, as before, the data presented in Figure 3.3 appear to again support the hypothesis that extroverted *S*s explore their interpersonal problems more and at deeper levels in a non-anxiety producing, "psychologically safe" environment, that is, with CC treatment, whereas the introverted *S*s seem to explore their personal problems more and at a deeper level in the context of a probing, confronting, and rather anxiety-inducing atmosphere, that is, with RT treatment.

Figure 3.4 presents weekly changes in the mean number of interpersonal contacts outside of the treatment setting for each of the treatment and no-treatment (placebo) control *S*s. The three interpretative restrictions imposed earlier remain relevant here as well. Furthermore, the generally quadratic shape of these graphs may have been the result of two additional factors. First, this was the beginning of a new school year for the returning sophomores (30 percent of the sample) and the beginning of university life *per se* for the new, incoming freshmen (70 percent of the sample). Consequently, the initially sharp rise in interpersonal activity by these *S*s probably reflects a natural process of "familiarization" among students. Second, in addition to slight drops around the third and sixth interviews, there is a marked decline in interpersonal contacts near the end of the treatment period. This probably reflects the more or less natural curtailment in interpersonal activity imposed by the restrictions inherent in preparing for and taking final examinations.

However, in addition to the aforementioned general influences, there appear to be some differential, specific effects due to the impact of the various treatment approaches. With regard to the introverted *S*s, simple attention and expectation of relief seems to have had little or no effect on the frequency of client interpersonal activity outside of treatment (post-test means, 2.0 and 2.2; mean pre-post changes, 0.1 and 0.2). Similarly, CC counselor C's introverts did not improve either (post-test mean, 2.2; mean pre-post change, 0.0), while counselor c's introverts showed some noticeable increase in interpersonal activity as treatment progressed (post-test mean, 3.0; mean pre-post change, 1.1). Once again, this appears to be consistent with the previous findings regarding the differential depth of self-exploration and anxiety reduction for these two groups during treatment. Finally, the most substantial gains in behavior change outside of treatment were obtained by the SD and RT counselor's introverted *S*s. The former groups doubled the frequency of their interpersonal activity (post-test means, 4.0 and 4.3; mean pre-post changes, 2.5 and 2.4), while the latter groups tripled theirs (post-test means, 5.1 and 5.2; mean pre-post changes, 3.2 and 3.6) by the time of post-testing.

While previous self-report measures seemed to indicate that the SD and RT treatment approaches were about equally effective in reducing interpersonal anxiety with introverted *S*s, in the terms of changes in target behaviors outside of the treatment setting, the RT treatment approach appears to have produced a *greater* increase in interpersonal activity. Part of this may be due to the fact that weekly homework assignments by the RT therapists "forced" these *S*s to interact more socially or at least report such interactions, since they were an integral part of the in-treatment, weekly discussions. In any event, the benefits which accrued from the RT treatment approach did appear to be more quickly implemented into activity outside of treatment than those resulting from the SD approach. It is unfortunate, however, that follow-up data on this variable could not be obtained to see if this pattern maintained itself.

With regard to the extroverts, there do not seem to be any consistent differences among the various treatments or between the treatment and control groups. Apparently, extroverts continue to remain quite active socially, in spite of their self-reported anxiety and discomfort in social situations. It seems that the extrovert's strong need for people and social activity (Eysenck, 1960; Eysenck & Rachman, 1965), generally overrides the anxiety generated by this same stimulus source.

Data on therapist variables

Table 3.7 presents the percent of time spent in conversation and silence by each of the CC and RT counselors and clients. Since the operations required in obtaining these gross time intervals were fairly objective, involving a minimum of judgment, and thus rater bias, these data were secured by the author. Each category (counselor, client, silence) was timed separately, by means of a stop watch, requiring three separate runs through the sampled segments. This entire procedure was performed twice, with a two-week interval between ratings, yielding a correlation of .946, across categories, for the two separate ratings. The tape samples employed in estimating these frequencies were the same as those used to secure the data presented in Figure 3.1 and Table 3.7.

Observation of these data reveals that regardless of client personality type both CC counselors tended to be less active verbally than either RT counselor. Furthermore, whereas this less active verbal stance on the part of the CC counselors tended to result in both increased speech activity and fewer silences on the part of the extroverted *S*s, it resulted in less speech activity and more silence on the part of the introverted *S*s. Conversely, the RT counselors' more active verbal stance yielded less speech activity and more silence from the extroverted *S*s but seemed to elicit more speech activity and a minimum of silence from the introverted *S*s.

A closer examination of the individual counselor effects reveals that whereas counselors C and r remained about as active verbally with both introverts and extroverts, counselors c and R changed their verbal activity level somewhat, counselor c becoming more active with his introverted *S*s and counselor R less active with his extroverted *S*s. These changes in therapist behavior produced proportional changes in the amount of client speech behavior and silence. The result was an increase in the former and a decrease in the latter. The differences in speech activity level between counselors c and R and counselors C and r may account partially for the increased effectiveness of the former with introverted and extroverted *S*s, in terms of client level of self-exploration (Figure

3.1), reduction in process measures of target symptoms and complaints (Figures 3.2 and 3.3), and increased interpersonal activity outside of treatment (Figure 3.4).

To gain a better qualitative appreciation for the kinds of counselor speech behaviors which comprised these gross frequency groupings, the counselor category was further divided into more specific responses and categorized by type and frequency of occurrence. Table 3.8 presents the frequency of use of specific techniques by each of the CC and RT therapists for each *S* personality type. This data was obtained from the same tape segments employed in securing the data presented in Figure 3.1 and Table 3.7. After each rater had rated those portions of the tape samples containing segments of the client's speech for level of self-exploration (see Figure 3.1), the same raters, still working independently of one another, went back and rated those portions of the same tape samples containing segments of the therapist's speech, categorizing according to the manual presented in Appendix I[3] each counselor's statement by content and frequency. The inter-rater reliability, computed on the raw frequency count, was .781. The data presented in Table 3.8 represents a pooled average of each rater's score for each content category.

Simple observation reveals that within-treatment differences among therapists were substantially less than between-treatment differences. The CC counselors relied most on reflection and clarification, suggestion, redirection of questions back to the group, and self-disclosure. The RT therapists, on the other hand, relied on direct confrontation, information and advice giving, and homework assignments. All counselors employed questioning, interpretation, and reinforcement with about equal frequency. A closer look at the points of emphasis of the CC and RT counselors reveals that the former group of

3. Neither rater was informed of this second rating of therapist verbal behavior until the first rating of client level of self-exploration was completed.

therapists tended to address their techniques to the client's feelings or feeling states, while the latter group addressed their techniques to the client's thinking and behavior.

An examination of the individual counselor effects reveals, once again, that while counselors C and r tended to behave almost identically with both introverted and extroverted *S*s, counselors c and R changed their approach or counseling style somewhat depending on the personality type of the group members. This change in counseling style resulted in counselor c becoming more active, directive, and leading with his introverts than counselor C, emphasizing cognitive rather than feeling states: while counselor R became more passive and nondirective with his extroverts than counselor r, emphasizing feeling rather than cognitive states.

Thus, while both CC and RT counselors behaved similarly and as predicted with extroverted and introverted *S*s, respectively, their behavior with the remaining *S* was quite variable. This variability appears to be the result of a change in in-treatment counselor behavior on the part of therapists c and R only. The direction of this change was to make therapist C's counseling style with introverted *S*s more like that expected of an RT counselor and to make therapist R's counseling style with extroverted *S*s more like that expected of a CC counselor.

In view of the information gained from Tables 3.7 and 3.8, the date presented in Figures 3.1 through 3.4 become somewhat more understandable. What seems to be suggested here is that the CC treatment approach produced the greatest amount of verbal activity with extroverted *S*s while the RT treatment approach produced the greatest amount of verbal activity with introverted *S*s. Furthermore, as treatment progressed, the content of these particular *S*s' increased speech activity seemed to move from silences and statements characterized as personally irrelevant, that is, not related to the presenting problem, to statements characterized by acceptance of the problem of interpersonal anxiety and exploration of its implications. Finally, as these *S*s became more active and probing, exploring their anxiety at a greater depth, they reported progressively fewer symptoms and complaints commonly viewed as indicative of anxiety and engaged in progressively more interpersonal activity outside of the treatment setting.

In order to better understand the therapist's role in initiating or failing to initiate this process of *S* self-exploration, the nine CC and RT treatment interviews were grouped into thirds with the data presented in Table 3.7 and the totals of each of the treatment techniques presented in Table 3.8 recalculated in terms of their frequency of occurrence in each of these three time periods. This data is presented in Tables 3.9 and 3.10.

Observation of these process data reveals that the initial treatment sessions were occupied predominantly by therapist speech activity. The nature and content of this activity seems to have been determined largely by the therapist's school affiliation, with the CC counselor's verbal activity consisting almost exclusively of reflection and clarification, suggestion, redirection of questions back to the group, and self-disclosure; and the RT counselor's verbal activity consisting predominantly of direct confrontation and information and advice giving. During the second phase, client speech activity tended to increase, while counselor speech activity in all but one category (reinforcement) tended to decrease somewhat. The final phase consisted of a predominance of client speech activity and a further decrease in all categories of therapist speech activity with the exception of reinforcement.

These data seem best explained in terms of the concepts of modeling and behavioral shaping (Bandura & Walters, 1963). During the initial treatment sessions, the therapist performs (that is, models) the behaviors which he wishes the *S*s to employ in exploring the problem of interpersonal anxiety. The behaviors he models are a product of his therapeutic model or particular school affiliation. As each *S* begins to explore his presenting problem, the therapist uses approval and disapproval to shape the *S*'s behavior so that it begins to successively approximate or match that which the counselor desires. During the final stages of treatment, the *S*s begin to explore, probe, and confront their own thoughts, feelings, and verbalizations, and the counselor simply encourages and reinforces this pattern of verbal behavior. Thus, in the final stages of successful treatment, the *S*s were doing to themselves what initially the counselors were doing for or to them.

A very similar sequential pattern has been noted by other investigators of the psychotherapeutic process (Bandura & Walters, 1963; Truax & Carkhuff, 1967). This same sequential process has been noted in the course of socialization during child development (Bandura & Walters, 1963).

An attempt to distinguish the most effective from the least effective counselors reveals that the sequence of therapist-*S* behaviors described above is clearly evident in those counseling relationships where the greatest amount of anxiety reduction was achieved with the widest variety of clients. The relative presence or absence of this sequence, then, does seem predictive of the amount of anxiety reduction reported by *S*s during the course of treatment. However, the so-called "central therapeutic ingredients" (Truax & Carkhuff, 1967) of accurate empathy, non-possessive warmth, genuineness, etc., did not distinguish between either treatment and no-treatment (placebo) control *S*s or among the various treatments (see Table 3.11). However, it should be noted that all of these mean scores were at or beyond the minimum level at which a relationship may be considered therapeutic (Carkhuff & Berenson, 1967; Truax & Carkhuff, 1967).

What is tentatively suggested here is that the central therapeutic ingredient in traditional, verbal counseling and psychotherapy is depth or level of client self-exploration and that a variety of treatment techniques are required to encourage *S*s to engage in this process, depending on their presenting problem and personality makeup. The variables of accurate empathy, nonpossessive warmth, genuineness, etc., are, at best, necessary but not sufficient conditions for therapeutic change.

• *Outcome Data*

Table 3.13 presents an analysis of variance of the post-test means using the individual scores as the unit of analysis. As indicated, all but the *Edwards Social Desirability Scale* (ESD) showed treatment and personality x treatment effects which were significant beyond the .05 level. No attempt was made to interpret the findings regarding the personality main effects since initial pretreatment differences make these comparisons invalid.

Treatment main effects

Table 3.16 presents the Scheffe post hoc comparisons for the treatment main effects. The unit of analysis was individual scores summed across counselor and *S* personality type, within treatment.

With the exception of the IIA, all of the treatments were significantly different from either of the control conditions. It appears, then, that any of these forms of counseling produces significantly greater decrements in interpersonal and general anxiety than simply the passage of time or the non-specific ancillary benefits derived from testing, interviewing, and the expectation of future treatment and relief. However, only the SD and RT treatment approaches were able to produce significantly greater changes in interpersonal activity outside of the treatment setting. The CC treatment approach produced no greater increase in interpersonal activity than the no-treatment (placebo) control condition.

An examination of the relative treatment effects reveals no significant differences between the CC and RT treatment approaches on any of the self-reports or behavior ratings of interpersonal and general anxiety. However, the SD treatment approach was significantly different from either of the CC or RT treatments. Thus, when *S* personality type and individual counselor effects are not considered, the SD treatment approach appears to result in the greatest amount of anxiety reduction. The RT and CC treatments were about equally as effective, producing significantly less anxiety reduction than the SD approach but significantly more anxiety reduction than either the no-treatment (placebo) control of the no-contact control conditions.

With regard to changes in interpersonal activity outside of treatment, the findings are somewhat reversed. The RT treatment approach produced the greatest increase in interpersonal activity outside of treatment with the SD approach showing a significantly smaller increment than the RT treatment but a significantly larger increment than either the CC or no-treatment (placebo) control conditions. The latter two groups showed no significant differences. This apparent contradiction will be better understood when *S* personality type is examined in closer detail.

Figure 3.5 presents a graphic representation of the mean reduction in self-reports and behavior ratings of interpersonal anxiety, general anxiety, and defensiveness from pre- to post-testing. These value were computed by subtracting the summed average of the post-test means across instruments, counselors, and *S* personality type from the summed average of the pre-test means.[4]

As can be seen from these graphs, the no-treatment (placebo) control condition was roughly twice as effective in

4. Interpersonal anxiety on all the remaining figures and graphs is operationally defined as the combined average of the post-test means on the IPAS and $S\text{-}R_I$ minus the combined average of the pre-test means of these same scales. Similarly, general anxiety is defined as the combined average of the post-test means on the TAI and $S\text{-}R_G$ minus the combined average of the pre-test means on these same scales.

reducing self-reports of anxiety as the no-contact control condition. Similarly, both the RT and CC treatments were about twice again as effective in reducing anxiety as the no-treatment (placebo) control conditions but only approximately two-thirds as effective as the SD treatment approach. Finally, whereas the CC and RT treatments were about four times as effective in reducing anxiety as the no-contact control condition, the SD treatment approach was roughly six times as effective as the simple passage of time.

In order to gain a better appreciation for the true impact of the various treatments administered, the effects of simple attention and expectation of future treatment and relief were subtracted from each of the treatment conditions. Figure 3.6 presents the mean reduction in self-reports and behavior ratings of interpersonal anxiety, general anxiety, and defensiveness from pre- to post-testing with placebo effects removed from each of the treatment conditions. The data reported here were derived in the same manner as the data presented in Figure 3.5.

Treatment x personality type effects

Table 3.17 presents the Scheffe post hoc comparisons for the treatment x *S* personality type interactions. The unit of analysis was individual scores summed across counselor within treatment. No attempt was made to interpret the italicized tabled values, that is, the second order interactions, since, with the exception of the S-R_G, differential starting position effects make these comparisons invalid.

TREATMENT X EXTROVERT PERSONALITY TYPE EFFECTS. With regard to the various measures of interpersonal and general anxiety, no significant differences were obtained between the no-treatment (placebo) control and the no-contact control extrovert groups. Similarly, no significant differences were found on any of these measures between extroverts treated by means of RT and those given only attention or no treatment at all. Finally, all extroverted *S*s treated by CC and SD improved significantly more than any of the control or RT extroverts, but did not differ significantly from each other.

Apparently, then, extroverted *S*s improve as much on their own as they do under conditions of attention, interviewing, etc., or when treated by means of RT. The only treatment regimes which had a significant impact on extroverted *S*s were the CC and SD approaches, which were equally effective in reducing interpersonal and general anxiety. Finally, in terms of changes in interpersonal activity outside of treatment (IIA), there were no significant differences among the various treatments or between treatment and control extroverts. All of these outcome results are consistent with the process data reported in the previous section.

TREATMENT X INTROVERT PERSONALITY TYPE EFFECTS. With regard to the various self-report measures of interpersonal and general anxiety, all scales showed a significant difference between the no-treatment (placebo) control and the no-contact control introverts. Similarly, significant differences were obtained on all of these measures between introverts treated by RT or SD and introverts given only attention or no treatment at all. Finally, while the introverts treated by means of the CC approach improved more than those given no treatment at all, they showed no significantly greater anxiety reduction than the no-treatment (placebo) control *S*s.

Thus, while introverts, unlike extroverts, showed significant decrements in interpersonal and general anxiety due to simple attention, interviewing, and expectation of future treatment and relief, they did not show any increased anxiety reduction when treated by means of CC counseling. The only treatment regimes which had a significant impact on introverted *S*s beyond simple attention, etc., were the RT and SD approaches, both of which were equally as effective in reducing self-reports and behavior ratings of interpersonal and general anxiety.

In terms of changes in behavior outside of the treatment setting (IIA), the RT approach produced significantly more increments in interpersonal activity than the SD approach. The SD approach, in turn, produced significantly more interpersonal activity outside of treatment than the CC or no-treatment (placebo) control conditions, the latter two showing no significant differences. These outcome results are consistent with the process data reported earlier.

Figure 3.7 presents a graphic representation of the mean pre-post reduction in self-reports and behavior ratings of interpersonal anxiety, general anxiety, and defensiveness for each treatment and *S* personality type. These values were computed by subtracting the summed average of the post-test means across instruments and counselors from the summed average of the pre-test means.

Clearly, the impact of simple attention and interviewing had no greater effect on extroverted *S*'s self-reports of anxiety than simply the passage of time. In contrast, the same placebo conditions resulted in approximately four times as much anxiety reduction in introverted *S*'s self-reports than no treatment at all. The fact that extroverts were so active socially, however, indicates that perhaps the no-contact control group was actually a placebo control in disguise, at least for the extroverted *S*s, and that the anxiety reduction noted here is not due simply to the passage of time but rather to uncontrolled placebo effects resulting from the extrovert's excessive interpersonal activity. Nevertheless, the fact that the no-contact control extroverts showed more improvement on their own and were less inhibited in their interpersonal activity outside of the treatment setting is consistent with their significantly lower pre-test self-reported anxiety level and suggests that perhaps the extroverts, at least the ones in this study, were "healthier" than the introverts prior to treatment.

The fact that extroverted *S*s improved most when treated by the CC and SD approaches is amply visible in Figure 3.7.

Each of these treatment regimes resulted in roughly three times as much anxiety reduction as either the no-treatment (placebo) control or no-contact control groups. Similarly, their nearest competitor, the RT treatment approach, was still only half as effective as either the CC or SD treatments in reducing *S* self-reports and behavior ratings of interpersonal and general anxiety. Finally, as indicated previously, no significant differences were obtained for any of the treatment x extrovert personality type interactions on the IIA.

Introverted *S*s, on the other hand, showed approximately four times as much anxiety reduction when treated by means of RT and SD, as compared to the no-treatment (placebo) control introverts, and ten times as much improvement, on the same criteria, as those introverts given no treatment at all. In addition, the CC treatment appeared only one-third as effective in reducing anxiety in introverts as the RT and SD approaches. Lastly, the clear superiority of the RT treatment with regard to changes in behavior outside of the therapy setting is also visibly evident here. The RT treatment approach was roughly twice as effective in increasing the interpersonal activity of introverted *S*s as either the CC or no-treatment (placebo) control conditions. Its nearest competitor, the SD treatment, was only two-thirds as effective as RT in increasing the interpersonal activity of introverts outside of treatment.

In order to test the within treatment x *S* personality type interactions, *t* tests were computed on the mean pre-post change scores. These *t* values, as well as their *p* levels, are reported in Table 3.18. As indicated, introverts and extroverts treated by means of either the CC or RT approaches, as well as those given no treatment at all, showed marked and significant differences. These differences, as shown in Figure 3.7, indicate that the CC treatment was about two and a half times more effective in reducing anxiety with extroverts as opposed to introverts, whereas the no-contact control condition was about five times more effective with extroverts than introverts.

Conversely, the RT treatment approach was almost three times more effective in reducing anxiety with introverts than with extroverts. Neither the SD nor the no-treatment (placebo) control conditions showed any significant introvert-extrovert differences on any of the self-reports or behavior ratings of interpersonal and general anxiety. However, in the case of both measures of anxiety, the means for the SD treatment were in the predicted direction, whereas in the case of the behavior ratings they were in the opposite direction, with extroverted *S*s showing slightly more improvement than introverted *S*s. Since no significant differences appeared among extroverted *S*s on the IIA, no further comparisons would be meaningful; and thus, none were made.

Once again, in order to gain a better appreciation of the true impact of the various treatment x *S* personality type interactions, the effects of simple attention and expectation of future treatment and relief were subtracted from each of the treatment conditions. Figure 3.8 presents the mean pre-post reduction in self-reports and behavior ratings of interpersonal anxiety, general anxiety, and defensiveness for each treatment and *S* personality type with placebo effects removed from each of the treatment conditions. These values were derived in the same manner as the data presented in Figure 3.7.

Counselor main effects

Table 3.19 presents the Scheffe post hoc comparisons for the counselor main effects. The unit of analysis was individual scores summed across *S* personality type within treatment. Since counselors were nested within-treatment, and only two therapists were employed as representative of each treatment approach, considerable caution should be exercised in interpreting these findings. However, as can be seen, the outcome results regarding individual differences in counselor effectiveness are consistent with the process data reported in the previous section. That is, there were no significant differences on any of the self-reports or behavior ratings of interpersonal and general anxiety between either the two no-contact control groups, the two no-treatment (placebo) control groups, or the two SD groups. However, the differences between the two RT and the two CC counselors were all significant at the .05 level.

Further analysis of the outcome results also indicates no significant differences, across "schools," between counselors C and r, on the one hand, and counselors c and R, on the other. Overall, then, the two SD counselors proved the most effective in reducing interpersonal and general anxiety, with counselors c and R significantly less effective than counselors B and b but significantly more effective than counselors C and r. These outcome results are identical to the process data reported earlier.

Since no significant differences were obtained on the IIA for any of the extroverted *S*s, the results obtained here on the IIA need no further explanation beyond that offered under the treatment x *S* personality type heading.

Figure 3.9 is a graphic representation of the mean pre-post reduction in self-reports and behavior ratings of interpersonal anxiety, general anxiety, and defensiveness for each treatment and counselor. These values were computed by subtracting the summed average of the post-test means across instruments and *S* personality type from the summed average of the pre-test means.

The clear superiority of the two SD counselors is visibly apparent here. Counselors B and b were roughly one-third more effective in reducing self-reports and behavior ratings of interpersonal and general anxiety than counselors c and R, tiwce as effective as counselors C and r, four times as effective as the no-treatment (placebo) control groups, and eight times as effective as the mere passage of time. As noted previously, this overwhelming success rate was due to the fact that the SD treatment was equally effective with introverted and extroverted *S*s.

Counselors c and R, the next most effective group, were approximately one fourth more effective than counselors C and r, three times as effective as the no-treatment (placebo) control condition, and six times as effective as the simple passage of time. As mentioned earlier, this phenomena was due to the fact that counselors c and R changed their counseling style with introverts and extroverts, producing increased anxiety reduction with these respective groups of *S*s.

Counselors C and r, the least effective group, were twice as effective as the no-treatment (placebo) control groups and four times as effective as the mere passage of time. Their inability to change counseling styles with different types of clients, resulted in significant amounts of anxiety reduction in only a limited number of the *S*s.

Finally, both of the no-treatment (placebo) control conditions were approximately twice as effective in reducing interpersonal and general anxiety as either of the no-contact control conditions. As noted before, the increased success of the placebo conditions over the mere passage of time was generally limited to introverted *S*s. Extroverts showed as much anxiety reduction on their own as they did when given the benefit of simple attention and expectation of future treatment and relief.

In order to gain a better appreciation for the true impact of the various counselors, the effects of simple attention and expectation of future treatment and relief were subtracted from each of the treatment conditions. Figure 3.10 presents the mean pre-post reduction in self-reports and behavior ratings of interpersonal anxiety, general anxiety, and defensiveness for each treatment and counselor with average placebo effects removed from each of the treatment conditions.

Counselor x personality type effects

Table 3.20 presents the Scheffe post hoc comparisons for the counselor x *S* personality type interactions. The unit of analysis was the individual scores for each *S*. No attempt was made to interpret the italicized tabled values, that is, the second order interactions, since, with the exception of the S-R_G, differential starting position effects make these comparisons invalid.

COUNSELOR X EXTROVERT PERSONALITY TYPE EFFECTS. Once again, no significant differences were obtained on any of the measures of interpersonal and general anxiety between the various no-treatment (placebo) control and no-contact control extroverts. However, all extroverted *S*s treated by counselors C, c, B, and b improved significantly more on all measures of anxiety than any of the control *S*s, although there were no significant differences between any of the former four counselors. Finally, whereas counselor R was able to produce significantly more anxiety reduction with extroverted *S*s than either of the controls, counselor r was no more effective in reducing self-reports and behavior ratings of interpersonal and general anxiety with extroverts than simple attention or no treatment at all.

With regard to the IIA, only counselor c was able to produce significant changes in behavior outside of treatment. However, since the overall treatment x extrovert personality type interaction was not significant at the .05 level, this one significant score should probably be disregarded.

Apparently, extroverted *S*s improve as much on their own as they do under conditions of simple attention etc., or when treated by counselor r. Counselors C, c, B, and b had equally significant impacts, producing the most anxiety reduction in extroverts, with counselor R significantly less effective than either of the CC or SD counselors but significantly more effective than either counselor r or any of the control conditions. These outcome results follow very closely the process data reported earlier.

COUNSELOR X INTROVERT PERSONALITY TYPE EFFECTS. With regard to the various self-report measures of interpersonal and general anxiety, all scales showed a significant difference between the two no-treatment (placebo) control introvert groups and the two no-contact control introvert groups. However, with the exception of the S-R_G for the no-contact control group, none of the within treatment x introvert personality type effects were significant at the .05 level.

All introverted *S*s treated by counselors B, b, R, and r improved significantly more on all measures of interpersonal and general anxiety than any of the control introverts. However, there were no significant differences between any of the four aforementioned counselors. Finally, whereas counselor c was able to produce significantly more anxiety reduction with introverted *S*s than either of the control introverts, counselor C was no more effective in reducing self-reports or behavior ratings of interpersonal and general anxiety than simple attention and expectation of future treatment and relief. In fact, counselor C's introverts showed significantly more behavioral manifestations of anxiety at post-testing than those introverts treated by means of the no-treatment (placebo) control condition.

While there were no significant differences between the four SD and RT counselors on any of the self-reports or behavior ratings of interpersonal and general anxiety, counselors R and r produced significantly greater increments in interpersonal activity on the IIA than either of the SD counselors. Furthermore, while counselor c's efforts in changing introverted *S*s' behavior outside of treatment were significantly less effective than any of the aforementioned counselors, they were significantly more effective than counselor C or either of the two introvert no-treatment (placebo) controls, the latter two groups showing no significant differences. However, both of the no-treatment (placebo) controls and counselor C were significantly more effective in increasing introverted *S*s interpersonal activity outside of treatment than simply the passage of time.

Thus, in terms of both reducing anxiety and increasing interpersonal activity, the RT counselors were by far the most effective with introverted *S*s. While both of the SD counselors were as effective as the two RT counselors in reducing cognitive complaints and behavioral manifestations of anxiety, they were unable to produce the rapid and pronounced increments in interpersonal activity outside of treatment noted in the introverts treated by RT. Finally, while counselor c was able to produce significantly more changes in all three of these areas than counselor C or either of the no-treatment (placebo) control conditions, his efforts were significantly less effective than those of counselors R, r, B, or b. All introverts, even those given only attention, etc., improved significantly more than those given no treatment at all. Once again, it should be noted that these outcome results follow very closely the process data reported earlier.

Figure 3.11 is a graphic representation of the mean pre-post reduction in self-reports and behavior ratings of interpersonal anxiety, general anxiety, and defensiveness for each counselor and *S* personality type. These values were computed by subtracting the summed average of the post-test means across instruments from the summed average of the pre-test means.

The data presented in Figure 3.11 follow very closely the counselor x *S* personality type process data reported earlier, in that introverts and extroverts treated by counselors C, c, R, and r, as well as those given no treatment at all, showed marked and significant differences.

While there were no significant differences between counselors C and c with extroverted *S*s, counselor c produced about twice as much anxiety reduction in introverts. Similarly, the no-contact control condition resulted in approximately four times as much anxiety reduction in extroverted *S*s as in introverted *S*s. Conversely, while there were no significant differences between counselors R and r with introverted *S*s, counselor R produced roughly twice as much anxiety reduction in extroverts.

None of the no-treatment (placebo) control introvert-extrovert differences were substantial enough to be significant. Similarly, none of the SD counselors' introvert-extrovert differences were of significant magnitude. Once again, the self-report questionnaires followed in the predicted direction, while the behavior ratings proceeded in the opposite direction to that predicted.

In order to gain a better appreciation of the true impact of the various counselor x *S* personality type interactions, the effects of simple attention and expectation of future treatment and relief were subtracted from each of the treatment conditions. Figure 3.12 presents the mean pre-post reduction in self-reports and behavior ratings of interpersonal anxiety, general anxiety, and defensiveness for each counselor and *S* personality type with average placebo effects removed from each of the treatment conditions. These values were derived in the same manner as the data presented in Figure 3.11.

Finally, as noted above, since counselors were nested within-treatment and only two counselors were employed as representative of each treatment approach, considerable caution should be exercised in interpreting the counselor and counselor x *S* personality type effects.

• *Follow-up Data*

Table 3.21 presents an analysis of variance of the follow-up means using the individual scores as the unit of analysis. As can be seen, all but the *Edwards Social Desirability Scale* (ESD) showed treatment and personality x treatment effects which were significant beyond the .05 level, indicating that the differences noted at post-testing were maintained at the time of the three-month follow-up. Once again, no attempt was made to interpret the findings regarding the personality main effects, since initial, pretreatment differences make these comparisons invalid.

Treatment main effects

Table 3.24 presents the Scheffe post hoc comparisons for the treatment main effects. The unit of analysis was individual scores summed across counselor and *S* personality type, within treatment. All of the treatments were significantly different from either of the control conditions. Thus, the clear superiority of all three of these forms of counseling over either the non-specific benefits derived from testing, interviewing, or simply the passage of time, noted at post-testing, was maintained at the time of the three-month follow-up.

As was also evidenced at post-testing, no significant differences were obtained at follow-up between the RT and CC treatments on any of the self-reports or behavior ratings of interpersonal and general anxiety. Similarly, the SD treatment approach, significantly more effective than either of the CC or RT treatments at post-testing, maintained its superior effectiveness at follow-up.

With regard to changes in introversion-extroversion, the findings are less clear. The no-contact control group was significantly more effective than the no-treatment (placebo) control group.[5] The RT and SD treatment did not differ from each other, while both were significantly different from the CC treatment approach. Also, the RT and SD treatments were equally as effective in producing a significantly better balance between introversion-extroversion than the CC treatment, which in turn, was significantly better than the no-treatment (placebo) control group but not the no-contact control group. This somewhat confusing finding will be better understood when *S* personality type is examined in closer detail.

Figure 3.13 presents a graphic representation of the mean reduction in self-reports and behavior ratings of interpersonal anxiety, general anxiety, and defensiveness from pre- to follow-up testing. These values were computed by subtracting the summed average of the follow-up test means across instruments, counselors, and *S* personality type from the summed average of the pre-test means.

As noted at post-testing, the no-treatment (placebo) control condition was again about twice as effective at follow-up

5. Smaller values on this scale indicate a better balance between introversion-extroversion.

in reducing self-reports of anxiety as the no-contact control condition. Similarly, both the RT and CC treatments were approximately twice again as effective as the no-treatment (placebo) control condition but only roughly two-thirds as effective as the SD treatment approach at the time of follow-up. Finally, whereas the CC and RT treatments were about four times more effective in reducing anxiety as the no-contact control condition, the SD treatment approach was roughly six times more effective as simply the passage of time. The fact that these follow-up data are identical to the post-test data reported earlier indicates that the results obtained at post-testing were maintained during the three-month follow-up period.

In order to gain a better appreciation for the true impact of the various treatments administered, the effects of simple attention and expectation of future treatment and relief were subtracted from each of the treatment conditions. Figure 3.14 presents the mean reduction in self-reports and behavior ratings of interpersonal anxiety, general anxiety, and defensiveness from pre- to follow-up testing with placebo effects removed from each of the treatment conditions. These data were derived in the same manner as the data presented in Figure 3.13.

Treatment x personality type effects

Table 3.25 presents the Scheffe post hoc comparisons for the treatment x *S* personality type interactions. The unit of analysis was individual scores summed across counselor within treatment. No attempt was made to interpret the italicized table values, that is, the second order interactions, since, with the exception of the S-R_G, differential starting position effects make these comparisons invalid.

TREATMENT X EXTROVERT PERSONALITY TYPE EFFECTS. As observed at post-testing, no significant differences were obtained at follow-up between the no-treatment (placebo) control and no-contact control extroverts on any of the self-reports or behavior ratings of interpersonal and general anxiety. Similarly, no significant differences were obtained on any of these measures between extroverts treated by means of RT and those given only attention or no treatment at all. In addition, all extroverted *S*s treated by means of CC and SD maintained the significant improvement over the control and RT extroverts noted at post-testing at the time of the three-month follow-up. Once again, the former two groups did not differ significantly from each other. Finally, in terms of changes in extroversion, there were no significant differences on the MBTI among the various treatments or between the treatment and control extroverts.

TREATMENT X INTROVERT PERSONALITY TYPE EFFECTS. As noted at post-testing, the no-treatment (placebo) control introverts showed significantly greater decrements in interpersonal and general anxiety at follow-up than the no-contact control introverts. Similarly, all introverted *S*s treated by means of RT and SD maintained the significant improvement evidenced at post-testing over both the control and CC introverts at the time of the three-month follow-up. Once again, no significant differences were obtained on any of these scales between introverts treated by either RT or SD. Finally, while the introverts treated by means of the CC approach maintained the significant improvement noted at post-testing over those introverts given no treatment at all, they were still no less anxious at follow-up than those introverts given only simple attention and the expectation of future treatment and relief.

In terms of changes in introversion, there were no significant differences between the no-treatment (placebo) control, the no-contact control, and the CC treatment. While no significant differences were obtained between introverts treated by either SD or RT, both of these treatment approaches produced significantly greater personality change in the direction of increased extroversion than either of the three aforementioned treatments.

Figure 3.15 is a graphic representation of the mean pre-follow-up reduction in self-reports and behavior ratings of interpersonal anxiety, general anxiety, and defensiveness for each treatment and *S* personality type. These values were computed by subtracting the summed average of the follow-up test means across instruments and counselors from the summed average of the pre-test means.

As noted at post-testing, the impact of simple attention and interviewing on extroverted *S*s' self-reports of anxiety had no greater effect than simply the passage of time. Similarly, introverts under these same placebo conditions maintained at the time of the three-month follow-up a level of anxiety reduction which was four times greater than that of the no-contact control group.

At follow-up, extroverted *S*s treated by CC and SD also maintained their threefold superiority in anxiety reduction over the no-treatment (placebo) control and no-contact control extroverts. In addition, while the RT treatment approach was once again about one third more effective in reducing interpersonal and general anxiety as either of the controls, it was only half as effective, as either the CC or SD treatments.

Introverted *S*s again showed approximately four times as much anxiety reduction when treated by means of RT or SD as compared to the no-treatment (placebo) control introverts, and ten times as much improvement, on the same criteria, as those introverts given no treatment at all. In addition, the CC treatment approach was once again only one third as effective in reducing anxiety in introverts as the RT or SD treatments and one third more effective, on the same criteria, as the no-treatment (placebo) control introverts.

Finally, while at follow-up the introverts treated by the CC approach were twice as extroverted as the no-treatment (placebo) control introverts and four times as extroverted as the no-contact control introverts, none of these differences were significant. However, the SD and RT introverts at follow-up were approximately five times more extroverted than the CC introverts, ten times more extroverted than the no-contact control introverts, and twenty times more extroverted than the no no-treatment (placebo) control introverts.

In order to test the within treatment x *S* personality type interactions, *t* tests were computed on the mean pre-follow-up change scores. These t values, as well as their *p* levels, are reported in Table 3.26.

As noted at post-testing, introverts and extroverts treated by means of either the CC or RT approaches, as well as those given no treatment at all, showed marked and significant differences. These differences, as shown in Figure 3.15, indicate that the CC treatment was about twice as effective in reducing anxiety with extroverts as opposed to introverts, whereas the no-contact control condition was approximately five times more effective with extroverts than introverts. Conversely, the RT treatment approach was nearly three times more effective in reducing anxiety with introverts as opposed to extroverts. Neither the SD nor the no-treatment (placebo) control condition showed any significant introvert-extrovert differences on any of the self-reports or behavior ratings of interpersonal and general anxiety.

On the MBTI both the RT and SD treatments showed large and significant introvert-extrovert differences. In both cases the introverts showed significantly more personality change than the extroverts. The direction of this change was such that the SD and RT introverts were far more extroverted at follow-up than any of the other treatment or control introverts. As expected, these findings parallel very closely the post-test changes in interpersonal activity outside of treatment (see Index of Interpersonal Activity).

All of these follow-up treatment x *S* personality type interactions are identical to the post-test treatment x *S* personality type interactions, indicating that the results obtained after treatment were maintained over the three-month period following the termination of treatment.

In order to gain a better appreciation for the true impact of the various treatment x *S* personality type interactions, the effects of simple attention and expectation of future treatment and relief were subtracted from each of the treatment conditions. Figure 3.16 presents the mean pre-follow-up reduction in self-reports and behavior ratings of interpersonal anxiety, general anxiety, and defensiveness for each treatment and *S* personality type with placebo effects removed from each of the treatment conditions. These values were computed in the same manner as the data presented in Figure 3.15.

Counselor main effects

Table 3.27 presents the Scheffe post hoc comparisons for the counselor main effects. The unit of analysis was individual scores summed across *S* personality type within treatment. The same interpretative restrictions imposed earlier relative to the counselor and counselor x *S* personality type effects are relevant here also.

The follow-up results concerning individual differences in counselor effectiveness are also consistent with the process and outcome data reported in previous sections. There were no significant differences on any of the self-reports or behavior ratings of interpersonal and general anxiety among the two no-contact control groups, the two no-treatment (placebo) control groups, and the two SD groups. However, the differences between the two RT and the two CC counselors were all significant at the .05 level.

Analysis of the above follow-up results once again indicates no significant differences, across "schools," between counselors C and r and counselors c and R. Overall, then, the two SD counselors again proved the most effective in maintaining their increased reduction in interpersonal and general anxiety, with counselors c and R significantly less effective than counselors B and b but significantly more effective than counselors C and r.

With only one exception, there were no significant differences on the MBTI between any of the four control groups or between the controls and the CC counselors. However, with only two exceptions the two RT and the two SD counselors' *S*s showed significantly more personality change on the MBTI than any of the control or CC counselor's *S*s.

Figure 3.17 presents a graphic representation of the mean pre-follow-up reduction in self-reports and behavior ratings of interpersonal anxiety, general anxiety, and defensiveness for each treatment and counselor. These values were computed by subtracting the summed average of the follow-up test means across instruments and *S* personality type from the summed average of the pre-test means.

The clear superiority of the two SD counselors, a fact noted at post-testing, is once again apparent here. Counselors B and b were roughly one-third more effective in reducing self-reports and behavior ratings of interpersonal and general anxiety than counselors c and R, twice as effective as counselors C and r, four times as effective as the no-treatment (placebo) controls, and eight times as effective as simply the passage of time. Counselors c and R, the next most effective group, were approximately one-fourth more effective as counselors C and r, three times more effective than the no-treatment (placebo) controls, and six times more effective than simply the passage of time. Counselors C and r, the least effective group, were about twice as effective as the no-treatment (placebo) controls and four times more effective than simply the passage of time. Finally, both of the no-treatment (placebo) control groups were approximately twice as effective in reducing interpersonal and general anxiety as either of the no-contact control groups.

In order to gain a better appreciation for the true impact of the various counselors, the effects of simple attention and expectation of future treatment and relief were subtracted from each of the treatment conditions. Figure 3.18 presents the mean pre-follow-up reduction in self-reports and behavior ratings of interpersonal anxiety, general anxiety, and defensiveness for each treatment and counselor with average placebo effects removed from each of the treatment conditions. These values were computed in the same manner as the data reported in Figure 3.17.

Counselor x personality type effects

Table 3.28 presents the Scheffe post hoc comparisons for the counselor x *S* personality type interactions. The unit of analysis was the individual scores for each *S*. No attempt was made to interpret the italicized tabled values, that is, the second order interactions, since, with the exception of the S-R_G, differential starting position effects make these comparisons invalid.

COUNSELOR X EXTROVERT PERSONALITY TYPE EFFECTS. Once again, no significant differences were obtained on any of the measures of interpersonal and general anxiety between the various no-treatment (placebo) control and no-contact control extroverts. Furthermore, the significantly greater reduction on all measures of anxiety between extroverts treated by counselors C, c, B, and b, and the control extroverts was maintained at the time of the three month follow-up also. Similarly, there were again no significant differences between counselors C, c, B, and b. In addition, whereas counselor R was able to maintain a significantly greater amount of anxiety reduction, noted at post-testing than either of the control extroverts, counselor r was again no more effective in reducing self-reports and behavior ratings of interpersonal and general anxiety with extroverts than simple attention or no treatment at all. Finally, in terms of changes in extroversion, there were no significant differences on the MBTI among the various counselor x extrovert personality type interactions or between the counseled and the control extroverted *S*s.

COUNSELOR X INTROVERT PERSONALITY TYPE EFFECTS. As at post-testing, all scales showed a significant difference between the two no-treatment (placebo) control groups and the two no-contact control introvert groups. None of the within treatment x introvert personality type effects were significant at the .05 level.

All introverted *S*s treated by counselors B, b, R, and r maintained their significantly greater amount of anxiety reduction over the control introverts, noted at post-testing, on all measures of interpersonal and general anxiety. Once again, however, there were no significant differences among any of these four counselors. Also, whereas counselor c was able to maintain a significantly greater amount of anxiety reduction, noted at post-testing, over either of the control introverts, counselor C was again no more effective in reducing self-reports or behavior ratings of interpersonal and general anxiety than simple attention and expectation of future treatment and relief.

In terms of changes in introversion, there were no significant differences on the MBTI between counselor C and any of the control introverts. In addition, while there were no significant differences between counselors R, r, B, and b, all of the introverted *S*s treated by these counselors were significantly more extroverted at follow-up than any of the aforementioned introvert groups. Finally, while counselor C's introverts showed no greater personality change than would be expected from the simple passage of time, counselor c's introverts showed as much change, in the direction of increased extroversion, as the no-treatment (placebo) control.

Figure 3.19 is a graphic representation of the mean pre-follow-up reduction in self-reports and behavior ratings of interpersonal anxiety, general anxiety, and defensiveness for each counselor and *S* personality type. These values were computed by subtracting the summed average of the follow-up test means across instruments from the summed average of the pre-test means.

The follow-up data presented in Figure 3.19 are nearly identical to the outcome results reported earlier. Introverted and extroverted *S*s treated by counselors C, c, R, and r, as well as those given no treatment at all, showed marked and significant differences.

While there were no significant differences between counselors C and c with regard to extroverted *S*s, counselor c produced about twice as much anxiety reduction in introverts as counselor C. Similarly, the no-contact control condition resulted in approximately four times as much anxiety reduction in extroverts as in introverts. Conversely, while there were no significant differences between counselors R and r with regard to introverted *S*s, counselor R produced about twice as much anxiety reduction in extroverts as counselor r.

None of the no-treatment (placebo) control introvert-extrovert differences were substantial enough to be significant. Similarly, none of the SD counselors introvert-extrovert differences were of significant magnitude. Once again, while the self-report questionnaires were in the predicted direction, the behavior ratings were in the direction opposite to that predicted.

Since none of the extroversion (MBTI) differences either among treatments or between treatment and control *S*s were significant at the .05 level, none of the introvert-extrovert differences on this scale could legitimately be compared from one counselor to the next. However, the data on changes in introversion follow very closely the various self-reports and behavior ratings of interpersonal and general anxiety.

Once again, in order to gain a better appreciation of the true impact of the various counselor x *S* personality type interactions, the effects of simple attention and expectation of future treatment and relief were subtracted from each of the treatment conditions. Figure 3.20 presents the mean pre-follow-up reduction in self-reports and behavior ratings of interpersonal anxiety, general anxiety, and defensiveness for each counselor and *S* personality type, with average placebo effects removed from each of the treatment conditions. These values were derived in the same manner as the data presented in Figure 3.19.

• *Summary*

In an attempt to compare the relative effectiveness of SD, RT, and CC group psychotherapy in the reduction of interpersonal and general anxiety in introverts and extroverts, it was found that there were significant sources of variance associated with treatment, counselor, and client variables, as well as with the interaction of each of the foregoing variables.

With regard to the treatment main effects, no significant differences were observed at post-testing between the CC and RT approaches. However, the SD treatment was significantly more effective than either of the CC or RT approached. *S*s treated by means of SD showed approximately 30 percent more anxiety reduction on both self-reports and behavior ratings at post-testing than either of the CC or RT *S*s.

Furthermore, the results of this study indicate that all of these forms of treatment produced significantly greater decrements in interpersonal and general anxiety than either simply the passage of time or the non-specific benefits derived from testing, interviewing, and expectation of future treatment and relief. Also, there were marked and significant differences on all of the self-reports and behavior ratings of anxiety between the two control groups, with those *S*s given the benefit of attention, interviewing, and the promise of future treatment and relief showing roughly twice as much anxiety reduction at post-testing as those *S*s given no treatment at all.

With regard to the treatment x *S* personality type effects, no significant within treatment differences were obtained on any of the self-reports or behavior ratings of anxiety between introverted and extroverted *S*s treated by either the SD or no-treatment (placebo) control conditions. However, introverts and extroverts treated by means of the CC and RT approaches, as well as those given no treatment at all, showed marked and significant differences. The CC treatment approach was about two and one-half times more effective in reducing anxiety with extroverts as opposed to introverts, whereas the no-contact control condition was about five times more effective with extroverts than introverts. Conversely, the RT treatment approach was nearly three times more effective in reducing anxiety with introverts than with extroverts.

A comparison of the treatment x *S* personality type effects across treatments revealed no significant post-test differences between extroverted *S*s treated by means of RT and any of the control extroverts. Similarly, while no significant differences were obtained between extroverts treated by the CC and SD approaches, both of these treatments showed significantly more anxiety reduction at post-testing than the three aforementioned approaches.

On the other hand, no significant differences were obtained between introverted *S*s in the no-treatment (placebo) control group and those introverts treated by the CC approach. However, both of these introvert groups were significantly different from the no-contact control introverts, the former groups showing roughly four times as much anxiety reduction at post-testing as the latter group. Finally, no significant differences were found at post-testing on any of the self-reports or behavior ratings of anxiety between the introverts treated by means of SD and RT. However, all introverts treated by these two approaches were significantly different from both the CC and control introverts, showing approximately four times as much anxiety reduction as the no-treatment (placebo) control introverts, ten times as much anxiety reduction as the no-contact control introverts, and twice as much anxiety reduction as the CC introverts.

While previous self-reports and behavior ratings indicated that the SD and RT treatments were equally effective in reducing cognitive complaints and behavioral manifestations of anxiety with introverted *S*s, in terms of changes in target behaviors outside of the treatment setting, the RT approach appears to have produced a significantly greater increase in interpersonal contacts. The RT treatment was roughly twice as effective in increasing the interpersonal activity of introverts outside of treatment as either the CC or no-treatment (placebo) control introverts and 30 percent more effective, on the same criteria, than the SD introverts. Finally, in terms of changes in interpersonal activity outside of treatment, there were no significant differences among the various treatments or between treatment and control extrovert *S*s.

With regard to the counselor main effects, there were no significant within treatment differences at post-testing on any of the self-reports or behavior ratings of anxiety between either the two no-contact control groups, the two no-treatment (placebo) control groups, or the two SD groups. However, the differences between the two RT and the two CC counselors were significant, with counselors c and R showing significantly more anxiety reduction at post-testing than counselors C and r.

A comparison of the counselor main effects across treatments or "schools" revealed no significant differences between counselors C and r and counselors c and R. Overall, the two SD counselors proved most effective in reducing anxiety, with counselors c and R significantly less effective than counselors B and b but significantly more effective than counselors C and r. Finally, the no-treatment (placebo) controls were significantly more effective than the no-contact controls.

With regard to the counselor x *S* personality type effects, no significant differences were found at post-testing between the various no-treatment (placebo) control and no-contact control extroverts. All extroverted *S*s treated by counselors B, b, C, and c showed significantly more anxiety reduction at post-testing than any of the control or RT extroverts, although there were no significant differences between the four SD and CC counselors. Also, whereas counselor R was able to produce significantly more anxiety reduction with extroverts than either of the control groups, counselor r was no more effective in reducing self-reports and behavior ratings of anxiety with extroverts than was simple attention or no treatment at all.

Both of the no-treatment (placebo) control introvert groups showed significantly more anxiety reduction at post-testing than either of the no-contact control introvert groups. Similarly, all introverted *S*s treated by counselors B, b, R, and r improved significantly more on all measures of anxiety than any of the control introverts. However, there were no significant differences between any of the four aforementioned counselors. Finally, whereas counselor c was able to produce significantly more anxiety reduction with introverted *S*s than was found in either of the control groups, counselor C was no more effective in reducing self-reports and behavior ratings of anxiety than was simple attention and expectation of future treatment and relief.

All of the above results remained virtually unchanged at the time of the three month (13 week) follow-up.

Table 3.1 • *Intercorrelations between the Interpersonal Anxiety Scales (IPAS)*, S-R Inventory of Anxiousness, *Interpersonal* $(S\text{-}R_I)$ *and General* $(S\text{-}R_G)$, Trait Anxiety Inventory *(TAI)*, *and* State Anxiety Inventory *(SAI)*

	IPAS B	$S\text{-}R_I$	$S\text{-}R_G$	TAI	SAI
IPAS A	.925	.782	.444	.479	.401
IPAS B		.757	.409	.437	.441
$S\text{-}R_I$			.498	.468	.379
$S\text{-}R_G$				.647	.502
TAI					.511

Table 3.2 • *Analysis of variance of pre-test data*

		IPAS A		IPAS B		$S\text{-}R_I$	
Source	*df*	MS	F	MS	F	MS	F
Personality	1	1315.44	175.44[a]	549.15	131.63[a]	3453.19	46.49[b]
Personality × Treatment	4	0.91	0.12	1.86	0.45	9.90	0.13
Pers. × Couns. + Pers. × Treat. × Couns.	5	7.50	—	4.17	—	74.28	—
Treatment	4	0.89	0.50	0.86	0.24	13.90	0.60
Remaining Error	5	1.80	—	3.64	—	23.28	—
TOTAL	19						

TAI		S-R$_G$		ESD		Bhv. Rts.		MBTI	
MS	F	MS	F	MS	F	MS (*df*)	F	MS	F
362.95	93.54[a]	0.16	0.01	101.25	52.35[b]	400.00 (1)	157.79[a]	1036.80	0.80
2.59	0.67	5.08	0.24	1.40	0.72	0.45 (3)	0.18	410.80	0.32
3.88	—	21.41	—	1.93	—	2.54 (4)	—	1304.00	—
1.82	0.47	26.02	1.29	7.80	0.94	0.55 (3)	0.31	305.20	0.16
3.90	—	20.10	—	8.31	—	1.78 (4)	—	1851.20	—
						15			

[a]$p < .0005$
[b]$p < .001$

Table 3.3 · Pre-test means and standard deviations for each

Treatment			IPAS A		IPAS B		$S\text{-}R_I$	
			Mean	SD	Mean	SD	Mean	SD
Client-Centered	C	E	61.2	11.39	62.8	11.45	171.2	33.04
		I	75.8	11.39	73.4	16.00	204.4	29.79
	c	E	63.2	11.95	63.0	14.95	177.8	23.11
		I	79.2	13.97	70.6	12.52	198.2	30.42
Desensitization	B	E	63.4	15.37	61.4	19.51	174.4	30.36
		I	78.6	12.97	74.4	13.13	205.4	27.72
	b	E	60.8	10.64	61.8	11.10	171.8	21.84
		I	81.0	10.46	74.0	10.39	198.6	31.93
Rational-Emotive	R	E	61.8	10.38	63.2	11.84	177.8	22.09
		I	77.4	14.22	72.4	16.32	198.8	33.57
	r	E	62.4	9.05	61.6	9.40	172.6	20.94
		I	79.0	11.49	72.8	14.84	210.8	28.74
No-Treatment (Placebo) Control		E	61.4	14.43	61.6	12.14	176.0	25.75
		I	80.8	15.20	76.6	17.40	205.6	33.16
		E	63.8	13.31	64.4	14.50	184.4	21.59
		I	77.4	12.20	71.2	12.37	199.8	32.25
No-Contact Control		E	60.4	10.88	60.2	10.26	177.0	24.60
		I	80.6	11.48	70.6	10.38	214.8	22.40
		E	64.6	11.33	64.8	14.04	182.2	28.17
		I	75.4	12.90	73.6	11.16	191.6	24.17

of the treatment and control groups

TAI		S-R$_G$		ESD		Bhv. Rts.		MBTI	
Mean	SD	Mean	SD	Mean	SD	Mean	SD	Mean	SD
45.2	7.57	160.2	34.33	28.8	5.85	54.4	6.84	25.4	6.54
52.4	12.93	159.2	25.45	20.0	6.20	41.4	5.46	31.8	10.92
42.4	8.73	157.6	37.06	28.6	8.32	52.4	9.91	34.6	10.43
52.0	9.92	158.8	43.23	25.0	7.58	44.2	5.54	33.4	8.41
44.4	11.17	159.0	43.81	31.6	5.90	54.6	11.74	35.0	16.73
50.0	9.90	160.2	40.38	25.6	4.83	42.8	11.43	29.8	14.18
43.6	6.84	154.0	27.90	31.8	5.26	51.2	6.83	27.8	9.65
55.0	9.03	159.2	38.28	28.4	5.68	42.2	7.85	29.8	12.54
43.8	11.03	160.4	28.80	28.8	6.30	54.2	9.36	25.4	9.63
56.4	10.43	156.8	43.44	24.6	5.98	43.2	7.69	27.4	15.19
42.4	9.21	161.8	27.48	31.6	5.90	51.4	7.23	30.2	12.21
52.0	13.95	165.2	38.52	27.4	5.81	42.6	10.16	33.0	14.07
46.4	10.01	160.4	31.05	28.2	6.38	53.8	9.20	33.4	11.26
54.2	8.07	160.4	32.58	26.4	6.02	43.6	6.73	31.8	14.32
45.2	6.46	168.4	32.00	31.2	6.42	52.4	6.35	26.6	11.61
53.2	10.99	166.2	32.46	27.2	5.76	44.4	11.49	29.0	8.25
46.0	7.84	167.4	33.61	31.8	4.97	—	—	30.6	15.45
50.0	7.18	155.0	37.87	27.4	5.27	—	—	28.2	11.28
45.0	11.55	162.2	29.11	27.2	6.14	—	—	25.4	6.71
54.4	10.09	168.6	35.18	22.6	5.81	—	—	34.6	9.21

Table 3.4 • ***Amount of treatment received by each of the treatment groups and amount of attention given the No-Treatment (Placebo) Control Ss***

Client Type \ Treatment Type	*Client-Centered Treatment*		*Desensitization Treatment*		*Rational-Emotive Treatment*		*No-Treatment (Placebo) Control*	
	C	c	B	b	R	r	*	*
Extroverts	11′46″	11′50″	11′39″	11′40″	11′11″	12′40″	11′00″	11′00″
Introverts	12′22″	12′04″	10′58″	11′00″	11′53″	11′37″	11′00″	11′00″

Note: These times were estimated from the tape recordings by determining the amount of time required for 50 feet of tape to pass through the tape counter, multiplying this figure by the amount of 50-foot segments of tape employed, and rounding to the nearest minute.

*These times were estimated as indicated in Chapter 3.

Table 3.5 • ***Number of sessions missed by each S during the treatment period***

Client Type \ Treatment Type	*Client-Centered Treatment*		*Desensitization Treatment*		*Rational-Emotive Treatment*		*No Treatment (Placebo) Control*	
	C	c	B	b	R	r		
Extroverts	2/1	2/1	2/1 1/2	4/1	1/1 1/2	4/1	1/1	1/1
Introverts	3/1	2/1	2/1	2/1	2/1	2/1	1/1	

Note: The numbers in each cell represent the number of *S*s followed by the number of sessions missed. For example 1/1 means one group member missed one session.

Table 3.6 • Additional treatment received by each S prior to treatment, during treatment, and during follow-up

Treatment Type	CC		SD		RT		NTC		NCC	
Client Type	C	c	B	b	R	r				
					Prior to Treatment					
Extroverts	1/1[a] 1/10 1/12		1/2[b]				1/3[ab]			1/5[a]
Introverts		1/8[a]	1/5 1/15		1/4[a]			1/1	1/3[a]	
					During Treatment					
Extroverts			1/3[b]		1/1[a] 1/1[a]	1/4 1/4[b]	1/1[b]		1/2[a]	
Introverts	1/6 1/4	1/3[b]	1/2	1/1	1/1[ab]					
					During Follow-up					
Extroverts				1/3		1/3[b]				1/2
Introverts	1/2						1/1		2/1	1/1

Note: The numbers in each cell represent the number of *S*s followed by the number of sessions missed. For example 1/1 means one group member missed one session.

[a]Extra interviews were sought for educational-vocational rather than personal-social reasons.

[b]Indicates the same *S* sought treatment in two of the three above periods.

Table 3.7 • Percent of time spent in conversation and silence by each of the Client-Centered (CC) and Rational-Emotive (RT) counselors and subjects

Client Type	*Speaker*	*Client-Centered* C	*Client-Centered* c	*Rational-Emotive* R	*Rational-Emotive* r
Extroverts	Counselor	26	25	35	44
	Client	59	58	42	25
	Silence	14	16	23	29
Introverts	Counselor	34	40	46	48
	Client	37	42	45	46
	Silence	28	18	10	05

Note: In order to avoid inclusion of natural pauses in speech, silences were defined as an interval of greater than five seconds during which neither counselor nor client spoke. Each tabled value was rounded to the nearest percent.

Table 3.8 · Frequency of use of specific techniques by each of the Client-Centered (CC) and Rational-Emotive (RT) therapists

	Per Cent of Use of Techniques by Counselor							
	C		c		R		r	
Technique	E	I	E	I	E	I	E	I
Reflection and Clarification of Feelings:	46	44	49	30	19	2	9	1
Reflection and Clarification of Thinking:	1	5	2	9	3	5	2	2
Reflection and Clarification of Content:	3	1	3	0	1	0	0	0
Reflection and Clarification of Behavior:	3	2	2	3	0	1	0	1
TOTALS:	53	52	56	42	23	8	11	4
Questioning of Feelings:	10	10	10	4	9	2	6	0
Questioning of Thinking:	0	3	1	8	5	14	4	11
Questioning of Content:	1	0	0	0	0	0	0	1
Questioning of Behavior:	1	0	1	2	1	0	3	3
TOTALS:	12	13	12	14	15	16	13	15
Interpretation of Feelings:	5	4	3	1	3	1	4	0
Interpretation of Thinking:	0	3	0	5	2	3	1	1
Interpretation of Content:	0	0	0	0	0	0	0	0
Interpretation of Behavior:	0	1	1	0	1	0	2	0
TOTALS:	5	8	4	6	6	4	7	1
Direct Confrontation with Feelings:	1	2	2	2	10	5	8	1
Direct Confrontation with Thinking:	0	3	0	14	20	40	41	51
Direct Confrontation with Content:	0	0	0	0	1	1	0	2
Direct Confrontation with Behavior	0	0	0	2	1	2	3	3
TOTALS:	1	5	2	18	32	48	52	57

Table 3.8 • *Continued*

Technique	*Per Cent of Use of Techniques by Counselor*							
	C		c		R		r	
	E	I	E	I	E	I	E	I
Suggestion:	4	5	2	0	1	0	0	0
Information and Advice Giving:	0	2	1	5	3	11	8	10
Redirecting Questions Back to the Group:	7	5	7	2	6	2	1	0
Self-disclosure:	8	2	8	0	3	1	1	0
Free Association:	0	0	0	0	0	0	0	0
Reinforcement (Approval-disapproval):	10	6	9	11	8	11	6	10
Home Work Assignments:*	0	0	3	6	4	8	7	9
Unclassifiable:**	2	1	2	1	3	1	2	4
TOTALS:	31	21	29	19	24	26	18	24

Note: This table is not identical to Table 3.4, since it was impossible to rate all of the items listed in the latter table from audio tapes only.

*This figure was not included in the frequency count presented above. The numbers here represent simply the number of times a homework assignment was given. For example, if a homework assignment was given each session, the entry would be 9, or 1 entry for each of the 9 sessions.

**This includes, in addition activities not clearly relevant to the tasks of therapy, for example, greetings, small talk, endings, etc. The very small entries in this category probably reflect the fact that both raters were instructed to avoid this classification unless therapist's statements could not be otherwise classified.

Table 3.9 • *Per cent of conversation and silence time for each CC and RT counselor and subject for each three-interview time period*

Client Type	*Speaker*	C *Period* 1	2	3	c *Period* 1	2	3	R *Period* 1	2	3	r *Period* 1	2	3
	Counselor	43	31	25	45	30	24	40	34	28	35	33	32
Extroverts	Client	22	30	49	24	35	42	28	35	36	33	37	28
	Silence	45	35	22	40	33	25	40	33	20	30	31	37
	Counselor	31	38	30	39	31	29	46	40	15	48	36	18
Introverts	Client	31	37	30	29	36	35	20	36	43	23	35	42
	Silence	31	34	36	39	31	30	39	35	26	41	33	24

Note: In order to avoid inclusion of natural pauses in speech, silences were defined as an interval of greater than five seconds during which neither counselor nor client spoke. Each tabled value was rounded to the nearest per cent.

Table 3.10 • Frequency of use of specific techniques by each of the

	Per Cent of Use of Techniques by Counselor								
	C						c		
	E			*I*			*E*		
	1	2	3	1	2	3	1	2	3
Reflection and Clarification (Totals):	48	30	21	56	10	35	43	32	24
Questioning (Totals):	40	31	28	32	36	33	41	31	26
Interpretation (Totals):	50	51	00	35	35	28	48	42	11
Direct Confrontation (Totals):	100	00	00	42	00	56	51	51	00
Suggestion:	80	18	04	58	12	31	40	35	25
Information and Advice Giving:	00	00	00	00	19	80	91	08	02
Redirecting Questions Back to the Group:	53	40	10	47	20	33	49	36	14
Self-disclosure:	61	28	11	50	00	50	53	37	10
Reinforcement:	08	44	48	28	34	36	11	43	48
Unclassifiable:	42	35	25	30	33	36	43	33	24

Table 3.11 • Analysis of variance of therapist variables of Accurate Overall Therapeutic Relationship (OTR), Intensity and Intimacy of

		AE		NPW	
Source	df	MS	F	MS	F
Personality	1	0.64	0.03	19.36	1.16
Personality × Treatment	3	26.68	1.46	9.32	0.56
Pers. × Couns. + Pers. × Treat. × Couns.	4	18.29	—	16.75	—
Treatment	3	38.19	3.13	103.16	5.72*
Remaining Error	4	12.19	—	18.05	—
TOTAL	15				

CC and RT therapists for each three-interview time period

Per Cent of Use of Techniques by Counselor														
c			R						r					
I			*E*			*I*			*E*			*I*		
1	2	3	1	2	3	1	2	3	1	2	3	1	2	3
40	30	29	39	35	28	45	44	11	12	41	48	03	80	15
37	35	29	36	35	29	42	33	25	33	33	33	46	32	21
41	36	21	51	12	37	63	31	05	39	31	32	48	11	43
48	29	23	49	30	23	48	30	21	57	18	26	47	30	23
00	00	00	00	100	00	00	00	00	00	00	00	00	00	00
51	30	20	100	00	00	44	33	23	53	17	29	44	35	20
100	00	00	40	30	28	32	60	07	00	00	100	00	00	00
00	00	00	80	09	11	100	00	00	00	100	00	00	00	00
20	39	40	22	39	40	10	38	53	30	34	38	13	40	50
40	30	29	39	31	28	45	32	22	35	31	33	41	34	25

Note: Each table value was rounded to the nearest per cent.

Empathy (AE), Nonpossessive Warmth (NPW), Genuineness (G), Interpersonal Contact (IIIC), and Concreteness (C)

G		OTR		IIIC		C	
MS	F	MS	F	MS	F	MS	F
2.65	0.23	22.09	0.40	0.36	0.02	0.02	0.00
12.26	1.11	52.94	0.96	15.65	0.77	8.26	0.55
11.05	—	54.87	—	20.25	—	14.89	—
29.56	1.51	334.97	5.35*	62.30	3.18	108.23	6.55*
19.63	—	62.65	—	19.57	—	16.51	—

*$p < .10$

Table 3.12 • *Post-test means and standard deviations for each of the*

Treatment	*Couns.*	*Pers. Type*	AE Means	AE SD	NPW Means	NPW SD
Client-Centered	C	E	33.8	5.07	58.6	9.10
		I	26.0	5.52	48.0	10.56
	c	E	33.2	9.52	62.0	3.24
		I	31.6	8.05	60.8	5.07
Desensitization	B	E	34.4	3.78	61.0	2.55
		I	24.2	4.55	53.8	5.67
	b	E	23.2	4.49	57.2	3.90
		I	26.8	4.71	58.2	2.59
Rational-Emotive	r	E	34.2	6.61	60.4	2.30
		I	36.2	11.50	61.8	11.03
	R	E	25.6	3.44	58.0	4.47
		I	35.0	9.67	59.2	11.39
No-Treatment (Placebo) Control		E	23.6	8.76	46.0	16.17
		I	29.0	8.40	50.2	15.99
		E	25.2	8.07	51.8	14.30
		I	27.6	7.92	45.4	13.43

Table 3.13 • *Analysis of variance of post-test data*

Source	*df*	IPAS A MS	IPAS A F	$S\text{-}R_I$ MS	$S\text{-}R_I$ F	TAI MS	TAI F
Personality	1	1235.59	70.14[e]	2817.94	50.09[d]	326.43	45.36[d]
Personality × Treatment	4	170.77	9.69[b]	468.99	8.33[b]	66.53	9.25[b]
Pers. × Couns. + Pers. × Treat. × Couns.	5	17.62	—	56.25	—	7.20	—
Treatment	4	525.75	42.13[e]	1784.07	49.21[e]	259.28	42.28[e]
Remaining Error	5	12.48	—	36.25	—	6.13	—
TOTAL	19						

[a] $p < .05$ [d] $p < .001$
[b] $p < .01$ [e] $p < .0005$
[c] $p < .005$

treatment and control groups

G		OTR		IIIC		C	
Means	SD	Means	SD	Means	SD	Means	SD
45.4	1.82	102.0	10.98	42.4	4.93	27.8	5.26
34.2	4.32	82.4	14.31	33.0	6.28	22.8	6.06
44.8	3.27	105.0	12.25	45.2	5.26	28.4	8.79
44.4	2.61	105.0	11.60	46.4	3.44	27.2	6.14
42.0	2.00	102.4	7.96	42.8	4.27	28.0	4.06
37.8	6.61	86.6	9.99	35.2	5.76	21.4	4.39
40.6	5.94	88.8	9.39	37.4	5.55	17.2	4.09
42.8	3.11	91.4	6.27	40.0	4.30	21.8	3.27
45.0	3.67	107.6	5.59	43.4	6.80	32.0	7.65
46.6	3.44	109.8	22.24	45.4	13.58	32.0	10.68
39.2	5.72	95.2	8.44	37.2	3.77	22.6	4.62
43.2	6.83	105.8	19.42	45.0	9.43	30.0	8.94
34.4	10.74	80.8	13.24	35.2	8.76	15.0	2.12
34.8	8.29	86.0	15.98	31.4	9.10	19.0	5.34
39.5	5.37	85.0	9.08	32.2	5.26	19.2	4.63
40.2	8.81	81.0	13.62	37.0	8.80	15.2	3.63

$S\text{-}R_G$		ESD		Bhv. Rts.			IIA		
MS	F	MS	F	MS	(*df*)	F	MS	(*df*)	F
39.20	2.11	78.41	7.02[a]	174.24	(1)	28.68[b]	1387.56	(1)	285.65[e]
249.43	13.42[b]	3.74	0.34	80.98	(3)	13.33[b]	128.18	(3)	26.39[c]
18.58	—	11.16	—	6.08	(4)	—	4.86	(4)	—
968.95	23.21[c]	5.60	0.61	117.36	(3)	13.48[b]	99.46	(3)	14.01[b]
41.76	—	9.23	—	8.71	(4)	—	7.10	(4)	—

Table 3.14 · *Pre- and post-test means and standard deviations for*

Treatment	*Couns.*	*Time*	IPAS A Means	IPAS A SD	S-R_I Means	S-R_I SD	TAI Means	TAI SD
Client-Centered	C	Pre	61.2	11.39	171.2	33.04	45.2	7.57
		Post	31.0	5.92	127.8	16.19	25.2	3.70
	c	Pre	63.2	11.95	177.8	23.11	42.4	8.73
		Post	31.4	5.41	131.8	11.38	24.6	4.62
Desensitization	B	Pre	63.4	15.37	174.4	30.36	44.4	11.17
		Post	33.0	7.52	130.4	16.04	24.4	2.20
	b	Pre	60.8	10.64	171.8	21.84	43.6	6.84
		Post	30.2	5.40	128.6	12.03	24.8	2.86
Rational-Emotive	R	Pre	61.8	10.38	177.8	22.09	43.8	11.03
		Post	40.2	7.19	145.4	17.71	32.2	8.32
	r	Pre	62.4	9.05	172.6	20.94	42.4	9.21
		Post	51.6	9.64	158.6	23.23	39.2	9.03
No-Treatment (Placebo) Control		Pre	61.4	14.43	176.0	25.75	46.4	10.01
		Post	48.0	12.01	165.8	22.74	40.8	7.88
		Pre	63.8	13.31	184.4	21.59	45.2	6.46
		Post	51.2	10.46	172.6	19.93	39.4	4.99
No-Contact Control		Pre	60.4	10.88	177.0	24.60	46.0	7.84
		Post	48.4	10.21	166.4	24.88	40.6	6.88
		Pre	64.6	11.33	182.2	28.17	45.0	11.55
		Post	53.6	10.67	171.2	29.35	39.4	10.67

each of the extrovert treatment and control groups

S-R_G		ESD		Bhv. Rts.		IIA	
Means	SD	Means	SD	Means	SD	Means	SD
160.2	34.33	28.8	5.85	54.4	6.84	—	—
127.4	22.54	28.4	5.94	34.2	3.03	51.2	10.45
157.6	37.06	28.6	8.32	52.4	9.91	—	—
123.2	24.26	31.8	6.53	33.6	4.34	56.0	14.76
159.0	43.81	31.6	5.90	54.6	11.74	—	—
123.0	19.59	32.0	6.78	33.4	5.13	50.2	6.72
154.0	27.90	31.8	5.26	51.2	6.83	—	—
119.2	15.55	26.8	5.45	32.6	4.16	53.6	14.15
160.4	28.80	28.8	6.30	54.2	9.36	—	—
138.2	21.79	29.2	7.59	42.2	7.69	50.8	6.64
161.8	27.48	31.6	5.90	51.4	7.23	—	—
153.2	25.58	28.8	4.97	46.4	7.26	52.4	9.84
160.4	31.05	28.2	6.38	53.8	9.20	—	—
151.0	24.81	23.6	5.55	47.4	6.07	55.0	15.94
168.4	32.00	31.2	6.42	52.4	6.35	—	—
154.0	26.80	27.6	7.73	46.8	6.14	50.2	9.28
167.4	33.61	31.8	4.97	—	—	—	—
157.4	36.62	32.4	4.61	—	—	—	—
162.2	29.11	27.2	6.14	—	—	—	—
152.6	33.28	25.4	4.33	—	—	—	—

Table 3.15 · Pre- and post-test means and standard deviations for

Treatment	Couns.	Time	IPAS A Means	IPAS A SD	S-R$_I$ Means	S-R$_I$ SD	TAI Means	TAI SD
Client-Centered	C	Pre	75.8	11.39	204.4	29.79	52.4	12.93
		Post	65.6	11.35	190.6	28.95	46.0	13.08
	c	Pre	79.2	13.97	198.2	30.42	52.0	9.92
		Post	55.2	10.99	170.6	25.79	38.0	6.54
Desensitization	B	Pre	78.6	12.97	205.4	27.72	50.0	9.90
		Post	40.0	7.04	146.4	16.47	29.4	5.41
	b	Pre	81.0	10.46	198.6	31.93	55.0	9.03
		Post	42.0	5.70	142.4	13.51	31.4	3.97
Rational-Emotive	R	Pre	77.3	14.22	198.8	33.57	56.4	10.43
		Post	42.8	6.61	145.0	21.14	32.6	5.08
	r	Pre	79.0	11.49	210.8	28.74	52.0	13.95
		Post	43.0	6.20	150.4	14.74	31.2	6.38
No-Treatment (Placebo) Control		Pre	80.8	15.20	205.6	33.16	54.2	8.07
		Post	68.0	12.48	189.4	28.11	46.0	7.48
		Pre	77.4	12.20	199.8	32.25	53.2	10.99
		Post	64.8	8.75	184.8	28.09	44.4	8.70
No-Contact Control		Pre	80.6	11.48	214.8	22.40	50.0	7.18
		Post	78.0	15.52	215.2	23.53	52.8	6.94
		Pre	75.4	12.90	191.6	24.17	54.5	10.09
		Post	76.4	13.58	201.2	22.11	55.6	10.99

each of the introvert treatment and control groups

S-R_G		ESD		Bhv. Rts.		IIA	
Means	SD	Means	SD	Means	SD	Means	SD
159.2	25.45	20.0	6.20	41.4	5.46	—	—
153.2	25.45	19.6	6.06	43.8	5.36	24.6	3.21
158.8	43.23	25.0	7.58	44.2	5.54	—	—
139.8	36.99	27.2	9.23	34.0	5.24	30.2	3.11
160.2	40.38	25.6	4.83	42.8	11.43	—	—
121.6	24.60	23.6	5.17	27.4	6.34	38.6	4.39
159.2	38.28	28.4	5.68	42.2	7.85	—	—
125.4	22.46	29.8	6.42	25.8	4.09	35.4	6.02
156.8	43.44	24.6	5.98	43.2	7.69	—	—
122.2	28.00	25.4	7.02	27.0	4.53	48.2	6.94
165.2	38.52	27.4	5.81	42.6	10.16	—	—
126.8	22.83	23.2	3.12	27.8	4.87	46.2	1.64
160.4	32.58	26.4	6.02	43.6	6.73	—	6.14
151.2	30.08	23.8	8.58	39.0	6.28	23.2	—
166.2	32.46	27.2	5.76	44.4	11.49	—	—
152.0	28.70	24.2	10.85	39.0	6.78	23.0	6.32
155.0	37.87	27.4	5.27	—	—	—	—
163.4	37.71	24.4	8.76	—	—	—	—
168.6	35.18	22.6	5.81	—	—	—	—
169.6	33.35	25.4	3.57	—	—	—	—

Table 3.16 • Scheffé post hoc comparisons of post-test means for treatment main effects

Groups		RT	SD	NT(P)C	NCC
			IPAS A		
	Means	44.40	36.30	58.00	64.10
CC	45.80	1.40	9.50	−12.20	−18.30
RT	44.40		8.10	−13.60	−19.70
SD	36.30			−21.70	−27.80
NT(P)C	58.00	[5.03]			− 6.10
			TAI		
	Means	33.80	27.50	42.65	47.10
CC	33.45	−0.35	5.95	− 9.20	−13.65
RT	33.80		6.30	− 8.85	−13.30
SD	27.50			−15.15	−19.60
NT(P)C	42.65	[3.55]			− 4.45
			Bhv. Rts.		
	Means	35.85	29.80	43.05	
CC	36.40	0.55	6.60	− 6.65	
RT	35.85		6.05	− 7.20	
SD	29.80	[4.12]		−13.25	
			$S\text{-}R_I$		
	Means	149.85	136.85	178.15	188.50
CC	155.20	5.35	18.25	−22.95	−33.30
RT	149.85		12.90	−28.30	−38.65
SD	136.95			−41.20	−51.55
NT(P)C	178.15	[8.63]			−10.35
			$S\text{-}R_G$		
	Means	135.10	122.30	152.05	160.75
CC	135.90	0.80	13.60	−16.15	−24.85
RT	135.10		12.80	−16.95	−25.65
SD	122.30	[8.26]		−29.75	−38.45
NT(P)C	152.05				− 8.70
			IIA (Index of Interpersonal Activity)		
	Means	49.40	44.45	37.85	
CC	40.75	−8.65	−3.70	2.90	
RT	49.40		4.95	11.55	
SD	44.45	[3.62]		6.60	

Note: Negative tabled values indicate that the row means are less than the column means, whereas positive values indicate that the column means are lower. Any differences which exceed the critical values enclosed in the brackets above are significant at the .05 level (two-sided tests).

Table 3.17 • Scheffé post hoc comparisons of post-test means for treatment X personality type effects

IPAS A

Groups		CC,I	RT,E	RT,I	SD,E	SD,I	NT(P) C,E	NT(P) C,I	NCC,E	NCC,I
	Means	60.4	45.9	42.9	31.6	41.0	51.1	64.9	51.0	77.2
CC,E	31.2	*−29.2*	−14.7	*−11.7*	−0.4	*−9.8*	−19.9	*−33.7*	−19.8	*−46.0*
CC,I	60.4		*14.5*	17.5	*28.8*	19.4	*9.3*	− 4.5	*9.4*	−16.8
RT,E	45.9			*3.0*	14.3	*4.9*	− 5.2	*−19.0*	− 5.1	*−31.3*
RT,I	42.9				*11.3*	1.9	*− 8.2*	−22.0	*− 8.1*	−34.3
SD,E	31.6					*−9.4*	−19.5	*−33.3*	−19.4	*−45.6*
SD,I	41.0						*−10.1*	−23.9	*−10.0*	−36.2
NT(P)C,E	51.1							*−13.8*	0.1	*−26.1*
NT(P)C,I	64.9	[12.13]							*13.9*	−12.3
NCC,E	51.0									*−26.2*

TAI

Groups		CC,I	RT,E	RT,I	SD,E	SD,I	NT(P) C,E	NT(P) C,I	NCC,E	NCC,I
	Means	42.0	35.7	31.9	24.6	30.4	40.1	45.2	40.0	54.2
CC,E	24.9	*−17.1*	−10.8	*− 7.0*	0.3	*5.5*	−15.2	*−20.3*	−15.1	*−23.9*
CC,I	42.0		*6.3*	10.1	*17.4*	11.6	*1.9*	− 3.2	*2.0*	−12.2
RT,E	35.7			*3.8*	11.1	*5.3*	− 4.4	*− 9.5*	− 4.3	*−18.5*
RT,I	31.9				*7.3*	1.5	*− 8.2*	−13.3	*− 8.1*	−22.3
SD,E	24.6					*− 5.8*	−15.5	*−20.6*	−15.4	*−29.6*
SD,I	30.4						*− 9.7*	−14.8	*9.6*	−23.8
NT(P)C,E	40.1							*− 5.1*	0.1	*−14.1*
NT(P)C,I	45.2	[8.10]							*5.2*	− 9.0
NCC,E	40.0									*−14.2*

Bhv. Rts.

Groups		CC,I	RT,E	RT,I	SD,E	SD,I	NT(P) C,E	NT(P) C,I
	Means	38.9	44.3	27.4	33.0	26.6	47.1	39.0
CC,E	33.9	−5.0	−10.4	*6.5*	0.9	*7.3*	−13.2	*− 5.1*
CC,I	38.9		*− 5.4*	11.5	*5.9*	12.3	*− 8.2*	− 0.1
RT,E	44.3			*16.9*	11.3	*17.7*	− 2.8	*− 5.3*
RT,I	27.4				*−5.6*	0.8	*−19.7*	−11.6
SD,E	33.0					*6.4*	−14.1	*− 6.0*
SD,I	26.6	[7.42]					*−20.5*	−12.4
NT(P)C,E	47.1							*8.1*

S-R$_I$

Groups		CC,I	RT,E	RT,I	SD,E	SD,I	NT(P) C,E	NT(P) C,I	NCC,E	NCC,I
	Means	180.6	152.0	147.7	129.5	144.4	169.2	187.1	168.8	208.2
CC,E	129.8	*−50.8*	−22.2	*−17.9*	0.3	−14.6	−39.4	*−57.3*	−39.0	*−78.4*
CC,I	180.6		*28.6*	32.9	*51.1*	36.2	*11.4*	− 6.5	*11.8*	−27.6
RT,E	152.0			*4.3*	22.5	*7.6*	−17.2	*−35.1*	−16.8	*−56.2*
RT,I	147.7				*18.2*	3.3	*−21.5*	−39.4	*−21.1*	−60.5
SD,E	129.5					*−14.9*	−39.7	*−57.6*	−39.3	*−78.7*
SD,I	144.4						*−24.8*	−42.7	*−24.4*	−63.8
NT(P)C,E	169.2							*−17.9*	0.4	*−39.0*
NT(P)C,I	187.1	[20.81]							*18.3*	−21.1
NCC,E	168.8									*−39.4*

Note: Negative tabled values indicate that the row means are less than the column means, whereas positive values indicate that the column means are lower. Any differences which exceed the critical values enclosed in the brackets above are significant at the .05 level (two-sided tests).

Table 3.17 · *Continued*

Groups		CC,I	RT,E	RT,I	SD,E	SD,I	NT(P) C,E	NT(P) C,I	NCC,E	NCC,I
						S-R$_G$				
	Means	146.5	145.7	124.5	121.1	123.5	152.0	152.1	155.0	166.5
CC,E	125.3	*−21.2*	−20.4	*0.8*	4.2	*1.8*	−26.7	*−28.8*	−29.7	*−41.2*
CC,I	146.5		*0.8*	22.0	*25.1*	23.0	− *5.5*	− 7.6	− *8.5*	−20.0
RT,E	145.7			*21.2*	24.6	*22.2*	− 6.3	− *8.4*	− 9.3	*−20.8*
RT,I	124.5				*3.4*	1.0	*−27.5*	−29.6	*−30.5*	−42.0
SD,E	121.1					− *2.4*	−30.9	*−33.0*	−33.9	*−45.4*
SD,I	123.5						*−28.5*	−30.6	*−31.5*	−43.0
NT(P)C,E	152.0	[13.14]						− *0.1*	− 3.0	*−14.5*
NT(P)C,I	152.1								− *2.9*	−14.4
NCC,E	155.0									*−11.5*

IIA
(Index of Interpersonal Activity)

	Means	27.9	51.6	47.2	51.9	37.0	52.6	23.1
CC,E	53.6	*25.7*	2.0	*6.4*	1.7	*16.6*	1.0	*30.5*
CC,I	27.9		*−23.7*	−19.3	*−24.0*	− 9.1	*−24.7*	4.8
RT,E	51.6			*4.4*	− 0.3	*14.6*	− 1.0	*28.5*
RT,I	47.2				− *4.7*	10.2	− *5.4*	24.1
SD,E	51.9					*14.9*	− 0.7	*28.8*
SD,I	37.0	[6.64]					*−15.6*	13.9
NT(P)C,E	52.6							*29.5*

Table 3.18 • Tests of significance of differences between introverts and extroverts, within treatment, with pre-post change scores as the unit of analysis

		CC,I	RT,I	SD,I	NCC,I	NT(P)C,I
	CC,E	3.64[c]				
	RT,E		3.70[c]			
IPAS A	SD,E			2.01[a]		
	NCC,E				4.01[c]	
	NT(P)C,E					—
	CC,E	2.85[b]				
	RT,E		3.14[b]			
S-R_I	SD,E			1.85[a]		
	NCC,E				4.44[c]	
	NT(P)C,E					—
	CC,E	3.29[c]				
	RT,E		4.56[c]			
TAI	SD,E			—		
	NCC,E				4.57[c]	
	NT(P)C,E					—
	CC,E	3.18[c]				
	RT,E		3.14[c]			
S-R_G	SD,E			—		
	NCC,E				4.49[c]	
	NT(P)C,E					—
	CC,E	6.24[d]				
	RT,E		2.91[b]			
Bhv.	SD,E			1.89[a]		
Rts.	NCC,E					
	NT(P)C,E					—

Note: Table entries are t values; t values, $t < 1$ are not entered. $N = 10$ for each of the treatment and control introvert and extrovert groups.

[a]$p < .10$
[b]$p < .05$
[c]$p < .01$
[d]$p < .001$

Table 3.19 · Scheffé post hoc comparisons of post-test means for

Groups		c	R	r	B	b	NT(P)C	nt(p)c	NCC	ncc
						IPAS A				
	Means	43.3	41.5	47.3	36.5	36.1	58.0	58.0	63.2	65.0
C	48.3	5.0	6.8	1.0	11.8	12.2	− 9.7	− 9.7	−14.9	−16.7
c	43.3		1.8	− 4.0	6.8	7.2	−14.7	−14.7	−19.9	−21.7
R	41.5			− 5.8	5.0	5.4	−16.5	−16.5	−21.7	−23.5
r	47.3				10.8	11.2	−10.7	−10.7	−15.9	−17.7
B	36.5					0.4	−21.5	−21.5	−26.7	−28.5
b	36.1						−21.9	−21.9	−27.1	−28.9
NT(P)C	58.0							0.0	− 5.2	− 7.0
nt(p)c	58.0	[2.96]							− 5.2	− 7.0
NCC	63.2									− 1.8
						TAI				
	Means	31.3	32.4	35.2	26.9	28.1	42.4	42.9	46.7	47.5
C	35.6	4.3	3.2	0.4	8.7	7.5	− 6.8	-- 7.3	−11.1	−11.9
c	31.3		− 1.1	− 3.9	4.4	3.2	−11.1	−11.6	−15.4	−16.2
R	32.4			− 2.8	5.5	4.3	−10.0	−10.5	−14.3	−15.1
r	35.2				8.3	7.1	− 7.2	− 7.7	−11.5	−12.3
B	26.9					− 1.2	−15.5	−16.0	−19.8	−20.6
b	28.1						−14.3	−14.8	−18.6	−19.4
NT(P)C	42.4	[1.50]						− 0.5	− 4.3	− 5.1
nt(p)c	42.9								− 3.8	− 4.6
NCC	46.7									− 0.8
						Bhv. Rts.				
	Means	33.8	34.6	37.1	30.4	29.2	43.2	42.9		
C	39.0	5.2	4.4	1.9	8.6	9.8	− 4.2	− 3.9		
c	33.8		− 0.8	− 3.3	3.4	4.6	− 9.4	− 9.1		
R	34.6			− 2.5	4.2	5.4	− 8.6	− 8.3		
r	37.1				6.7	7.9	− 6.1	− 5.8		
B	30.4					1.2	−12.8	−12.5		
b	29.2						−14.0	−13.7		
NT(P)C	43.2	[2.10]						0.3		

counselor main effects

Groups	c	R	r	B	b	NT(P)	Cnt(p)c	NCC	ncc
					S-R$_I$				
Means	151.2	145.2	154.5	138.4	135.5	177.6	178.7	190.8	186.2
159.2	8.0	14.0	4.7	20.8	23.7	−18.4	−19.5	−31.6	−27.0
151.2		6.0	− 3.3	12.8	15.7	−26.4	−27.5	−39.6	−35.0
145.2			− 9.3	6.8	9.7	−32.4	−33.5	−45.6	−41.0
154.5				16.1	19.0	−23.1	−24.2	−36.3	−31.7
138.4					2.9	−39.2	−40.3	−52.4	−47.8
135.5						−42.1	−43.2	−55.3	−50.7
177.6							− 1.1	−13.2	− 8.6
178.7	[4.92]							−12.1	− 7.5
190.8									4.6
					S-R$_G$				
Means	131.5	130.2	140.0	122.3	122.3	152.1	152.0	160.4	161.1
140.3	8.8	10.1	0.3	18.0	18.0	−11.8	−11.7	−20.1	−20.8
131.5		1.3	− 8.5	9.2	9.2	−20.6	−20.5	−28.9	−29.6
130.2			− 9.8	7.9	7.9	−21.9	−21.8	−30.2	−30.9
140.0				17.7	17.7	−12.1	−12.0	−20.4	−21.1
122.3					0.0	−29.8	−29.7	−38.1	−38.8
122.3						−29.8	−29.7	−38.1	−38.8
152.1	[5.64]						0.1	− 8.3	− 9.0
152.0								− 8.4	− 9.1
160.4									− 0.7
					IIA (Index of Interpersonal Activity)				
Means	43.1	49.5	49.3	44.4	44.5	39.1	36.6		
38.4	−4.7	−11.1	−10.9	− 6.0	− 6.1	− 0.7	1.8		
43.1		− 6.2	− 6.3	− 1.3	− 1.4	4.0	6.5		
49.5			0.2	5.1	5.0	10.4	12.9		
49.3				4.9	4.8	10.2	12.7		
44.4					− 0.1	5.3	7.8		
44.5	[2.85]					5.4	7.9		
39.1							2.5		

Note: Negative tabled values indicate that the row means are less than the column means, whereas positive values indicate that the column means are lower. Any differences which exceed the critical values enclosed in the brackets above are significant at the .05 level (two-sided tests).

Table 3.20 · Scheffé post hoc comparisons of post-test means for

Groups		C,I	c,E	c,I	R,E	R,I	r,E	r,I	B,E
					IPAS A				
	Means	65.6	31.4	55.2	40.2	42.8	51.6	43.0	33.0
C,E	31.0	*−34.6*	− 0.4	*−24.2*	− 9.2	*−11.8*	−20.6	*−12.0*	− 2.0
C,I	65.6		*34.2*	10.4	*25.4*	22.8	*14.0*	22.6	*32.6*
c,E	31.4			*−23.8*	− 8.8	−11.4	−20.2	*−11.6*	− 1.6
c,I	55.2				*15.0*	12.4	*3.6*	12.2	*22.2*
R,E	40.2					*− 2.6*	−11.4	*− 2.8*	7.2
R,I	42.8						*− 8.8*	− 0.2	*9.8*
r,E	51.6							*8.6*	18.6
r,I	43.0								*10.0*
B,E	33.0								
B,I	40.0								
b,E	30.2								
b,I	42.0								
NT(P)C,E	48.0								
NT(P)C,I	68.0								
nt(p)c,E	51.2	[5.82]							
nt(p)c,I	64.8								
NCC,E	48.4								
NCC,I	78.0								
ncc,E	53.6								

Note: Negative tabled values indicate that the row means are less than the column means, whereas positive values indicate that the column means are lower. Any differences which

Groups		C,I	c,E	c,I	R,E	R,I	r,E	r,I	B,E
					S-R_I				
	Means	190.6	131.8	170.6	145.4	145.0	158.6	150.4	130.4
C,E	127.8	*−62.8*	− 4.0	*−42.8*	−17.6	*−17.2*	−30.8	*−22.6*	− 2.6
C,I	190.6		*58.8*	20.0	*45.2*	45.6	*32.0*	40.2	*60.2*
c,E	131.8			*−38.8*	−13.6	*−13.2*	−26.8	*−18.6*	1.4
c,I	170.6				*25.2*	25.6	*12.0*	20.2	*40.2*
R,E	145.4					*0.4*	−13.2	*− 5.0*	15.0
R,I	145.0						*−13.6*	− 5.4	*14.6*
r,E	158.6							*8.2*	28.2
r,I	150.4								*20.0*
B,E	130.4								
B,I	146.4								
b,E	128.6								
b,I	142.4								
NT(P)C,E	165.8								
NT(P)C,I	189.4								
nt(p)c,E	172.6	[9.04]							
nt(p)c,I	184.8								
NCC,E	166.4								
NCC,I	215.2								
ncc,E	171.2								

counselor X personality type effects

B,I	b,E	b,I	NT(P) C,E	NT(P) C,I	nt(p) c,E	nt(p) c,I	NCC,E	NCC,I	ncc,E	ncc,I
					IPAS A					
40.0	30.2	42.0	48.0	68.0	51.2	64.8	48.4	78.0	53.6	76.4
−9.0	0.8	−11.0	−17.0	−37.0	−20.2	−33.2	−17.4	−47.0	−22.6	−45.4
25.6	35.4	23.6	17.6	−2.4	14.4	0.8	17.2	−12.4	12.0	−11.0
−8.6	1.2	−10.6	−16.6	−36.6	−19.8	−33.4	−17.0	−46.4	−22.2	−45.0
15.2	25.0	13.2	7.2	−12.8	4.0	−9.6	6.8	−22.8	1.6	−21.2
0.2	10.0	−1.8	−7.8	−27.8	−11.0	−24.6	−8.2	−37.8	−13.4	−36.2
2.8	12.6	0.8	−5.2	−25.2	−8.4	−22.0	−5.6	−35.2	−10.8	−33.6
11.6	21.4	9.6	3.6	−16.4	0.4	−13.2	3.2	−26.4	−2.0	−24.8
3.0	12.8	1.0	−5.0	−25.0	−8.2	−20.8	−5.4	−35.0	−10.6	−33.4
−7.0	2.8	−9.0	−15.0	−35.0	−18.2	−31.8	−15.4	−45.0	−20.6	−43.4
	9.8	−2.0	−8.0	−28.0	−11.2	−24.8	−8.4	−38.0	−13.6	−36.4
		−11.8	−17.8	−37.8	−21.0	−34.6	−18.2	−48.0	−23.4	−46.2
			−6.0	−26.0	−9.2	−22.8	−6.4	−46.0	−11.6	−34.4
				−20.0	−3.2	−16.8	−0.4	−30.0	−5.6	−28.4
					16.8	3.2	19.6	−10.0	14.4	−8.4
						−13.6	2.8	−26.8	−2.4	−25.2
							16.4	−13.2	11.2	−11.6
								−29.6	−5.2	−28.0
									24.4	1.6
										−22.8

exceed the critical values enclosed in the brackets above are significant at the 0.5 level (two-sided tests).

B,I	b,E	b,I	NT(P) C,E	NT(P) C,I	nt(p) c,E	nt(p) c,I	NCC,E	NCC,I	ncc,E	ncc,I
					S-R$_I$					
146.4	128.6	142.4	165.8	189.4	172.6	184.8	166.4	215.2	171.2	201.2
−18.6	−0.8	−14.6	−38.0	−61.6	−44.8	−57.0	−38.6	−87.4	−43.4	−73.4
44.2	62.0	48.2	24.8	1.2	18.0	5.8	24.2	−24.6	19.4	−10.6
−14.6	3.2	−10.6	−34.0	−57.6	−40.8	−53.0	−34.6	−83.4	−39.4	−69.4
24.2	42.0	28.2	4.8	−18.8	−2.0	−14.2	4.2	−44.6	−1.2	−30.6
−1.0	16.8	3.0	−20.4	−44.0	−27.2	−39.4	−21.0	−69.8	−25.8	−55.8
−1.4	16.4	2.6	−20.8	−44.4	−27.6	−39.8	−21.4	−70.2	−26.2	−56.2
12.2	30.0	16.2	−7.2	−30.8	−14.0	−26.2	−7.8	−56.6	−12.6	−42.6
4.0	21.8	8.0	−15.4	−39.0	−22.2	−34.4	−16.0	−64.8	−20.8	−50.8
−16.0	1.8	−12.0	−35.4	−59.0	−42.2	−54.4	−36.0	−84.8	−40.8	−70.8
	17.8	4.0	−19.4	−43.0	−26.2	−38.4	−20.0	−68.3	−24.8	−54.8
		−13.8	−37.2	−60.8	−44.0	−56.2	−37.8	−86.6	−42.6	−72.6
			−23.4	−47.0	−30.2	−42.4	−24.0	−72.8	−28.8	−58.8
				−23.6	−6.8	−19.0	−0.6	−49.4	−5.4	−35.4
					−16.8	4.6	23.0	−25.8	18.2	−11.8
						−12.2	6.2	−42.6	1.4	−28.6
							18.4	−30.4	13.6	−16.4
								−48.8	−4.8	−34.8
									−44.0	14.0
										−30.0

Table 3.20 · *Continued*

Groups		C,I	c,E	c,I	R,E	R,I	r,E	r,I	B,E
					TAI				
	Means	46.0	24.6	38.0	32.2	32.6	39.2	31.2	24.4
C,E	25.2	*−20.8*	0.6	*−12.8*	− 7.0	*− 7.4*	−14.0	*− 6.0*	0.8
C,I	46.0		*21.4*	8.0	*13.8*	13.4	*6.8*	14.8	*21.6*
c,E	24.6			*−13.4*	− 7.6	*− 8.0*	−14.6	*− 6.6*	0.2
c,I	38.0				*5.8*	5.4	*− 1.2*	6.8	*13.6*
R,E	32.2					*− 0.4*	− 7.0	*1.0*	7.8
R,I	32.6						*− 6.6*	1.4	*8.2*
r,E	39.2							*8.0*	14.8
r,I	31.2								*6.8*
B,E	24.4								
B,I	29.4								
b,E	24.8								
b,I	31.4								
NT(P)C,E	40.8								
NT(P)C,I	46.0								
nt(p)c,E	39.4	[3.50]							
nt(p)c,I	44.4								
NCC,E	40.6								
NCC,I	52.8								
ncc,E	39.4								

Groups		C,I	c,E	c,I	R,E	R,I	r,E	r,I	B,E
					$S\text{-}R_G$				
	Means	153.2	123.2	139.8	138.2	122.2	153.2	126.8	123.0
C,E	127.4	*−25.8*	4.2	*−12.4*	−10.8	*− 5.2*	−25.8	*0.6*	4.4
C,I	153.2		*30.0*	13.4	*15.0*	31.0	*0.0*	26.4	*30.2*
c,E	123.2			*−16.6*	−15.0	*1.0*	−30.0	*− 3.6*	0.2
c,I	139.8				*1.6*	17.6	*−13.4*	13.0	*16.8*
R,E	138.2					*16.0*	−15.0	*11.4*	15.2
R,I	122.2						*−31.0*	− 4.6	*− 0.8*
r,E	153.2							*26.4*	30.2
r,I	126.8								*3.8*
B,E	123.0								
B,I	121.6								
b,E	119.2								
b,I	125.4								
NT(P)C,E	151.0	[10.57]							
NT(P)C,I	151.2								
nt(p)c,E	154.0								
nt(p)c,I	152.0								
NCC,E	157.4								
NCC,I	163.4								
ncc,E	152.6								

Table 3.20 • *Continued*

B,I	b,E	b,I	NT(P) C,E	NT(P) C,I	nt(p) c,E	nt(p) c,I	NCC,E	NCC,I	ncc,E	ncc,I
					TAI					
29.4	24.8	31.4	40.8	46.0	39.4	44.4	40.6	52.8	39.4	55.6
−4.2	0.4	*−6.2*	−15.6	*−20.8*	−14.2	*−19.2*	−15.4	*−27.6*	−14.2	*−30.4*
16.6	*21.2*	14.6	*5.2*	−0.0	*6.6*	1.6	*5.4*	−6.8	*6.6*	−9.6
−4.8	−0.2	*−6.8*	−16.2	*−21.4*	−14.8	*−19.8*	−16.0	*−28.2*	−14.8	*−31.0*
8.6	*13.2*	6.6	*−2.8*	−8.0	*−1.4*	−6.4	*−2.6*	−14.8	*−1.4*	−17.6
2.8	7.4	*0.8*	−8.6	*−13.8*	−7.2	*−12.2*	−8.4	*−20.6*	−7.2	*−23.4*
3.2	*7.8*	1.2	*−8.2*	−13.4	*−6.8*	−11.8	*−8.0*	−20.2	*−6.8*	−23.0
9.8	14.4	*7.8*	−1.6	*−6.8*	−0.2	*−5.2*	−1.4	*−13.6*	−0.2	*−16.4*
1.8	*6.4*	−0.2	*−9.6*	−14.8	*−8.2*	−13.2	*−9.4*	−21.6	*−8.2*	−24.4
−5.0	−0.4	*−7.0*	−16.4	*−21.6*	−15.0	*−20.0*	−16.2	*−28.4*	−15.0	*−31.2*
	4.6	−2.0	*−11.4*	−16.6	*−10.0*	−15.0	*−11.2*	−23.4	*−10.0*	−26.2
		−6.6	−16.0	*−21.2*	−14.6	*−19.6*	−15.8	*−28.0*	−14.6	*−30.8*
			−9.4	−14.6	*−8.0*	−13.0	*−9.2*	−21.4	*−8.0*	−24.2
				−5.2	1.4	*−3.6*	0.2	*−12.0*	1.4	*−14.8*
					6.6	1.6	*5.4*	−6.8	*6.6*	−9.6
						−5.8	−1.2	*−13.4*	0.0	*−16.2*
							1.8	−8.4	*5.0*	−11.2
								−12.2	1.2	*−15.0*
									13.4	−2.8
										−16.2

B,I	b,E	b,I	NT(P) C,E	NT(P) C,I	nt(p) c,E	nt(p) c,I	NCC,E	NCC,I	ncc,E	ncc,I
					S-R_a					
121.6	119.2	125.4	151.0	151.2	154.0	152.0	157.4	163.4	152.6	169.6
5.8	7.6	*2.0*	−23.6	*−23.8*	−26.6	*−24.6*	−30.0	*−36.0*	−25.2	*−42.2*
31.6	*34.0*	27.8	*2.2*	2.0	*−0.8*	1.2	*−4.2*	−14.4	*0.6*	−16.4
1.6	4.0	*−2.2*	−27.8	*−28.0*	−30.8	*−28.8*	−34.2	*−40.2*	−29.4	*−46.4*
18.2	*20.6*	14.4	*−11.2*	−11.4	*−14.2*	−12.2	*−17.6*	−23.6	*−12.8*	−29.8
16.6	19.0	*12.8*	−12.8	*−13.0*	−15.8	*−13.8*	−19.2	*−25.2*	−14.4	*−31.4*
0.6	*3.0*	−3.2	*−28.2*	−28.0	*−31.8*	−29.8	*−35.2*	−41.2	*−30.4*	−47.4
31.6	34.0	*27.8*	2.2	*2.0*	−0.8	*1.2*	−4.2	*−14.4*	0.6	*−16.4*
5.2	*7.6*	1.4	*−24.2*	−24.4	*−27.2*	−25.2	*−30.6*	−36.6	*−25.8*	−42.8
1.4	3.8	*−2.4*	−28.0	*−28.2*	−31.0	*−29.0*	−34.4	*−40.4*	−29.6	*−46.6*
	2.4	−3.8	*−29.4*	−29.6	*−32.4*	−30.4	*−35.8*	−41.8	*−31.0*	−48.0
		−6.2	−31.8	*−32.0*	−34.8	*−32.8*	−38.2	*−44.2*	−33.4	*−50.4*
			−25.6	−25.8	*−28.6*	−26.6	*−32.0*	−38.0	*−27.2*	−44.2
				−0.2	−3.0	*−1.0*	−6.4	*−12.4*	−1.6	*−18.6*
					−2.8	−0.8	*−6.2*	−12.2	*−1.4*	−18.4
						2.0	−3.4	*−9.4*	1.4	*−15.6*
							−5.4	−11.4	*−0.6*	−17.6
								−6.0	4.8	*−12.2*
									10.8	−6.2
										−17.0

Table 3.20 · *Continued*

Groups		C,I	c,E	c,I	R,E	R,I	r,E
			Bhv. Rts.				
	Means	43.8	33.6	34.0	42.2	27.0	46.4
C,E	34.2	*– 9.6*	0.6	*0.2*	– 8.0	*7.2*	–12.2
C,I	43.8		*10.2*	9.8	*1.6*	16.8	– *2.6*
c,E	33.6			– *0.4*	– 8.6	*6.6*	–12.8
c,I	34.0				– *8.2*	7.0	*–12.4*
R,E	42.2					*15.2*	– 4.2
R,I	27.0						*–19.4*
r,E	46.4						
r,I	27.8						
B,E	33.4						
B,I	27.4						
b,E	32.6						
b,I	25.8	[2.58]					
NT(P)C,E	47.4						
NT(P)C,I	39.0						
nt(p)c,E	46.8						

Group		C,I	C,E	c,I	R,E	R,I	r,E
			IIA (Index of Interpersonal Activity)				
	Means	24.6	56.0	30.2	50.8	48.2	52.4
C,E	51.2	*26.6*	4.8	*21.0*	0.4	*3.0*	– 1.2
C,I	24.6		*–31.4*	– 5.6	*–26.2*	–23.6	*–27.8*
c,E	56.0			*25.8*	5.2	*7.8*	3.6
c,I	30.2				*–20.6*	–18.0	*–22.2*
R,E	50.8					*2.6*	– 1.6
R,I	48.2						– *4.2*
r,E	52.4						
r,I	46.2						
B,E	50.2						
B,I	38.6						
b,E	53.6						
b,I	35.4						
NT(P)C,E	55.0		[4.84]				
NT(P)C,I	23.2						
Nt(p)c,E	50.2						

Table 3.20 • *Continued*

r,I	B,E	B,I	b,E	b,I	NT(P) C,E	NT(P) C,I	nt(p) c,E	nt(p) c,I
				Bhv. Rts.				
27.8	33.4	27.4	32.6	25.8	47.4	39.0	46.8	39.0
6.4	0.8	*6.8*	1.6	*8.4*	−13.2	− *4.8*	−12.6	− *4.8*
16.0	*10.4*	16.4	*11.2*	18.0	− *3.6*	4.8	− *3.0*	4.8
5.8	0.2	*6.2*	1.0	*7.8*	−13.8	− *5.4*	−13.2	− *5.4*
6.2	*0.6*	6.6	*1.4*	8.2	−*13.4*	− 5.0	−*13.8*	− 5.0
14.4	8.8	*14.8*	9.6	*16.4*	− 5.2	*3.2*	− 4.6	*3.2*
− 0.8	− *6.4*	− 0.4	− *5.6*	1.2	−*20.4*	−12.0	−*19.8*	−12.0
18.6	13.0	*19.0*	13.8	*20.6*	− 1.0	*7.4*	− 0.4	*7.4*
	− *5.6*	0.4	− *4.8*	2.0	−*19.6*	−11.2	−*19.0*	−11.2
		6.0	0.8	*7.6*	−14.0	− *5.6*	−13.4	− *5.6*
			− *5.2*	1.6	−*20.0*	−11.6	−*19.4*	−11.6
				6.8	−14.8	− *6.4*	−14.2	− *6.4*
					−*21.6*	−13.2	−*21.0*	−13.2
						8.4	0.6	*8.4*
							− *7.8*	0.0
								7.8

r,I	B,E	B,I	b,E	b,I	NT(P) C,E	NT(P) C,I	c,E nt(p)	nt(p) c,I
				IIA (Index of Interpersonal Activity)				
46.2	50.2	38.6	53.6	35.4	55.0	23.2	50.2	23.0
5.0	1.0	*12.6*	− 2.4	*15.8*	− 3.8	*28.0*	−*25.6*	*28.2*
−21.6	−*25.6*	−14.0	−*29.0*	−10.8	−*30.4*	1.4	5.8	1.6
9.8	5.8	*17.4*	2.4	*20.6*	1.0	*32.8*	−*20.0*	*33.0*
−16.0	−*20.0*	− 8.4	−*23.4*	− 5.2	−*24.8*	7.0	0.6	7.2
4.6	0.6	*12.2*	− 2.8	*15.4*	− 4.2	*27.6*	− *2.0*	*27.8*
2.0	− *2.0*	9.6	− *5.4*	12.8	− *6.8*	25.0	2.2	25.2
6.2	2.2	*13.8*	− 1.2	*17.0*	− 2.6	*29.2*	− *4.0*	*29.4*
	− *4.0*	7.6	− *7.4*	10.8	− *8.8*	23.0	0.0	23.2
		11.6	− 3.4	*14.8*	− 4.8	*27.0*	−*11.6*	*27.2*
			−*15.0*	3.2	−*16.4*	15.4	3.4	15.6
				18.2	− 1.4	*30.4*	−*14.8*	*30.6*
					−*19.6*	12.2	1.0	12.4
						31.8	4.8	*32.0*
							−*27.0*	0.2
								−*27.2*

Table 3.21 • *Analysis of variance of follow-up data*

Source		IPAS B MS	IPAS B F	$S\text{-}R_I$ MS	$S\text{-}R_I$ F	TAI MS	TAI F
Personality	1	793.80	52.90[d]	3220.72	35.61[c]	449.35	47.50[d]
Personality × Treatment	4	165.68	11.04[b]	584.02	6.46[a]	73.24	7.74[a]
Pers. × Couns. + Pers. × Treat. × Couns.	5	15.00	—	90.43	—	9.46	—
Treatment	4	476.30	29.61[d]	2183.65	45.99[e]	271.87	38.25[d]
Remaining Error	5	16.08	—	47.48	—	7.11	—
TOTAL	19						

Table 3.22 • *Pre-, post-, and follow-up test means and standard*

Treatment	*Couns.*	*Time*	IPAS A Means	IPAS A SD	IPAS B Means	IPAS B SD	$S\text{-}R_I$ Means	$S\text{-}R_I$ SD
Client-Centered	C	Pre	61.2	11.39	62.8	11.45	171.2	33.04
		Post	31.0	5.92	—	—	127.8	16.19
		FU	—	—	31.4	7.02	121.8	18.70
	c	Pre	63.2	11.95	63.0	14.95	177.8	23.11
		Post	31.4	5.41	—	—	131.8	11.38
		FU	—	—	32.0	6.40	126.6	11.85
Desensitization	B	Pre	63.4	15.37	61.4	19.51	174.4	30.36
		Post	33.0	7.52	—	—	130.4	16.04
		FU	—	—	30.2	9.81	127.6	15.80
	b	Pre	60.8	10.64	61.8	11.10	171.8	21.84
		Post	30.2	5.40	—	—	128.6	12.03
		FU	—	—	32.8	5.63	121.2	11.82
Rational-Emotive	R	Pre	61.8	10.38	63.2	11.84	177.8	22.09
		Post	40.2	7.19	—	—	145.4	17.71
		FU	—	—	39.8	8.14	142.2	17.54
	r	Pre	62.4	9.05	61.6	9.40	172.6	20.94
		Post	51.6	9.64	—	—	158.6	23.23
		FU	—	—	50.6	8.88	160.4	20.88
No-Treatment (Placebo) Control		Pre	61.4	14.43	61.6	12.14	176.0	25.75
		Post	48.0	12.01	—	—	165.8	22.74
		FU	—	—	48.2	8.70	164.2	23.52
		Pre	63.8	13.31	64.4	14.50	184.4	21.59
		Post	51.2	10.46	—	—	172.6	19.93
		FU	—	—	50.2	10.54	170.4	16.85
No-Contact Control Group		Pre	60.4	10.88	60.2	10.26	177.0	24.60
		Post	48.4	10.21	—	—	166.4	24.88
		FU	—	—	47.2	10.08	163.0	25.06
		Pre	64.6	11.33	64.8	14.04	182.2	28.17
		Post	53.6	10.67	—	—	171.2	29.35
		FU	—	—	50.2	11.99	171.0	28.20

S-R$_G$		ESD		Bhv. Rts.			MBTI	
MS	F	MS	F	MS	(*df*)	F	MS	F
22.05	1.05	97.68	10.23[a]	244.92	(1)	33.09[c]	1479.20	1.38
276.22	13.17[b]	3.14	0.33	115.47	(3)	15.60[b]	8336.70	7.79[a]
20.97	—	9.54	—	7.40	(4)	—	1070.80	—
970.30	20.20[c]	9.01	3.32	168.34	(3)	21.69[b]	5697.30	6.84[a]
48.03	—	2.71	—	7.76	(4)	—	832.40	—
					15			

[a]$p < .05$ [b]$p < .01$ [c]$p < .005$ [d]$p < .001$ [e]$p < .0005$

deviations for each of the extrovert treatment and control groups

TAI		S-R$_G$		ESD		Bhv. Rts.		MBTI	
Means	SD	Means	SD	Means	SD	Means	SD	Means	SD
45.2	7.57	160.2	34.33	28.8	5.85	54.4	6.84	25.4	6.54
25.2	3.70	127.4	22.54	28.4	5.94	34.2	3.03	—	—
22.6	2.41	122.4	21.34	27.2	9.83	32.2	3.70	20.6	6.23
42.4	8.73	157.6	37.06	28.6	8.32	52.4	9.91	34.6	10.43
24.6	4.62	123.2	24.26	31.8	6.53	33.6	4.34	—	—
23.2	3.77	121.0	19.94	28.6	7.30	30.8	5.21	31.0	6.78
44.4	11.17	159.0	43.81	31.6	5.90	54.6	11.74	35.0	16.73
24.4	2.20	123.0	19.59	32.0	6.78	33.4	5.13	—	—
23.0	3.94	121.6	24.20	32.2	5.63	30.8	5.85	29.4	11.43
43.6	6.84	154.0	27.90	31.8	5.26	51.2	6.83	27.8	9.65
24.8	2.86	119.2	15.55	26.8	5.45	32.6	4.16	—	—
24.0	3.39	118.0	15.61	29.0	4.47	29.2	3.11	25.8	8.67
43.8	11.03	160.4	28.80	28.8	6.30	54.2	9.36	25.4	9.63
32.2	8.32	138.2	21.79	29.2	7.59	42.2	7.69	—	—
30.2	7.26	134.6	20.23	31.0	3.40	41.0	6.78	26.6	7.13
42.2	9.21	161.8	27.48	31.6	5.90	51.4	7.23	30.2	12.21
39.2	9.03	153.2	25.58	28.8	4.97	46.4	7.26	—	—
38.8	8.67	151.6	26.36	29.2	4.60	47.6	7.80	27.4	9.53
46.4	10.01	160.4	31.05	28.2	6.38	53.8	9.20	33.4	11.26
40.8	7.88	151.0	24.81	23.6	5.55	47.4	6.07	—	—
39.4	7.83	146.8	26.70	24.4	5.03	46.0	8.69	30.2	7.56
45.2	6.46	168.4	32.00	31.2	6.42	52.4	6.35	26.6	11.61
39.4	4.99	154.0	26.80	27.6	7.73	46.8	6.14	—	—
37.8	6.61	149.8	30.74	29.8	4.21	45.2	4.44	27.8	5.02
46.0	7.84	167.4	33.61	31.8	4.97	—	—	30.6	15.45
40.6	6.88	157.4	36.62	32.4	4.61	—	—	—	—
38.6	8.29	151.6	31.04	27.8	6.10	—	—	25.6	13.45
45.0	11.55	162.2	29.11	27.2	6.14	—	—	25.4	6.71
39.4	10.67	152.6	33.28	25.4	4.33	—	—	—	—
37.2	10.23	149.0	27.36	26.2	4.44	—	—	21.4	5.37

Table 3.23 · *Pre-, post-, and follow-up test means and standard*

			IPAS A		IPAS B		S-R$_I$	
			Means	SD	Means	SD	Means	SD
Client-Centered	C	Pre	75.8	11.39	73.4	16.00	204.4	29.7
		Post	65.6	11.35	—	—	190.6	28.9
		FU	—	—	61.6	13.18	190.0	29.8
	c	Pre	79.2	13.97	70.6	12.52	198.2	30.4
		Post	55.2	10.99	—	—	170.6	25.7
		FU	—	—	49.4	9.40	162.8	24.9
Desensitization	B	Pre	78.6	12.97	74.4	13.13	205.4	27.7
		Post	40.0	7.04	—	—	146.4	16.4
		FU	—	—	38.0	6.52	141.6	12.6
	b	Pre	81.0	10.46	74.0	10.39	198.6	31.9
		Post	42.0	5.70	—	—	142.4	13.5
		FU	—	—	36.8	7.80	140.8	18.8
Rational-Emotive	R	Pre	77.4	14.22	72.4	16.32	198.8	33.5
		Post	42.8	6.61	—	—	145.0	21.1
		FU	—	—	38.0	8.86	142.6	20.9
	r	Pre	79.0	11.49	72.8	14.84	210.8	28.7
		Post	43.0	6.20	—	—	150.4	14.7
		FU	—	—	40.8	9.01	144.2	14.4
Treatment (Placebo) Control		Pre	80.8	15.20	76.6	17.40	205.6	33.16
		Post	68.0	12.48	—	—	189.4	28.11
		FU	—	—	62.6	14.62	190.6	29.29
		Pre	77.4	12.20	71.2	12.37	199.8	32.25
		Post	64.8	8.75	—	—	184.8	28.09
		FU	—	—	60.2	11.05	184.4	27.80
o-Contact Control		Pre	80.6	11.48	70.6	10.38	214.8	22.40
		Post	78.0	15.52	—	—	215.2	23.53
		FU	—	—	75.2	9.91	217.6	22.41
		Pre	75.4	12.90	73.6	11.15	191.6	24.17
		Post	76.4	13.58	—	—	201.2	22.11
		FU	—	—	72.0	9.82	207.6	24.36

deviations for each of the introvert treatment and control groups

TAI		S-R_G		ESD		Bhv. Rts.		MBTI	
Means	SD	Means	SD	Means	SD	Means	SD	Means	SD
52.4	12.93	159.2	25.45	20.0	6.20	41.4	5.46	31.8	10.92
46.0	13.08	153.2	25.45	19.6	6.06	43.8	5.36	—	—
45.0	12.72	150.4	24.41	19.4	4.04	40.0	7.52	30.4	8.44
52.0	9.92	158.8	43.23	25.0	7.58	44.2	5.54	33.4	8.41
38.0	6.54	139.8	36.99	27.2	9.23	34.0	5.24	—	—
37.0	6.04	134.2	37.67	23.6	7.47	31.8	5.07	26.4	7.13
50.0	9.90	160.2	40.38	25.6	4.83	42.8	11.43	29.8	14.18
29.4	5.41	121.6	24.60	23.6	5.17	27.4	6.34	—	—
30.2	4.87	120.2	23.50	22.6	6.39	23.0	5.48	17.6	5.27
55.0	9.03	159.2	38.28	28.4	5.68	42.2	7.85	29.8	12.54
31.4	3.97	125.4	22.46	29.8	6.42	25.8	4.09	—	—
29.2	2.95	116.6	24.05	29.2	7.12	22.6	5.41	15.0	5.83
56.4	10.43	156.8	43.44	24.6	5.98	43.2	7.69	27.4	15.19
32.6	5.08	122.2	28.00	25.4	7.02	27.0	4.53	—	—
31.6	3.78	117.6	27.17	23.8	6.22	23.2	3.84	15.6	6.62
52.0	13.95	165.2	38.52	27.4	5.81	42.6	10.16	33.0	14.07
31.2	6.38	126.8	22.83	23.2	3.12	27.8	4.87	—	—
31.4	4.04	122.2	24.10	25.6	4.22	21.8	4.38	16.4	4.22
54.2	8.07	160.4	32.58	26.4	6.02	43.6	6.73	31.8	14.32
46.0	7.48	151.2	30.08	23.8	8.58	39.0	6.28	—	—
45.6	6.03	147.0	29.44	26.4	8.08	38.0	6.28	32.6	14.59
53.2	10.99	166.2	32.46	27.2	5.76	44.4	11.49	29.0	8.25
44.4	8.70	152.0	28.70	24.2	10.85	39.0	6.78	—	—
46.4	8.85	147.4	30.65	24.2	7.12	39.8	9.57	28.6	16.94
50.0	7.18	155.0	37.87	27.4	5.27	—	—	28.2	11.28
52.8	6.94	163.4	37.71	24.4	8.76	—	—	—	—
52.4	7.23	160.8	37.44	22.0	4.30	—	—	34.2	9.65
54.4	10.09	168.6	35.18	22.6	5.81	—	—	34.6	9.21
55.6	10.99	169.6	33.35	25.4	3.57	—	—	—	—
56.8	8.64	165.0	34.14	24.6	5.61	—	—	31.8	9.86

Table 3.24 · Scheffé post hoc comparisons of follow-up test means for treatment main effects

Groups		RT	SD	NT(P)C	NCC
			IPAS B		
	Means	42.30	34.45	55.30	61.15
CC	43.60	1.30	9.15	−11.70	−17.55
RT	42.30		7.85	−13.00	−18.85
SD	34.45			−20.85	−26.70
NT(P)C	55.30	[5.62]			− 5.85
			TAI		
	Means	33.00	26.60	42.30	46.25
CC	31.95	− 1.05	5.36	−10.35	−14.30
RT	33.00		6.40	− 9.30	−13.25
SD	26.60	[3.82]		−15.70	−19.65
NT(P)C	42.30				− 3.95
			Bhv. Rts.		
	Means	33.40	26.40	42.25	
CC	33.70	0.30	7.30	− 8.55	
RT	33.40		7.00	− 8.85	
SD	26.40	[3.98]		−15.85	
			S-R$_I$		
	Means	147.35	132.80	177.40	189.80
CC	150.30	2.95	17.50	−27.10	−39.50
RT	147.35		14.55	−30.05	−42.45
SD	132.80			−44.60	−57.00
NT(P)C	177.40	[9.85]			−12.40
			S-R$_G$		
	Means	131.50	119.10	147.75	156.60
CC	132.00	0.50	12.90	−15.75	−24.60
RT	131.50		12.40	−16.25	−25.10
SD	119.19			−28.65	−37.50
NT(P)C	147.75	[8.74]			− 8.85
			MBTI (Introversion-Extroversion)		
	Means	21.50	21.95	29.80	28.25
CC	27.10	5.60	5.15	− 2.70	− 1.15
RT	21.50		− 0.40	− 8.30	− 6.75
SD	21.95	[1.31]		− 7.85	− 6.30
	29.80				1.55

Note: Negative tabled values indicate that the row means are less than the column means, whereas positive values indicate the column means are lower. Any differences which exceed the critical values enclosed in the brackets above are significant at the .05 level (two-sided tests).

Table 3.25 • Scheffé post hoc comparisons of follow-up means for treatment X personality type effects

Groups		CC,I	RT,E	RT,I	SD,E	SD,I	NT(P) C,E	NT(P) C,I	NCC,E	NCC,I
						IPAS B				
	Means	55.5	45.2	39.4	31.5	37.4	49.2	61.4	48.7	73.6
CC,E	31.7	*-23.8*	-13.5	*-7.7*	0.2	*-5.7*	-17.5	*-29.7*	-17.0	*-41.9*
CC,I	55.5		*10.3*	16.1	*24.0*	18.1	*6.3*	-5.9	*6.8*	-18.1
RT,E	45.2			*5.8*	13.7	*7.8*	-4.0	*-16.2*	-3.5	*-28.4*
RT,I	39.4				*7.9*	2.0	*-9.8*	-22.0	*-9.3*	-34.2
SD,E	31.5					*-5.9*	-17.7	*-29.9*	-17.2	*-42.1*
SD,I	37.4						*-11.8*	-24.0	*-11.3*	-36.2
NT(P)C,E	49.2	[11.78]						*-12.2*	0.5	*-24.4*
NT(P)C,I	61.4								*12.7*	-12.2
NCC,E	48.7									*-24.9*
						TAI				
	Means	41.0	34.5	31.5	23.5	29.7	38.6	46.0	37.9	54.6
CC,E	22.9	*-18.1*	-11.6	*-8.6*	-0.6	*-6.8*	-15.7	*-23.1*	-15.0	*-31.7*
CC,I	41.0		*6.5*	9.5	*17.5*	11.3	*2.4*	-5.0	*3.1*	-13.6
RT,E	34.5			*3.0*	11.0	*4.8*	-4.2	*-11.5*	-3.4	*-20.1*
RT,I	31.5				*8.0*	1.8	*-7.1*	-14.5	*-6.4*	-23.1
SD,E	23.5					*-6.2*	-15.1	*-22.5*	-14.4	*-31.1*
SD,I	29.7						*-8.9*	-16.3	*-8.2*	-24.9
NT(P)C,E	38.6	[8.32]						*-7.4*	0.7	*-16.0*
NT(P)C,I	46.0								*8.1*	-8.6
NCC,E	37.9									*-16.7*
						Bhv. Rts.				
	Means	35.9	44.3	22.5	30.0	22.8	45.6	38.9		
CC,E	31.5	*-4.4*	-12.8	*9.0*	1.5	*8.7*	-14.1	*-7.4*		
CC,I	35.9		*-8.4*	13.4	*5.9*	13.1	*-9.7*	-3.0		
RT,E	44.3			*21.8*	14.3	*21.5*	-1.3	*5.4*		
RT,I	22.5				*-7.5*	-0.3	*-23.1*	-16.4		
SD,E	30.0					*7.2*	-15.6	*-8.9*		
SD,I	22.8	[8.16]					*-22.8*	-16.1		
NT(P)C,E	45.6							*6.7*		
NT(P)C,I										
NCC,E										

Note: Negative tabled values indicate that the row means are less than the column means, whereas positive values indicate that the column means are lower. Any differences which exceed the critical values enclosed in the brackets above are significant at the .05 level (two-sided tests).

Table 3.25 · *Continued*

Groups		CC,I	RT,E	RT,I	SD,E	SD,I	NT(P) C,E	NT(P) C,I	NCC,E	NCC,I
							$S\text{-}R_I$			
Means		176.4	151.3	143.4	124.4	141.2	167.3	187.5	167.0	212.6
CC,E	124.2	*−52.5*	−27.1	*−19.2*	− 0.2	*−17.0*	−43.1	*−63.3*	−42.8	*−88.4*
CC,I	176.4		*25.1*	33.0	*52.0*	35.2	*9.1*	−11.1	*9.4*	−36.2
RT,E	151.3			*7.9*	26.9	*10.1*	−16.0	*−36.2*	−15.7	*−61.3*
RT,I	143.4				*19.0*	2.2	*−23.9*	−44.1	*−23.6*	−69.2
SD,E	124.4					*−16.8*	−42.9	*−63.1*	−42.6	*−88.2*
SD,I	141.2						*−26.1*	−46.3	*−25.8*	−71.4
NT(P)C,E	167.3	[24.85]						*−20.3*	0.3	*−45.3*
NT(P)C,I	187.5								*20.5*	−25.1
NCC,E	167.0									*−45.6*
							$S\text{-}R_G$			
Means		142.3	143.1	119.9	119.8	118.4	148.8	146.7	150.3	162.9
CC,E	121.7	*−20.6*	−21.4	*1.8*	1.9	*3.3*	−27.1	*−25.0*	−28.6	*−41.2*
CC,I	142.3		− *0.8*	22.4	*22.5*	23.9	− *6.5*	− 4.4	− *8.0*	−20.6
RT,E	143.1			*23.2*	23.3	*24.7*	− 5.7	− *3.6*	−7.2	*−19.8*
RT,I	119.9				*0.1*	1.5	*−28.9*	−26.8	*−30.4*	−43.0
SD,E	119.8					*1.4*	−29.0	*−26.9*	−30.5	*−43.1*
SD,I	118.4						*−30.4*	−28.3	*−31.9*	−44.5
NT(P)C,E	148.8	[13.89]						*2.1*	− 2.5	*−14.1*
NT(P)C,I	146.7								− *3.6*	−16.2
NCC,E	150.3									*−12.6*
							MBTI			
Means		28.4	27.0	16.0	27.6	16.3	29.0	30.6	23.5	33.0
CC,E	25.8	− *2.6*	− 1.2	*9.8*	− 1.8	*9.5*	− 3.2	− *4.8*	2.3	− *7.2*
CC,I	28.4		*1.4*	12.4	*0.8*	12.1	− *0.6*	− 2.2	*4.9*	− 4.6
RT,E	27.0			*11.0*	− 0.6	*10.7*	− 2.0	− *3.6*	3.5	− *6.0*
RT,I	16.0				*11.6*	− 0.3	*−13.0*	−14.3	*−7.5*	−17.0
SD,E	27.6					*11.3*	− 1.4	− *3.0*	4.1	− *5.4*
SD,I	16.3						*−12.7*	−14.3	− 7.2	−16.7
NT(P)C,E	29.0	[9.94]						− *1.6*	5.5	− *4.0*
NT(P)C,I	30.6								*7.1*	− *2.4*
NCC,E	23.5									− *9.5*

Table 3.26 • *Tests of significance of differences between introverts and extroverts, within treatment, with pre-follow-up change scores as the unit of analysis*

		CC,I	RT,I	SD,I	NCC,I	NT(P)C,I
	CC,E	3.56[c]				
	RT,E		3.61[c]			
IPAS A	SD,E			1.89[a]		
	NCC,E				6.21[d]	
	NT(P)C,E					—
	CC,E	2.98[b]				
	RT,E		3.01[b]			
$S\text{-}R_I$	SD,E			1.85[a]		
	NCC,E				6.10[d]	
	NT(P)C,E					—
	CC,E	3.35[c]				
	RT,E		4.44[c]			
TAI	SD,E			—		
	NCC,E				4.15[c]	
	NT(P)C,E					—
	CC,E	3.19[c]				
	RT,E		3.11			
$S\text{-}R_G$	SD,E			—		
	NCC,E				3.89[c]	
	NT(P)C,E					—
	CC,E	5.51[d]				
Bhv.	RT,E		4.21[c]			
Rts.	SD,E			2.21[a]		
	NCC,E					
	NT(P)C,E					—

Note: Table entries are t values: t values, $t < 1$ are not entered. N = 10 for each of the treatment and control introvert and extrovert groups.

[a] $p < .10$
[b] $p < .05$
[c] $p < .01$
[d] $p < .001$

Table 3.27 · Scheffé post hoc comparisons of follow-up means for

Groups		c	R	r	B	b	NT(P) C	nt(p)c	NCC	ncc
						IPAS B				
	Means	40.7	38.9	45.7	34.1	34.8	55.4	55.2	61.2	61.1
C	46.5	5.8	7.6	0.8	12.4	11.7	− 8.9	− 8.7	−14.7	−14.6
c	40.7		1.8	− 5.0	6.6	5.9	−14.7	−14.5	−20.5	−20.4
R	38.9			− 6.8	4.8	4.1	−16.5	−16.3	−22.3	−22.2
r	45.7				11.6	10.9	− 9.7	− 9.5	−15.5	−15.4
B	34.1					0.7	−21.3	−21.1	−21.1	−27.0
b	34.8						−20.6	−20.4	−26.4	−26.3
NT(P)C	55.4							0.2	− 5.8	− 5.7
nt(p)c	55.2	[1.98]							− 6.0	− 5.9
NCC	61.2									
						TAI				
	Means	30.1	30.9	35.1	26.6	26.6	42.0	42.6	45.5	47.0
C	33.8	3.7	2.9	− 1.3	7.2	7.2	− 8.2	− 8.8	−11.7	−13.2
c	30.1		− 0.8	− 5.0	3.5	3.5	−11.9	−12.5	−15.4	−16.9
R	30.9			− 4.2	4.3	4.3	−11.1	−11.7	−14.6	−16.1
r	35.1				8.5	8.5	− 6.9	− 7.5	−10.4	−11.9
B	26.6					0.0	−15.4	−16.0	−18.9	−20.4
b	26.6						−15.4	−16.0	−18.9	−20.4
NT(P)C	42.0	[1.52]						− 0.6	− 3.5	− 5.0
nt(p)c	42.6								− 2.9	− 4.4
NCC	45.5									− 1.5
						Bhv. Rts.				
	Means	31.3	32.1	34.7	26.9	25.9	42.0	42.5		
C	36.1	4.8	4.0	1.4	9.2	10.2	− 5.9	− 6.4		
c	31.3		− 0.8	− 3.4	4.4	5.4	−10.7	−11.2		
R	32.1			− 2.6	5.2	6.2	− 9.9	−10.4		
r	34.7				7.8	8.8	− 7.3	− 7.8		
B	26.9					1.0	−15.1	−15.6		
b	25.9	[1.54]					−16.1	−16.6		
NT(P)C	42.0							− 0.5		

Note: Negative tabled values indicate that the row means are less than the column means, whereas positive values indicate that the column means are lower. Any differences that exceed the critical values enclosed in the brackets above are significant at the .05 level (two-sided tests).

counselor main effects

Groups		c	R	r	B	b	NT(P) C	nt(p)c	NCC	ncc
						S-R$_I$				
	Means	144.7	142.4	152.3	134.6	131.0	177.4	177.4	190.3	189.3
C	155.9	11.2	13.5	3.6	21.3	24.9	−21.5	−21.5	−34.4	−33.4
c	144.7		2.3	− 7.6	10.1	13.7	−32.7	−32.7	−45.6	−44.6
R	142.4			− 9.9	7.8	11.4	−35.0	−35.0	−47.9	−46.9
r	152.3				17.7	21.3	−25.1	−25.1	−38.0	−37.0
B	134.6					3.6	−42.8	−42.8	−55.7	−54.7
b	131.0						−46.4	−46.4	−59.3	−58.3
NT(P)C	177.4							0.0	−12.9	−11.9
nt(p)c	177.4	[4.42]							−12.9	−11.9
NCC	190.3									1.0
						S-R$_{II}$				
	Means	127.6	126.1	136.9	120.9	117.3	146.9	148.6	156.2	157.0
C	136.4	8.8	10.3	− 0.5	16.5	19.1	−10.5	−12.2	−19.8	−20.6
c	127.6		1.5	− 9.3	6.7	10.3	−19.3	−21.0	−28.6	−29.4
R	126.1			−10.8	5.2	8.8	−20.8	−22.5	−30.1	−30.9
r	136.9				16.0	19.6	−10.0	−11.7	−19.3	−20.1
B	120.9					3.6	−26.0	−27.7	−35.3	−36.1
b	117.3						−29.6	−31.3	−38.9	−39.7
NT(P)C	146.9	[5.09]						− 1.7	− 9.3	−10.1
nt(p)c	148.6								− 7.6	− 8.4
NCC	156.2									− 0.8
						MBTI				
	Means	28.7	21.1	21.9	23.5	20.4	31.4	28.2	29.9	26.6
C	25.5	−3.2	4.4	3.6	2.0	5.1	− 5.9	− 2.7	− 4.4	− 1.1
c	28.7		7.6	6.8	5.2	8.3	− 2.7	0.5	− 1.2	2.1
R	21.1			− 0.8	− 2.4	0.7	−10.3	− 7.1	− 8.8	− 5.5
r	21.9				− 1.6	1.5	− 9.5	− 6.3	− 8.0	− 4.7
B	23.5					3.1	− 7.9	− 4.7	− 6.4	− 3.1
b	20.4						−11.0	− 7.8	− 9.5	− 6.2
NT(P)C	31.4							3.2	1.5	4.8
nt(p)c	28.2	[5.12]							− 1.7	1.6
NCC	29.9									3.3

Table 3.28 • Scheffé post hoc comparison of follow-up test means for

Groups		C,I	c,E	c,I	R,E	R,I	r,E	r,I	B,E
					IPAS B				
	Means	61.6	32.0	49.4	39.8	38.0	50.6	40.8	30.2
C,E	31.4	*−30.2*	− 0.6	*−18.0*	− 8.4	*− 6.6*	−19.2	*− 9.4*	1.2
C,I	61.6		*29.6*	12.2	*21.8*	23.6	*−11.0*	20.8	*31.4*
c,E	32.0			*−17.4*	− 7.7	*− 6.0*	−18.6	*− 8.8*	1.8
c,I	49.4				*9.6*	11.4	*− 1.2*	8.6	*19.2*
R,E	39.8					*1.8*	−10.8	*− 1.0*	9.6
R,I	38.0						*−12.6*	− 2.3	*7.8*
r,E	50.6							*9.8*	20.4
r,I	40.8								*10.6*
B,E	30.2								
B,I	38.0								
b,E	32.8								
b,I	36.8								
NT(P)C,E	48.2		[4.04]						
NT(P)C,I	62.6								
nt(p)c,E	50.2								
nt(p)c,I	60.2								
NCC,E	47.2								
NCC,I	75.2								
ncc,E	50.2								

Note: Negative tabled values indicate that the row means are less than the column means, whereas positive values indicate that the column means are lower. Any differences that ex-

Groups		C,I	c,E	c,I	R,E	R,I	r,E	r,I	B,E
				S-R_1					
	Means	190.0	126.6	162.8	142.2	142.6	160.4	144.2	127.6
C,E	121.8	*−68.2*	− 4.8	*−41.0*	−20.4	*−20.8*	−38.6	*−22.4*	− 5.8
C,I	190.0		*63.4*	27.2	*47.8*	47.4	*29.6*	45.8	*62.4*
c,E	126.6			*−36.2*	−15.6	*−16.0*	−33.8	*−17.6*	− 1.0
c,I	162.8				*20.6*	20.2	*2.4*	18.6	*35.2*
R,E	142.2					*− 0.4*	−18.2	*− 2.0*	14.6
R,I	142.6						*−17.8*	− 1.6	*15.0*
r,E	160.4							*16.2*	32.8
r,I	144.2								*16.6*
B,E	127.6								
B,I	141.6								
b,E	121.2								
b,I	140.8			[10.09]					
NT(P)C,E	164.2								
NT(P)C,I	190.6								
nt(p)c,E	170.4								
nt(p)c,I	184.4								
NCC,E	163.0								
NCC,I	217.6								
ncc,E	171.0								

counselor X personality type effects

B,I	b,E	b,I.	NT(P) C,E	NT(P) C,I	nt(p) c,E	nt(p) c,I	NCC,E	NCC,I	ncc,E	ncc,I
					IPAS B					
38.0	32.8	36.8	48.2	62.6	50.2	60.2	47.2	75.2	50.2	72.0
−6.6	−1.4	*−5.4*	−16.8	*−31.2*	−18.8	*−28.8*	−15.8	*−43.8*	−18.8	*−40.6*
23.6	*28.8*	24.8	*13.4*	−1.0	*11.4*	1.4	*14.4*	−13.6	*11.4*	−10.4
−6.0	−0.8	*−4.8*	−16.2	*−30.6*	−18.2	*−28.2*	−15.2	−14.2	−18.2	*−40.0*
11.4	*16.6*	12.6	*1.2*	−13.2	*−0.8*	−10.8	*2.4*	−25.8	*−0.8*	−22.6
1.8	7.0	*3.0*	−8.4	*−22.8*	−10.4	*−20.4*	−7.4	*−35.4*	−10.4	*−32.2*
0.0	*5.2*	1.2	*−10.2*	−24.6	*−12.2*	−22.2	*−9.2*	−37.2	*−12.2*	−34.0
12.6	17.8	*13.8*	2.4	*−12.0*	0.4	*−9.6*	3.4	*−24.6*	0.4	*−21.4*
2.8	*8.0*	4.0	*−7.4*	−21.8	*−9.4*	−19.4	*−6.4*	−34.4	*−9.4*	−31.2
−7.8	−2.6	*−6.6*	−18.0	*−32.4*	−20.0	*−30.0*	−17.0	*−45.0*	−20.0	*−41.8*
	5.2	1.2	*−10.2*	−24.6	*−12.2*	−22.2	*−9.2*	−37.2	*−12.2*	−34.0
		−4.0	−15.4	*−29.8*	−17.4	*−27.4*	−14.4	*−42.8*	−17.4	*−39.2*
			−11.4	−25.8	*−13.4*	−23.4	*−10.4*	−38.4	*−13.4*	−35.2
				−14.4	−2.0	*−12.0*	1.0	*−27.0*	−2.0	*−23.8*
					−12.4	0.4	*15.4*	−12.6	*12.4*	−9.4
						−10.0	3.0	*−25.0*	0.0	*−21.8*
							13.0	−15.0	*10.0*	−11.8
								−28.0	3.0	*−24.8*
									25.0	3.2
										−21.8

ceed the critical values enclosed in the brackets above are significant at the .05 level (two-sided tests).

B,I	b,E	b,I	NT(P) C,E	NT(P) C,I	nt(p) c,E	NT(P) C,I	NCC,E	NCC,I	ncc.E	ncc.I
					S-R$_I$					
141.6	121.2	140.8	164.2	190.6	170.4	184.4	163.0	217.6	171.0	207.6
−19.8	0.6	*−19.0*	−42.4	*−68.8*	−48.6	*−62.6*	−41.2	*−95.8*	−49.2	*−85.8*
48.4	*68.8*	49.2	*25.8*	−0.6	*19.6*	5.6	*27.0*	−27.6	*19.0*	−17.6
−15.0	5.4	*−14.2*	−37.6	*−64.0*	−43.8	*−57.8*	−36.4	*−91.0*	−44.4	*−81.0*
21.2	*41.6*	22.8	*−1.4*	−27.8	*−7.6*	−21.6	*−0.2*	−54.8	*−8.2*	−44.8
0.6	21.0	*1.4*	−22.0	*−48.4*	−28.2	*−42.2*	−20.8	*−75.4*	−28.8	*−65.4*
1.0	*21.4*	1.8	*−21.6*	−48.0	−27.8	−41.8	*−20.4*	−75.0	*−28.4*	−65.0
18.8	39.2	*19.6*	−3.8	*−30.2*	−10.0	*−24.0*	−2.6	−57.2	−10.6	*−47.2*
2.6	*23.0*	3.4	*−20.0*	−46.4	*−26.2*	−40.2	*−18.8*	−73.4	*−26.8*	−63.4
−14.0	6.4	*−13.2*	−36.6	−63.0	−42.8	*−56.8*	−35.4	*−90.0*	−43.4	*−80.0*
	20.4	0.8	*−22.6*	−49.0	*−28.8*	−42.8	*−21.4*	−76.0	*−29.4*	−66.0
		−19.6	−43.0	*−69.4*	−49.2	*−63.2*	−41.9	*−96.4*	−49.8	*−86.4*
			−23.4	−49.6	*−29.6*	−43.6	−22.2	−76.8	*−30.2*	−66.8
				−26.4	−6.2	*−20.2*	1.2	*−53.4*	−6.8	*−43.4*
					20.2	6.2	*27.6*	−27.0	*−19.6*	−17.0
						−14.0	7.4	*−47.2*	−0.6	*−37.2*
							21.4	−33.2	*13.4*	−23.2
								−54.6	−8.0	*−44.6*
									46.6	10.0
										−36.6

Table 3.28 • *Continued*

Groups		C,I	c,E	c,I	R,E	R,I	r,E	r,I	B,E
					TAI				
	Means	45.0	23.2	37.0	30.2	31.6	38.8	31.4	23.0
C,E	22.6	*−22.4*	− 0.6	*−14.4*	− 7.6	*− 9.0*	−16.2	*− 8.8*	− 0.4
C,I	45.0		*21.8*	8.0	*14.8*	13.4	*6.2*	13.6	*22.0*
c,E	23.2			*−13.8*	− 7.0	*− 8.4*	−15.6	*− 8.2*	0.2
c,I	37.0				*6.8*	5.4	*− 1.8*	5.6	*14.0*
R,E	30.2					*− 1.4*	− 8.6	*− 1.2*	7.2
R,I	31.6						*− 7.2*	0.2	*8.6*
r,E	38.8							*7.4*	15.8
r,I	31.4								*8.4*
B,E	23.0								
B,I	30.2								
b,E	24.0								
b,I	29.2								
NT(P)C,E	39.4								
NT(P)C,I	45.6								
nt(p)c,E	37.8		[4.50]						
nt(p)c,I	46.4								
NCC,E	38.6								
NCC,I	52.4								
ncc,E	37.2								

Groups		C,I	c,E	c,I	R,E	R,I	r,E	r,I	B,E
					S-R$_G$				
	Means	150.4	121.0	134.2	134.6	117.6	151.6	122.2	121.6
C,E	122.4	*−28.0*	1.4	*−11.8*	−12.2	*4.8*	−29.2	*0.2*	0.8
C,I	150.4		*29.4*	16.2	*15.8*	32.8	*− 1.2*	28.2	*28.8*
c,E	121.0			*−13.2*	−13.6	*3.4*	−30.6	*− 1.2*	− 0.6
c,I	134.2				*− 0.4*	16.6	*−17.4*	12.0	*12.6*
R,E	134.6					*17.0*	−17.0	*12.4*	13.0
R,I	117.6						*−34.0*	− 4.6	*− 4.0*
r,E	151.6							*29.4*	30.0
r,I	122.2								*0.6*
B,E	121.6								
B,I	120.2								
b,E	118.0								
b,I	116.6								
NT(P)C,E	146.8								
NT(P)C,I	147.0		[11.50]						
nt(p)c,E	149.8								
nt(p)c,I	147.4								
NCC,E	151.6								
NCC,I	160.8								
ncc,E	149.0								

Table 3.28 • *Continued*

B,I	b,E	b,I	NT(P) C,E	NT(P) C,I	nt(p) c,E	nt(p) c,I	NCC,E	NCC,I	ncc,E	ncc,I
					TAI					
30.2	24.0	29.2	39.4	45.6	37.8	46.4	38.6	52.4	37.2	56.8
−7.6	−1.4	*−6.6*	−16.8	*−23.0*	−15.2	*−23.8*	−16.0	*−29.8*	−14.6	*−34.2*
14.8	*21.0*	15.8	*5.6*	−0.6	*7.2*	−1.4	*6.4*	−7.4	*7.8*	−11.8
−7.0	−0.8	*−6.0*	−16.2	*−22.4*	−14.6	*−23.2*	−15.4	*−29.2*	−14.0	*−33.6*
6.8	*13.0*	7.8	*−2.4*	−8.6	*−0.8*	−9.4	*−1.6*	−15.4	*−0.2*	−19.8
0.0	6.2	*−1.0*	−9.2	*−15.4*	−7.6	*−16.2*	−8.6	*−22.2*	−7.0	*−26.6*
1.4	*7.6*	2.4	*−7.8*	−14.0	*−6.2*	−14.8	*−7.0*	−20.8	*−5.6*	−25.2
8.6	14.8	*9.6*	−0.5	*−6.8*	1.0	*−7.6*	0.2	*−13.6*	1.6	*−18.0*
1.2	*7.4*	2.2	*−8.0*	−14.2	*−6.4*	−15.0	*−7.2*	−21.0	*−5.8*	−25.4
−7.2	−1.0	*−6.2*	−16.4	−22.6	−14.8	*−23.4*	−15.6	*−29.4*	−14.2	*−33.8*
	6.2	1.0	*−9.2*	−15.4	*−7.6*	−16.2	*−8.6*	−22.2	*−7.0*	−26.6
		−5.2	−15.4	*−21.6*	−13.8	*−22.4*	−14.6	*−28.4*	−13.2	*−32.8*
			−10.2	−16.4	*−8.6*	−17.2	*−9.4*	−23.2	*−8.0*	−27.6
				−6.2	1.6	*−7.0*	0.8	*−13.0*	2.2	*−17.4*
					7.8	−0.8	*7.0*	−6.8	*8.4*	−11.2
						−8.6	−0.8	*−14.6*	0.6	*−19.0*
							7.8	−6.0	*9.2*	−10.4
								−13.8	1.4	*−18.2*
									15.2	−4.4
										−19.6

B,I	b,E	b,I	NT(P) C,E	NT(P) C,I	nt(p) c,E	nt(p) c,I	NCC,E	NCC,I	ncc,E	ncc,I
					S-R$_G$					
120.2	118.0	116.6	146.8	147.0	149.8	147.4	151.6	160.8	149.0	165.0
2.2	4.4	*5.8*	−24.4	*−24.6*	−27.4	*−25.0*	−29.2	*−38.4*	−26.6	*−42.6*
30.2	*32.4*	33.8	*1.6*	3.4	*0.6*	3.0	*−1.2*	−10.4	*1.4*	−14.6
0.8	3.0	*4.4*	−25.8	*−26.0*	−27.8	*−26.4*	−30.6	*−39.8*	−28.0	*−44.0*
14.0	*16.2*	17.6	*−12.6*	−12.8	*−15.6*	−13.2	*−17.4*	−26.6	*−14.8*	−30.8
14.4	16.6	*18.0*	−12.2	*−12.4*	−15.2	*−12.8*	−17.0	*−26.2*	−14.4	*−30.4*
−2.6	*−0.4*	1.0	*−29.2*	−29.4	*−32.2*	−29.8	*−34.0*	−43.2	*−31.4*	−47.4
31.4	33.6	*35.0*	2.8	*4.6*	1.8	*4.2*	0.0	*−9.2*	2.6	*−13.4*
2.0	*4.2*	5.6	*−24.6*	−24.8	*−27.6*	−25.2	*−29.0*	−38.6	*−26.8*	−42.8
1.4	3.6	*5.0*	−25.2	*−25.4*	−28.2	*−25.8*	−30.0	*−39.2*	−27.4	*−43.4*
	2.2	3.6	*−26.6*	−26.8	*29.6*	−27.2	*−31.4*	−40.6	*−28.8*	−44.8
		1.4	−28.8	*−29.0*	−31.8	*−29.4*	−33.6	*−42.8*	−31.0	*−47.0*
			−30.2	−30.4	*−33.2*	−30.8	*35.0*	−44.2	*−32.4*	−48.4
				−0.2	−3.0	*0.6*	−4.8	*−14.0*	−2.2	*−18.2*
					−2.8	−0.4	*−4.6*	−13.8	*−2.0*	−18.0
						2.4	1.8	*−11.0*	0.8	*−15.2*
							4.2	−13.4	*−1.6*	−17.6
								−9.2	2.6	*−13.4*
									11.8	−4.2
										−16.0

Table 3.28 · Continued

Groups		C,I	c,E	c,I	R,E	R,I	r,E	r,I	B,E
					Bhv. Rts.				
	Means	40.0	30.8	31.8	41.0	23.2	47.6	21.8	30.8
C,E	32.2	*—7.8*	1.4	*0.4*	—8.8	*9.0*	—15.4	*10.4*	1.4
C,I	40.0		*9.2*	8.2	*—1.0*	16.8	*—7.6*	18.2	*9.2*
c,E	30.8			*—1.0*	—10.2	*7.6*	—16.8	*9.0*	0.0
c,I	31.8				*—9.2*	8.6	*—15.8*	10.0	*1.0*
R,E	41.0					*17.8*	—6.6	*19.2*	10.2
R,I	23.2						*—24.4*	1.4	*—7.6*
r,E	47.6							*25.8*	16.8
r,I	21.8								*9.0*
B,E	30.8								
B,I	23.0								
b,E	29.2								
b,I	22.6	[3.29]							
NT(P)C,E	46.0								
NT(P)C,I	38.0								
nt(p)c,E	45.2								

Groups		C,I	c,E	c,I	R,E	R,I	r,E	r,I	B,E
				MBTI					
	Means	30.4	31.0	26.4	26.6	15.6	27.4	16.4	29.4
C,E	20.6	*—9.8*	—10.4	*—5.8*	—6.0	*5.0*	—6.8	*4.2*	—8.8
C,I	30.4		*0.6*	4.0	*3.8*	14.8	*3.0*	14.0	*1.0*
c,E	31.0			*4.6*	4.4	*15.4*	3.6	*14.6*	1.6
c,I	26.4				*—0.2*	10.8	*—1.0*	10.0	*—3.0*
R,E	26.6					*11.0*	—0.8	*10.2*	—2.8
R,I	15.6						*—11.8*	—0.8	*—13.8*
r,E	27.4							*11.0*	—2.0
r,I	16.4								*—13.0*
B,E	29.4								
B,I	17.6								
b,E	25.8								
b,I	15.0								
NT(P)C,E	30.2								
NT(P)C,I	32.6								
nt(p)c,E	27.8	[10.00]							
nt(p)c,I	28.6								
NCC,E	25.6								
NCC,I	34.2								
ncc,E	21.4								

Table 3.28 • *Continued*

B,I	b,E	b,I	NT(P) C,E	NT(P) C,I	nt(p) c,E	nt(p) c,I	NCC,E	NCC,I	ncc,E	ncc,I
					Bhv. Rts.					
23.0	29.2	22.6	46.0	38.0	45.2	39.8				
9.2	3.0	*9.6*	−13.8	− *5.8*	−13.0	− *7.6*				
17.0	*10.8*	17.4	− *6.0*	2.0	− *5.2*	0.2				
7.8	1.6	*8.2*	−15.2	− *7.2*	−14.4	− *9.0*				
8.8	*2.6*	9.2	−*14.2*	− 6.2	−*13.4*	− *8.0*				
18.0	11.8	*18.4*	− 5.0	*3.0*	− 4.2	*1.2*				
0.2	− *6.0*	0.6	−*22.8*	−14.8	−*22.0*	−16.6				
24.6	18.4	*25.0*	1.6	*9.6*	2.4	*7.8*				
− 1.2	− *7.4*	− 0.8	−*24.2*	−16.2	−*23.4*	−18.0				
7.8	1.6	*8.2*	−15.2	− *7.2*	−14.4	− *9.0*				
	− *6.2*	0.4	−*23.0*	−16.0	−*23.2*	−16.8				
		6.6	−16.8	− *8.8*	−16.0	−*10.6*				
			−*23.4*	−15.4	−*22.6*	−17.2				
				8.0	0.8	*6.2*				
					− *7.2*	− 1.8				
						5.4				

B,I	b,E	b,I	NT(P) C,E	NT(P) C,I	nt(p) c,E	nt(p) c,I	NCC,E	NCC,I	ncc,E	ncc,I
					MBTI					
17.6	25.8	15.0	30.2	32.6	27.8	28.6	25.6	34.2	21.4	31.8
3.0	− 5.2	*5.6*	− 9.6	−*12.0*	− 7.2	− *8.0*	− 5.0	−*13.6*	− 0.8	−*11.2*
12.8	*4.6*	15.4	*0.2*	− 2.2	*2.6*	1.8	*4.8*	3.8	*9.0*	− 1.4
13.4	5.2	*16.0*	0.8	− *1.6*	3.2	*2.4*	5.4	−*3.2*	9.6	− *0.8*
8.8	*0.6*	11.4	− *3.8*	− 6.2	− *1.4*	− 2.2	*0.8*	− 7.8	*5.0*	− 5.4
9.0	0.8	*11.6*	− 3.6	− *6.0*	− 1.2	− *2.0*	1.0	− *7.6*	5.2	− *5.2*
− 2.0	−*10.2*	0.6	−*14.6*	−17.0	−*12.2*	−13.0	−*10.0*	−18.6	*5.8*	−16.2
9.8	1.6	*12.4*	− 2.8	− *5.2*	− 0.4	− 1.2	1.8	− *6.8*	6.0	− *4.4*
− 1.2	− *9.4*	1.4	−*13.8*	−16.2	−*11.4*	−12.2	− *9.2*	−17.8	− *5.0*	−15.4
11.8	4.0	*14.4*	− 0.8	− 3.2	1.6	*0.8*	3.8	− *4.8*	8.0	− 2.4
	− *8.2*	2.6	−*12.6*	−15.0	−*10.2*	−11.0	− *8.0*	−16.6	− *3.8*	−14.2
		10.8	− 4.4	− *6.6*	− 2.0	− *2.8*	0.2	− *8.4*	4.4	− *6.0*
			−*15.2*	−17.6	−*12.8*	−13.6	−*10.6*	−19.2	− *6.4*	−16.8
				− *2.4*	*2.4*	*1.6*	4.6	− *4.0*	8.8	− *1.6*
					4.8	4.0	*7.0*	− 1.6	*11.2*	0.8
						− *0.8*	2.2	− *6.4*	6.4	− *4.0*
							3.0	− 5.6	*7.2*	− 3.2
								− *8.6*	4.2	− *6.2*
									12.8	2.4
										−*10.4*

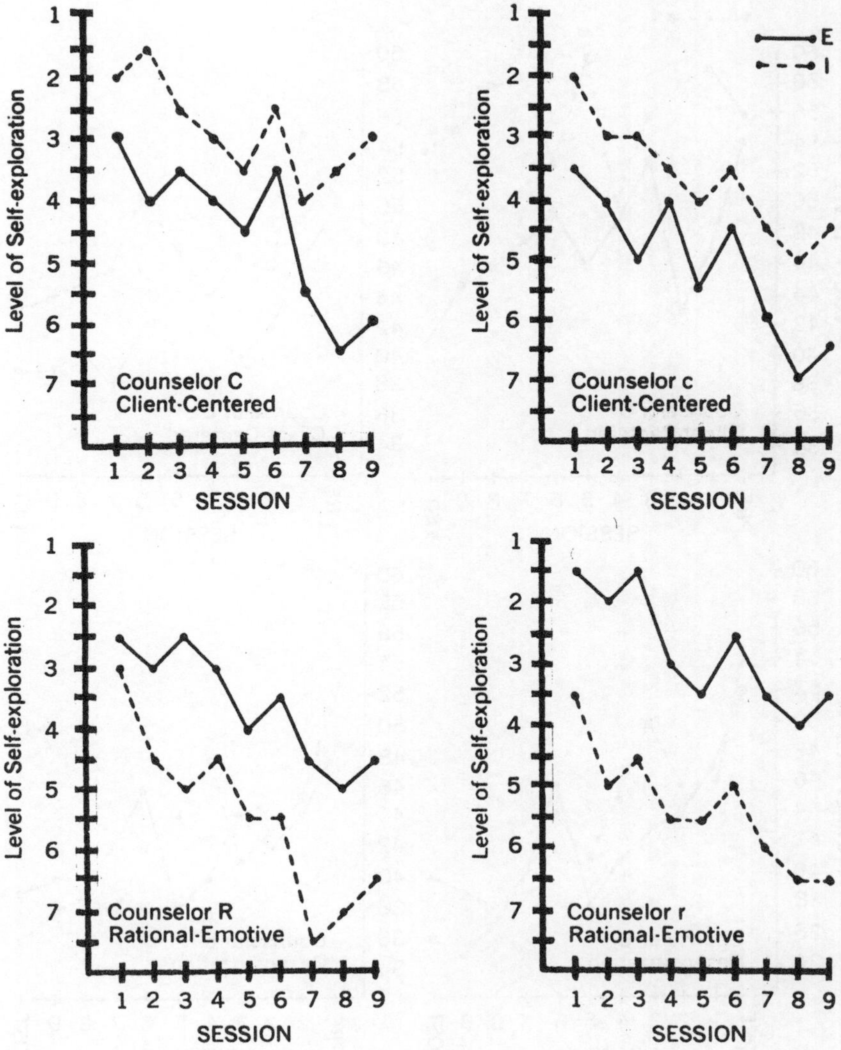

Figure 3.1 · Weekly changes in mean level of client self-exploration of each of the client-centered (CC) and rational-emotive (RT) treatment groups (E = Extrovert, I = Introvert)

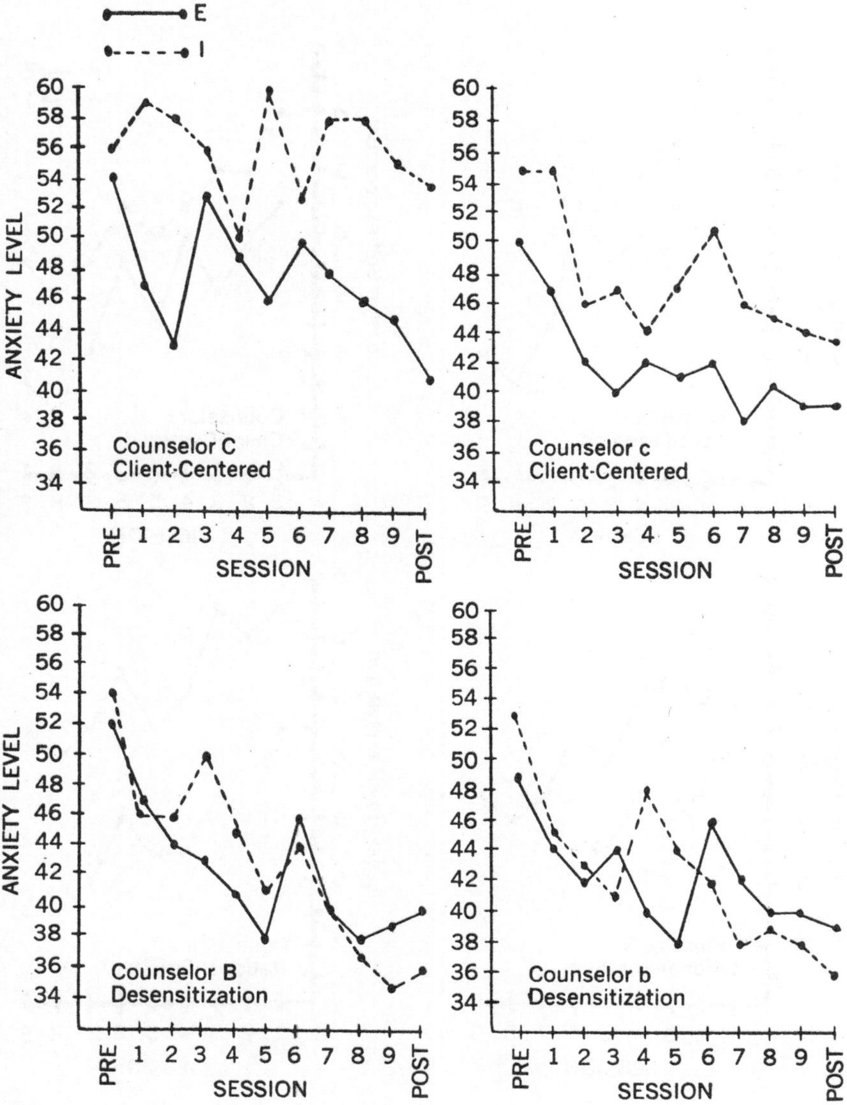

Figure 3.2 · *Weekly changes in group mean on the* State Anxiety Inventory *for each treatment, each counselor, and each client personality type (E = Extrovert, I = Introvert)*

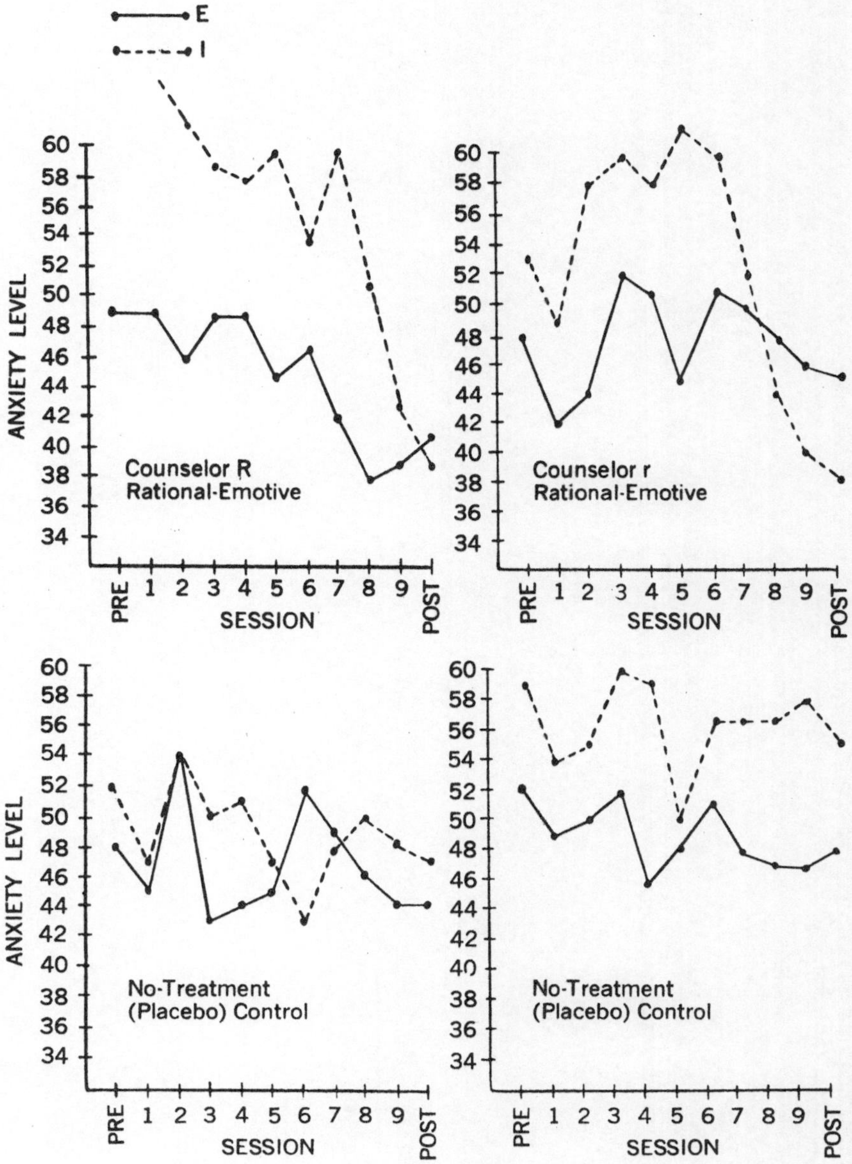
E
I
ANXIETY LEVEL
SESSION
PRE 1 2 3 4 5 6 7 8 9 POST
Counselor R
Rational-Emotive
Counselor r
Rational-Emotive
No-Treatment
(Placebo) Control
No-Treatment
(Placebo) Control

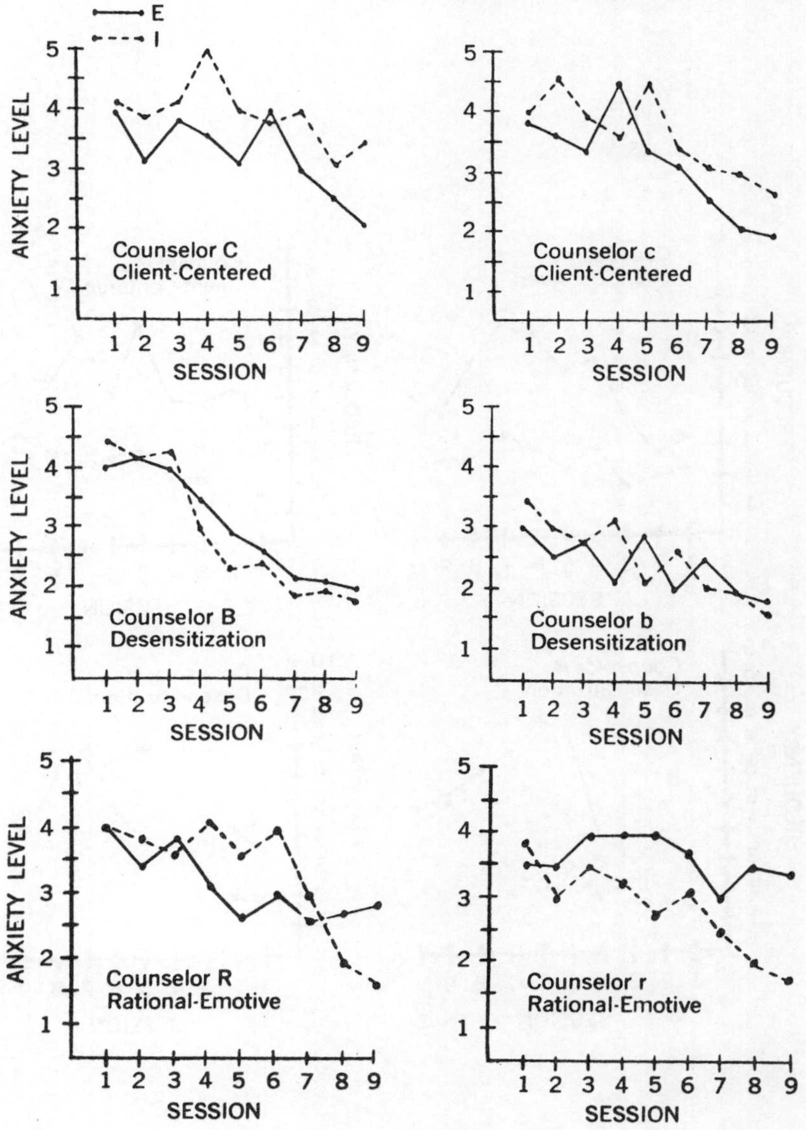

Figure 3.3 • *Weekly changes in group mean on Therapist Rating Sheet for each of the client-centered (CC), rational-emotive (RT), and systematic desensitization (SD) treatment groups (E = Extrovert, I = Introvert)*

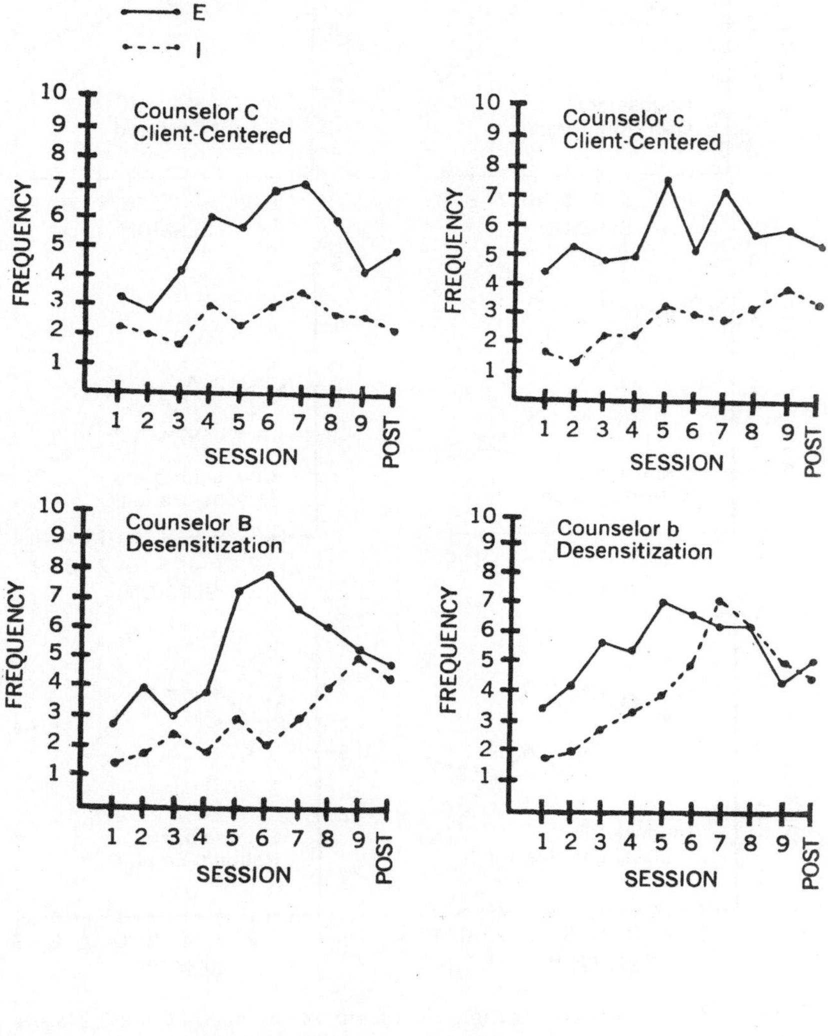

Figure 3.4 · Weekly changes in group mean on the Index of Interpersonal Activity for each treatment, each counselor, and each client personality type (E = Extrovert, I = Introvert)

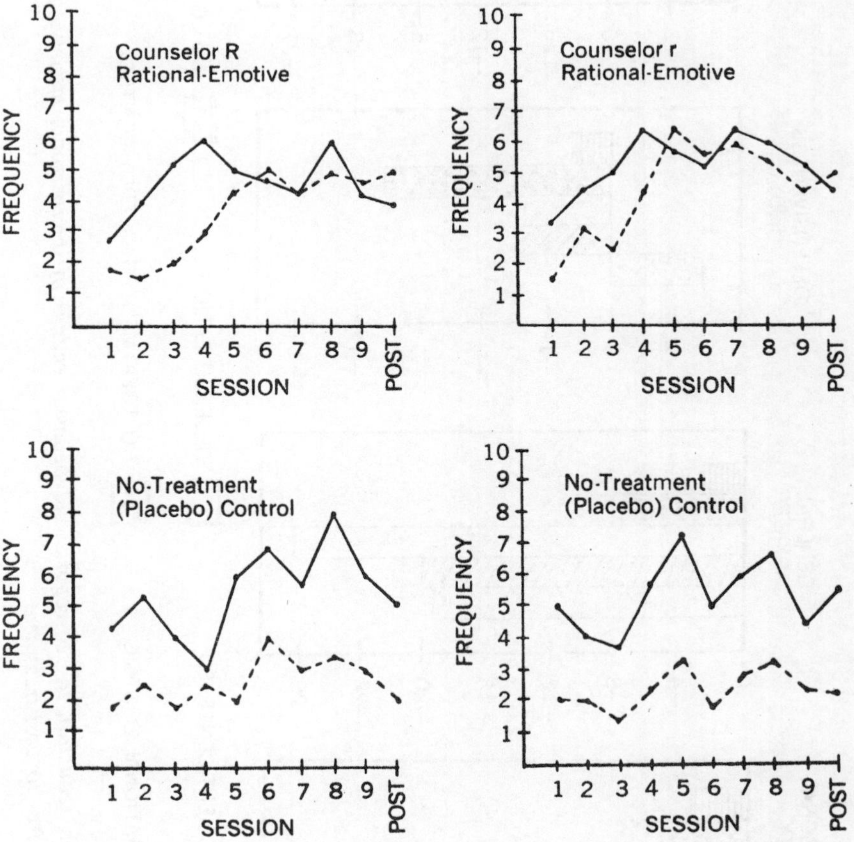
Counselor R
Rational-Emotive
Counselor r
Rational-Emotive
No-Treatment
(Placebo) Control
No-Treatment
(Placebo) Control
FREQUENCY
SESSION
1 2 3 4 5 6 7 8 9 POST
10 9 8 7 6 5 4 3 2 1

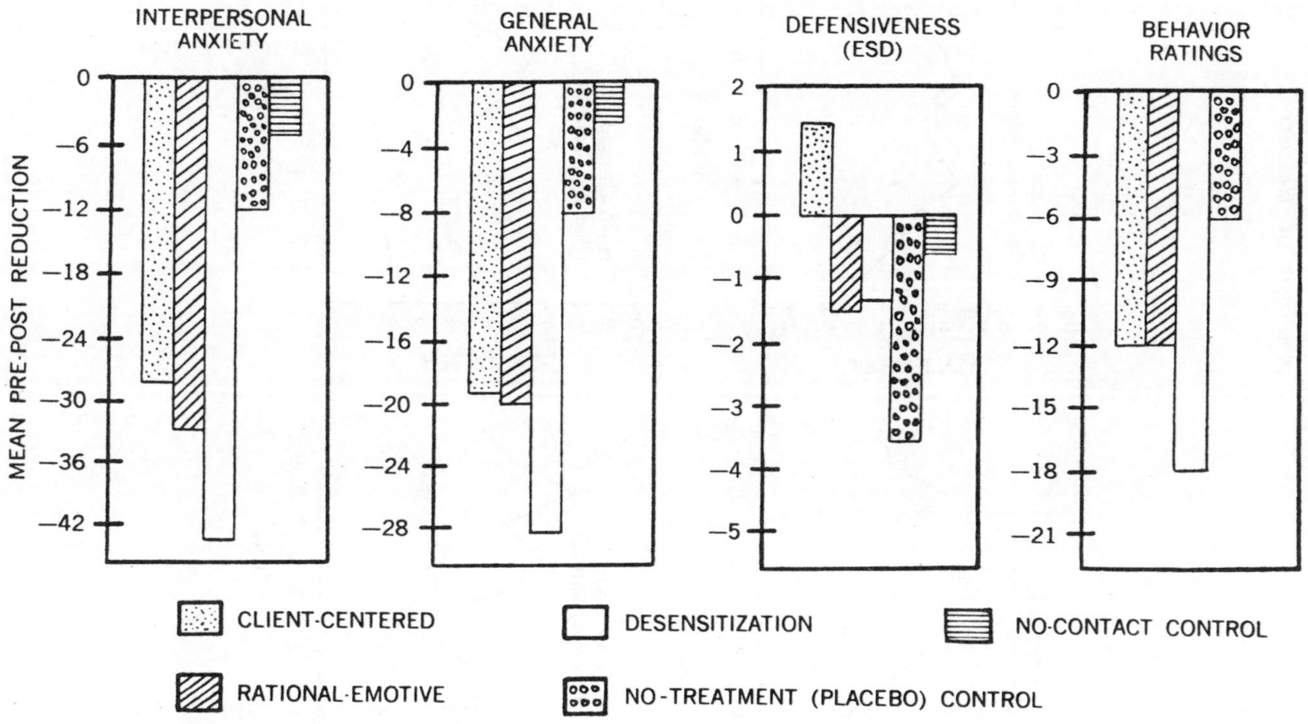

Figure 3.5 • *Mean reduction in self-reports and behavior ratings of interpersonal anxiety, general anxiety, and defensiveness from pre- to post-treatment*

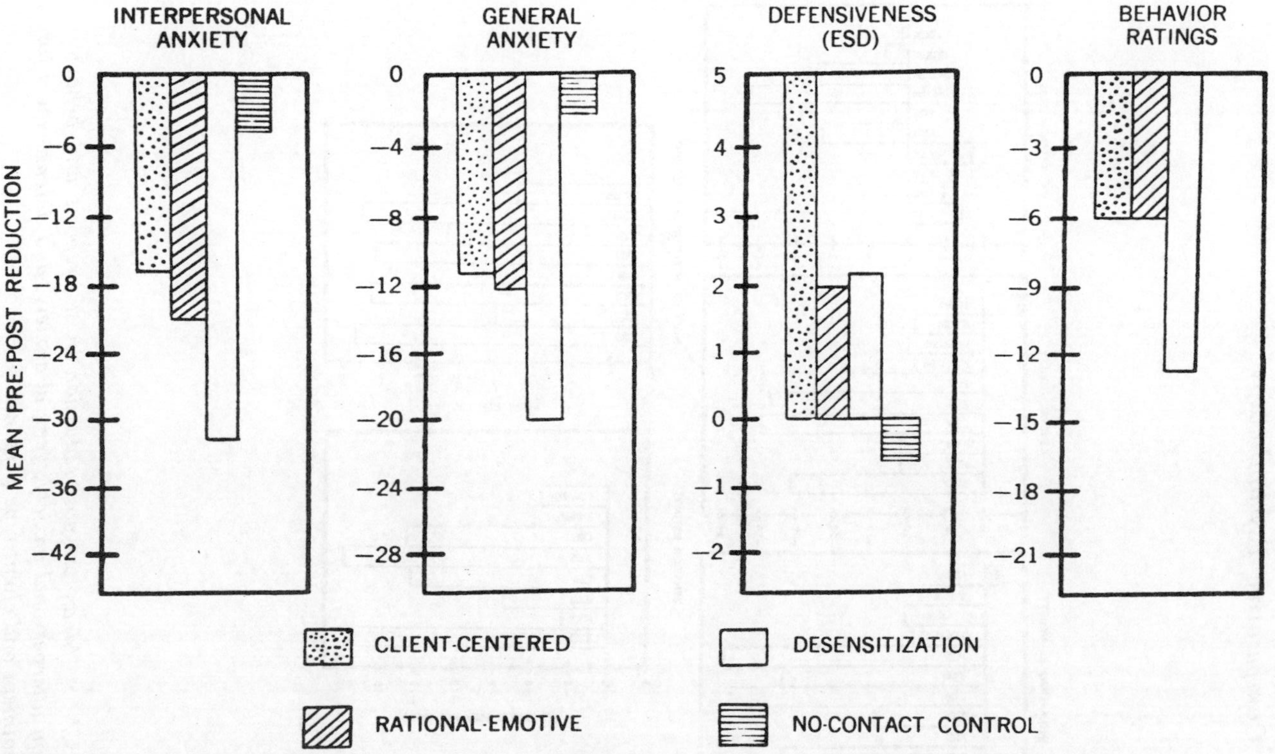

Figure 3.6 • *Mean reduction in self-reports and behavior ratings of interpersonal anxiety, general anxiety, and defensiveness from pre- to post-treatment with placebo effects removed from each of the treatment conditions*

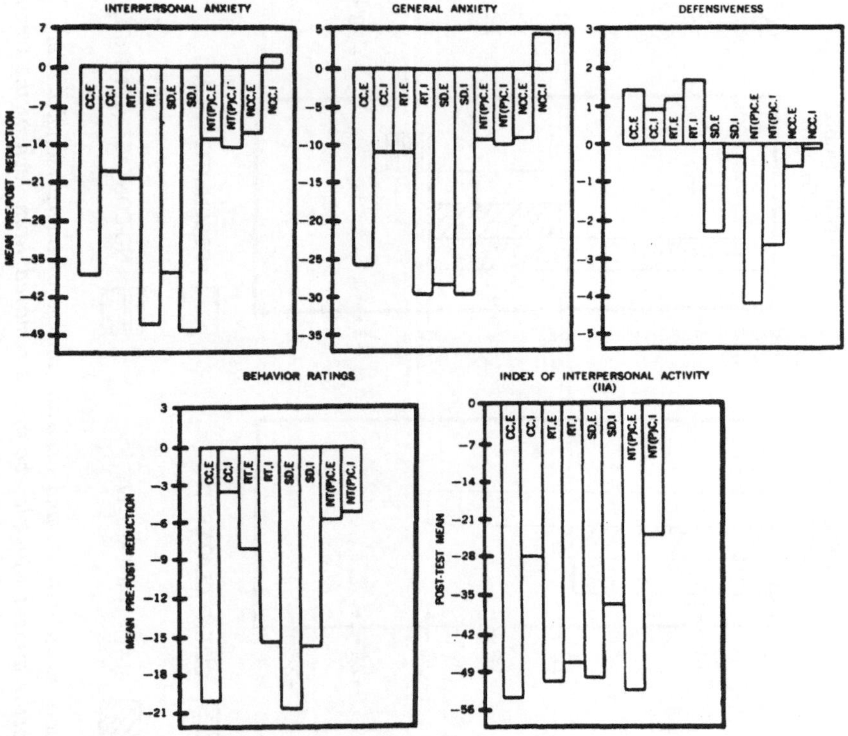

Figure 3.7 · Mean pre-post reduction in self-reports and behavior ratings on interpersonal anxiety, general anxiety, and defensiveness for each treatment and client type personality

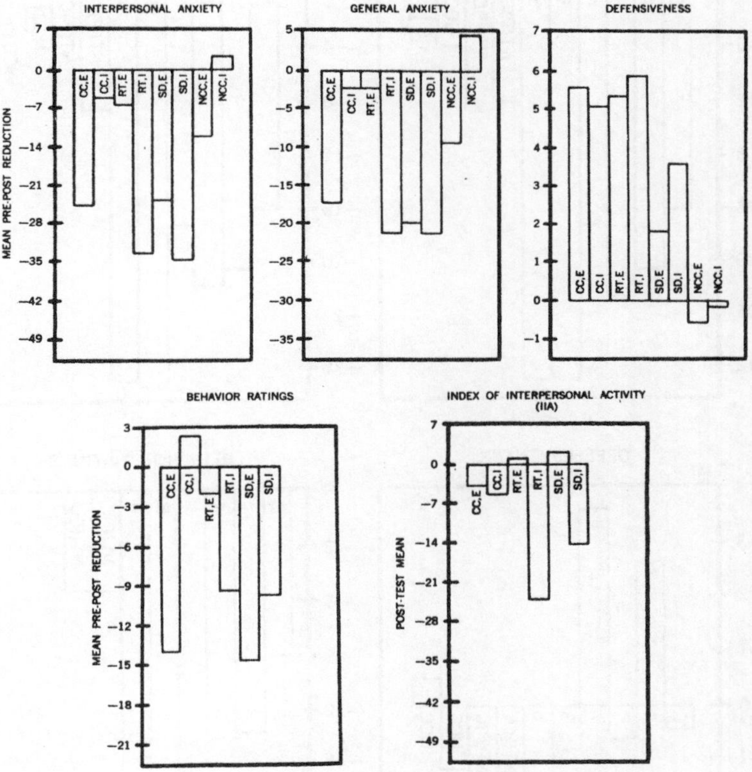

Figure 3.8 · Mean pre-post reduction in self-reports and behavior ratings of interpersonal anxiety, general anxiety, and defensiveness for each treatment and client personality type with placebo effects removed from each of the treatment conditions

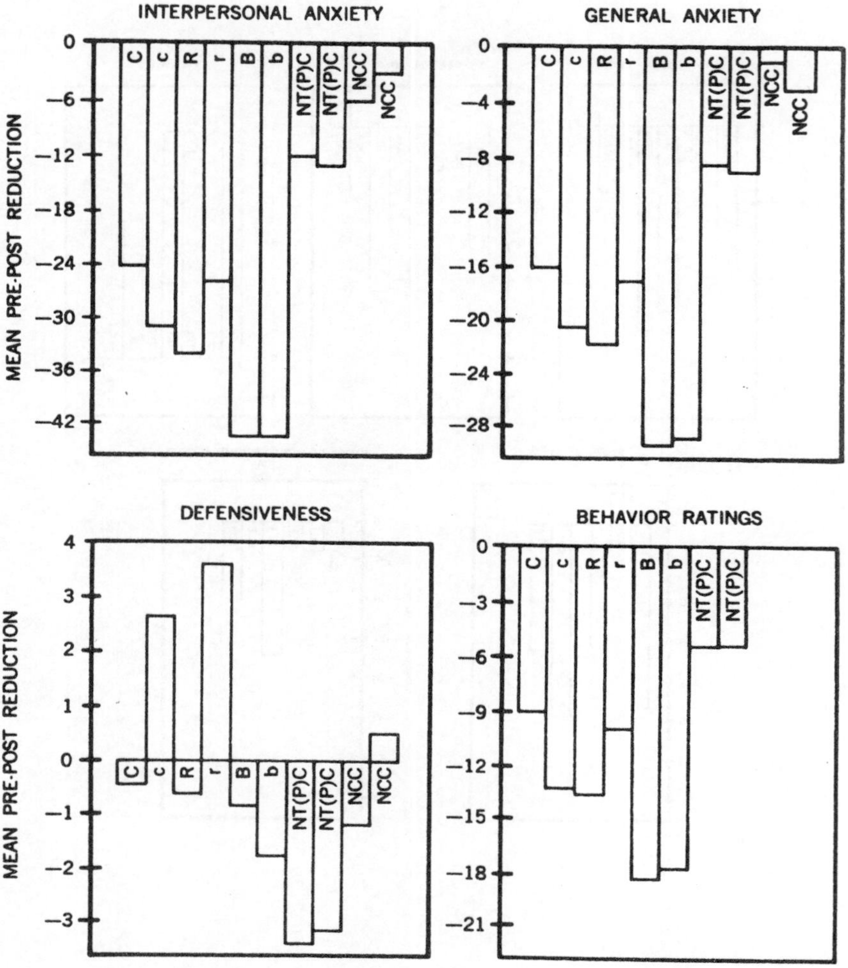

Figure 3.9 · Mean pre-post reduction in self-reports and behavior ratings of interpersonal anxiety, general anxiety, and defensiveness for each treatment and each counselor

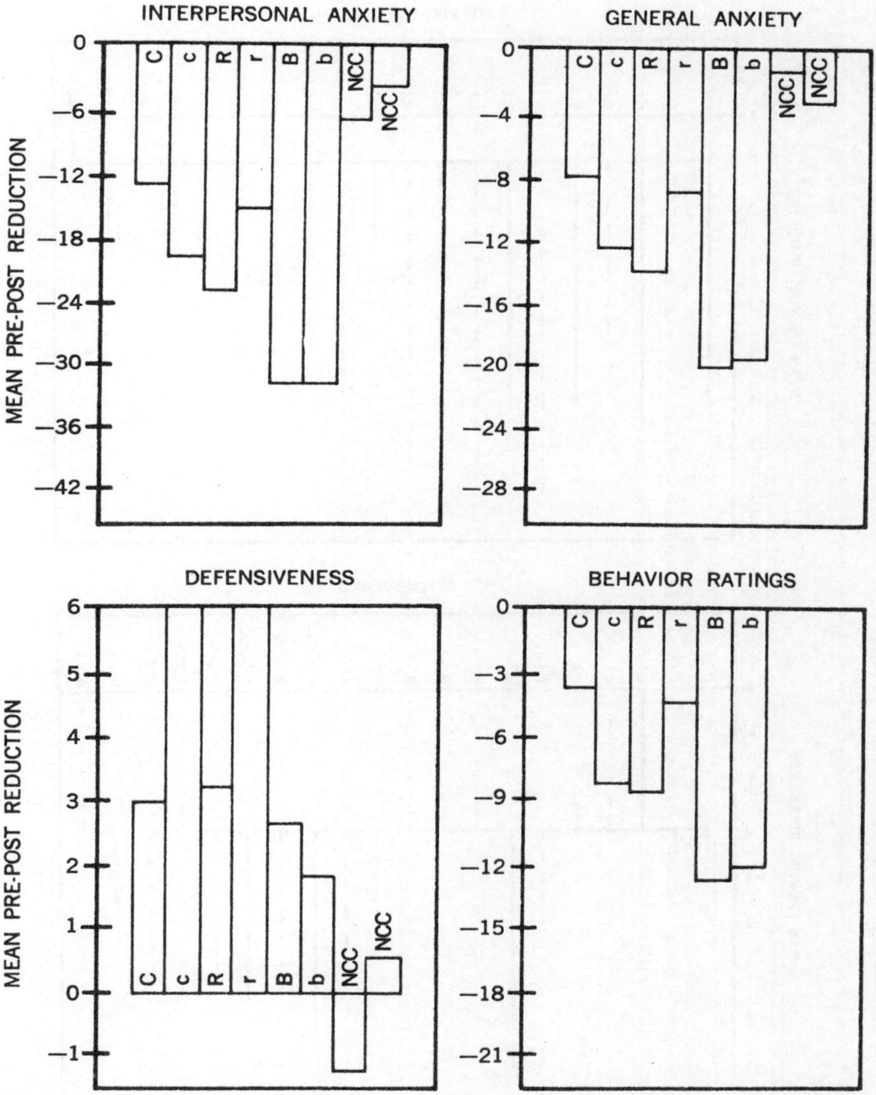

Figure 3.10 · Mean pre-post reduction in self-reports and behavior ratings of interpersonal anxiety, general anxiety, and defensiveness for each treatment and each counselor with average placebo effects removed from each of the treatment conditions

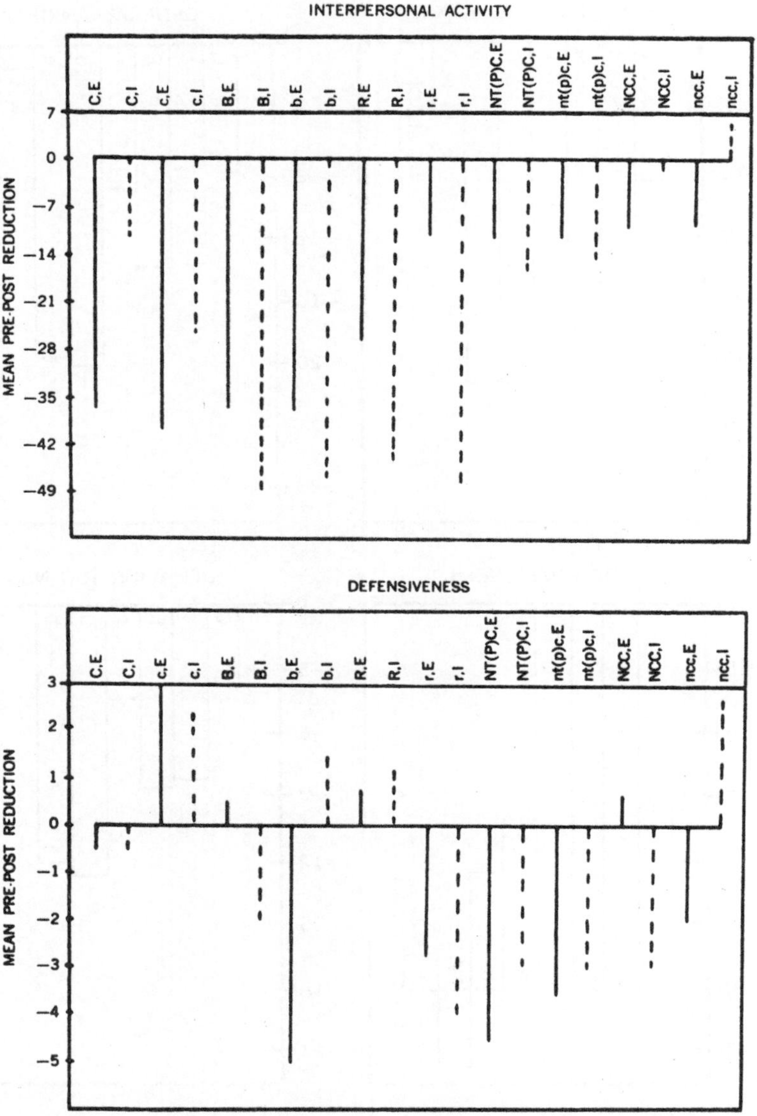

Figure 3.11 • *Mean pre-post reduction in self-reports and behavior ratings on interpersonal anxiety, general anxiety, and defensiveness for each counselor and client personality type*

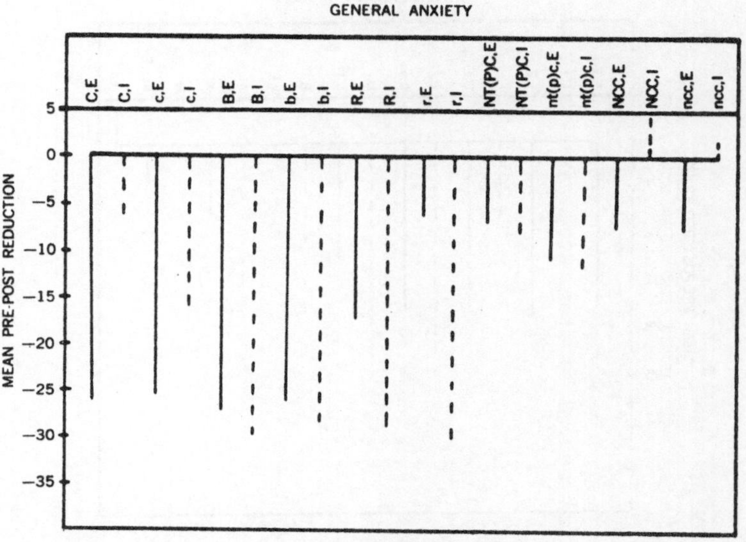
GENERAL ANXIETY
MEAN PRE-POST REDUCTION
5
0
−5
−10
−15
−20
−25
−30
−35
C,E
C,I
c,E
c,I
B,E
B,I
b,E
b,I
R,E
R,I
r,E
r,I
NT(P)C,E
NT(P)C,I
nt(p)c,E
nt(p)c,I
NCC,E
NCC,I
ncc,E
ncc,I

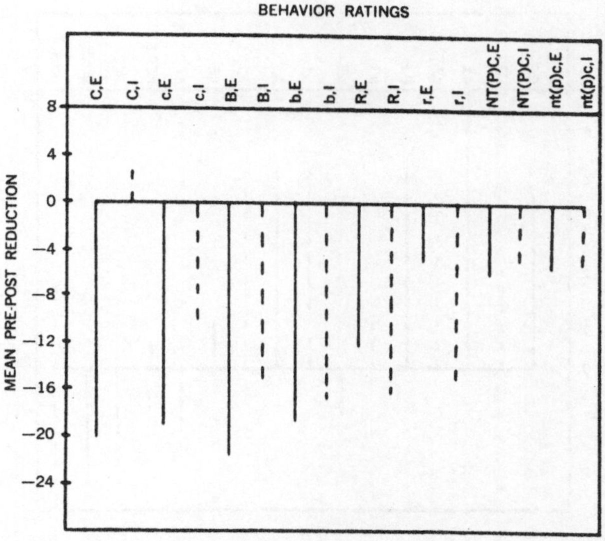
BEHAVIOR RATINGS
MEAN PRE-POST REDUCTION
8
4
0
−4
−8
−12
−16
−20
−24
C,E
C,I
c,E
c,I
B,E
B,I
b,E
b,I
R,E
R,I
r,E
r,I
NT(P)C,E
NT(P)C,I
nt(p)c,E
nt(p)c,I

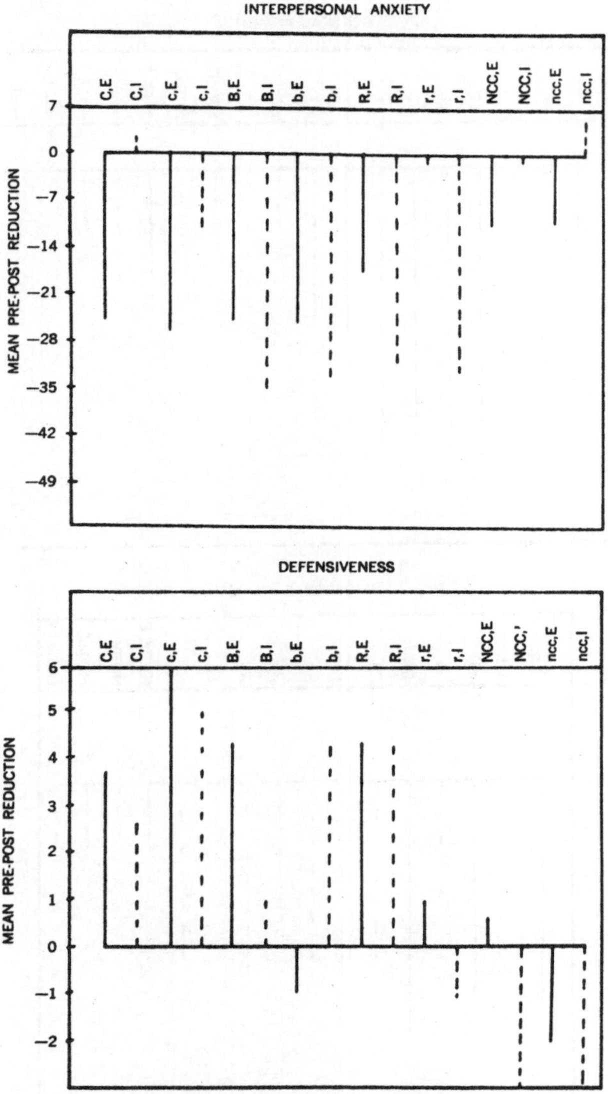

Figure 3.12 • Mean pre-post reduction in self-reports and behavior ratings of interpersonal anxiety, general anxiety, and defensiveness for each counselor and client personality type with average placebo effects removed from each of the treatment conditions

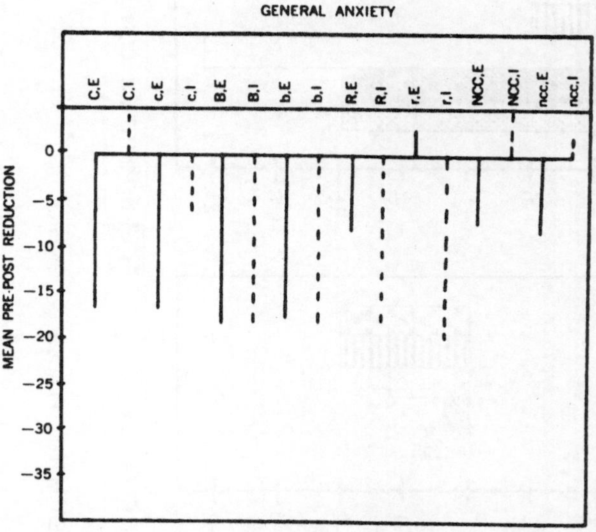
GENERAL ANXIETY
MEAN PRE-POST REDUCTION
0
−5
−10
−15
−20
−25
−30
−35
C,E
C,I
c,E
c,I
B,E
B,I
b,E
b,I
R,E
R,I
r,E
r,I
NCC,E
NCC,I
ncc,E
ncc,I

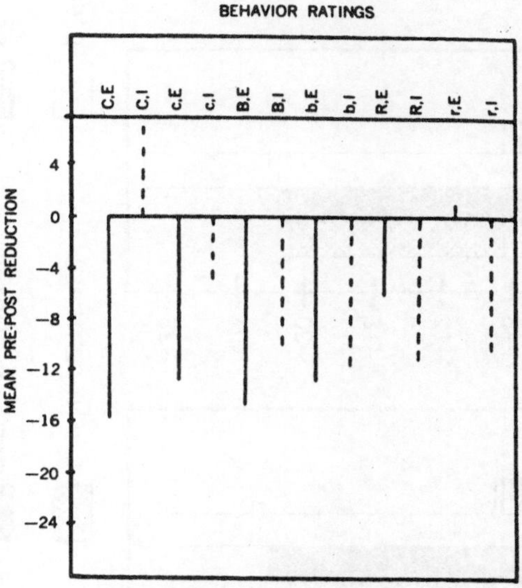
BEHAVIOR RATINGS
MEAN PRE-POST REDUCTION
4
0
−4
−8
−12
−16
−20
−24
C,E
C,I
c,E
c,I
B,E
B,I
b,E
b,I
R,E
R,I
r,E
r,I

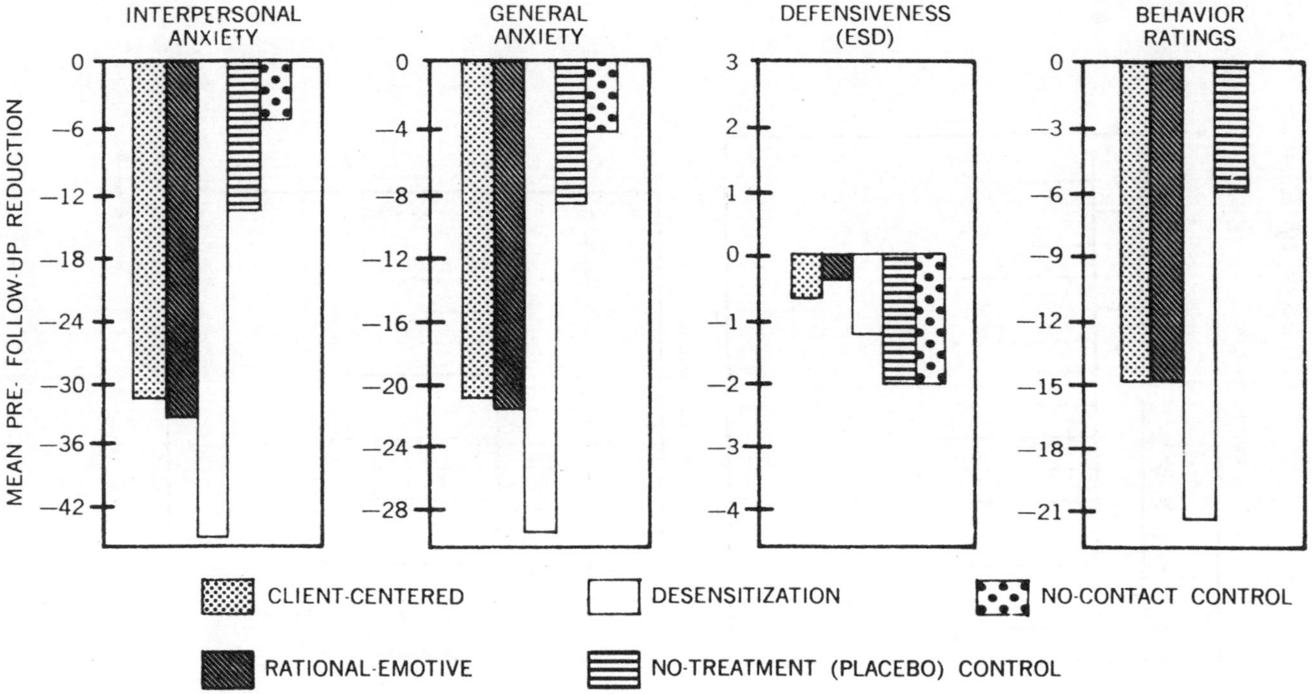

Figure 3.13 • Mean reduction in self-reports and behavior ratings of interpersonal anxiety, general anxiety, and defensiveness from pre- to follow-up testing

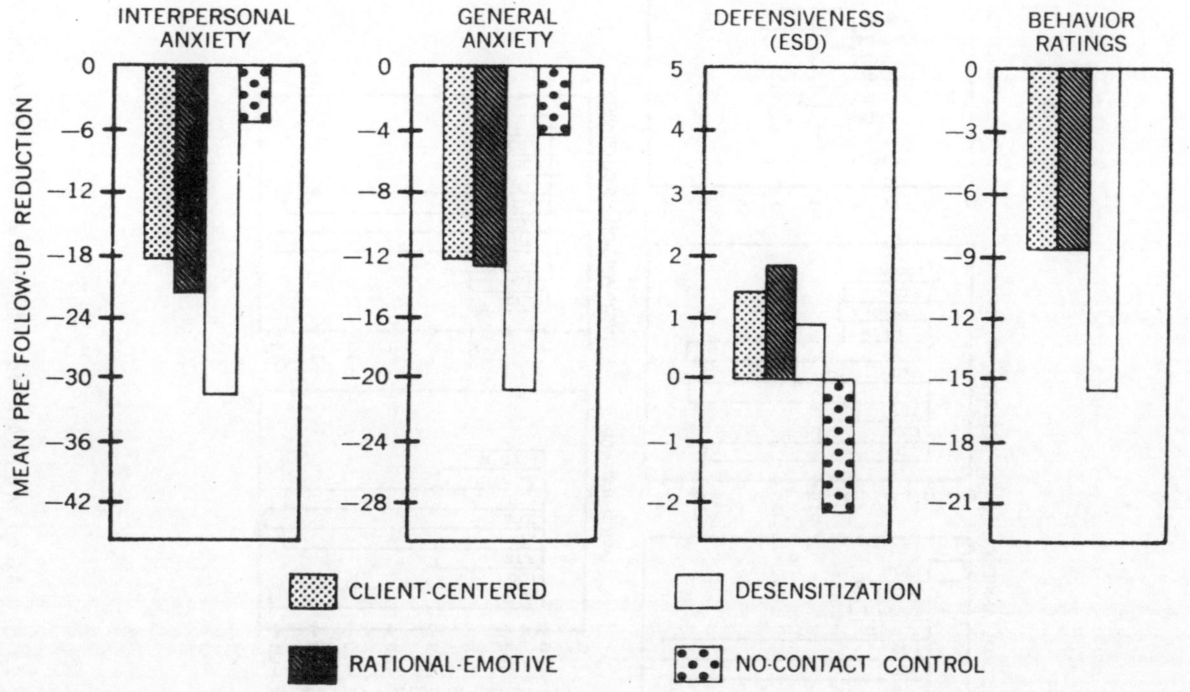

Figure 3.14 • Mean reduction in self-reports and behavior ratings of interpersonal anxiety, general anxiety, and defensiveness from pre- to follow-up testing with placebo effects removed from each of the treatment conditions

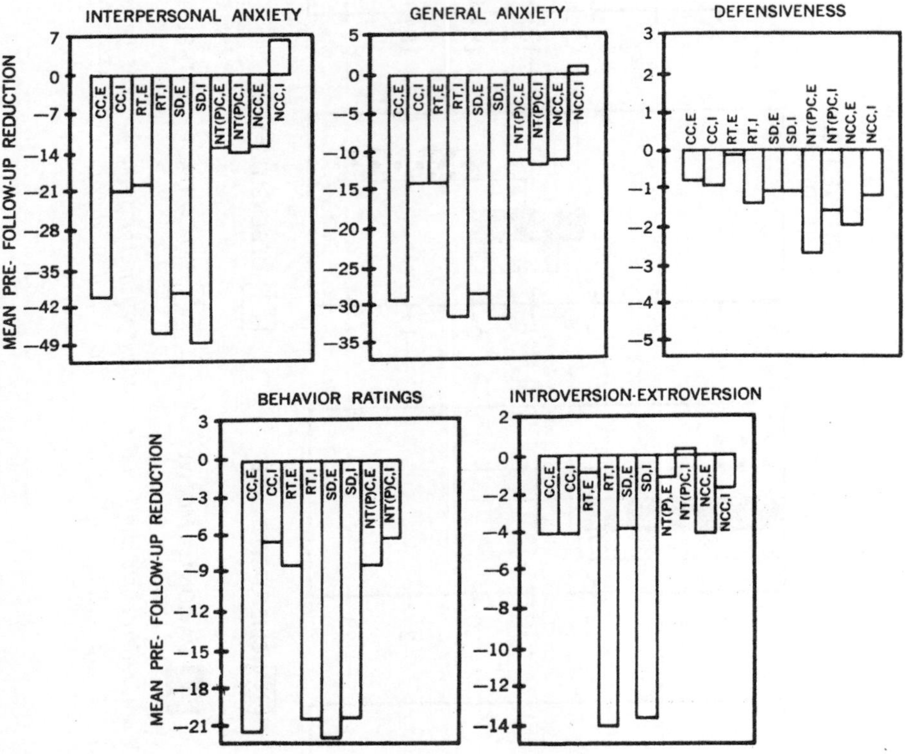

Figure 3.15 • Mean pre-follow-up reduction in self-reports and behavior ratings of interpersonal anxiety, general anxiety, and defensiveness for each treatment and client personality type

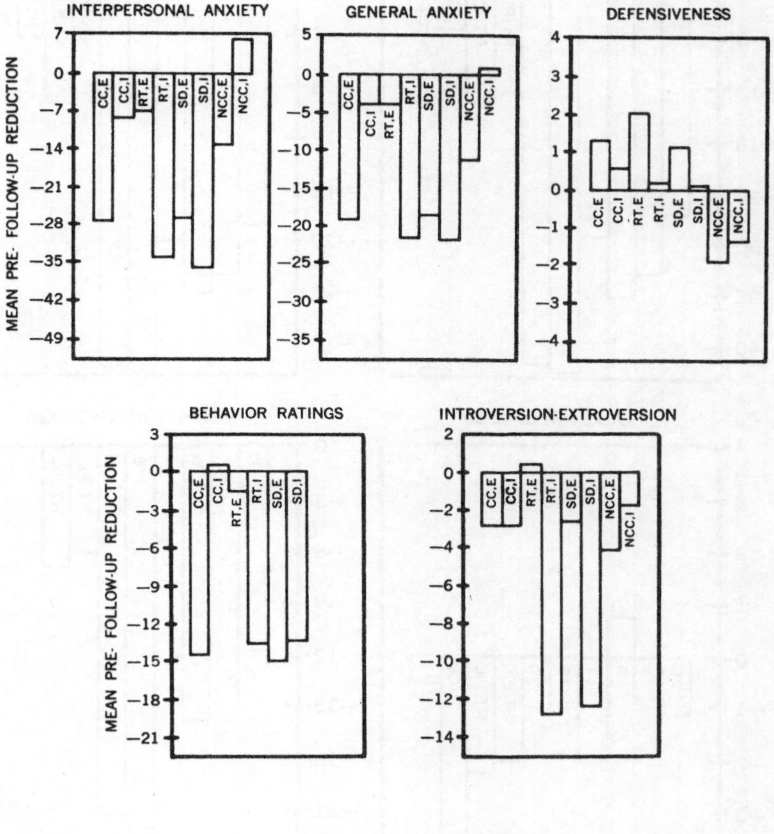

Figure 3.16 · Mean pre-follow-up reduction in self-reports and behavior ratings of interpersonal anxiety, general anxiety, and defensiveness for each treatment and client personality type with placebo effects removed from each of the treatment conditions

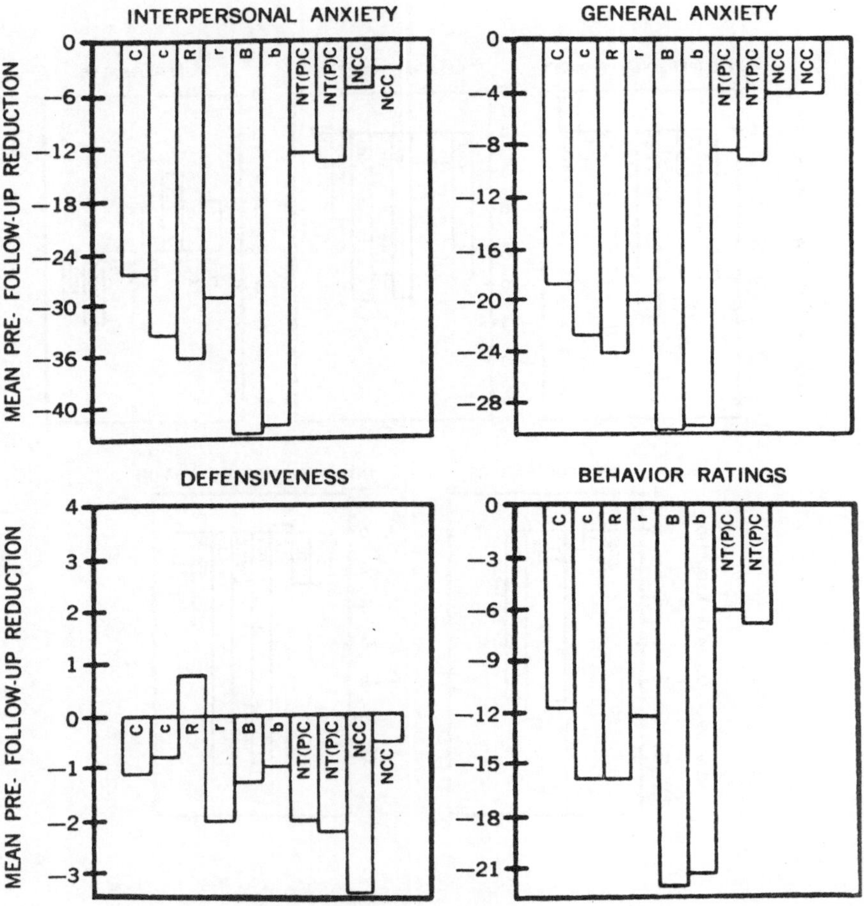

Figure 3.17 • Mean pre-follow-up reductions in self-reports and behavior ratings of interpersonal anxiety, general anxiety, and defensiveness for each treatment and each counselor

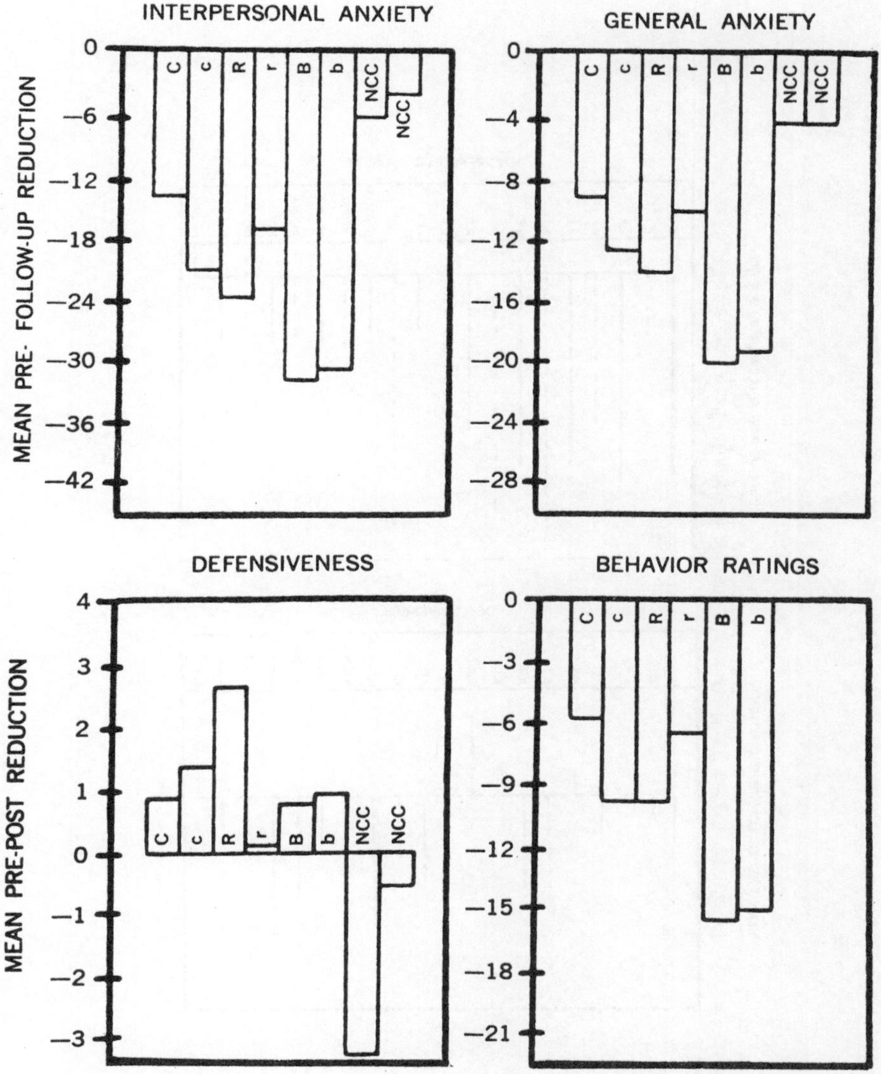

Figure 3.18 • Mean pre-follow-up reduction in self-reports and behavior ratings of interpersonal anxiety, general anxiety, and defensiveness for each treatment and each counselor with average placebo effects removed from each of the treatment conditions

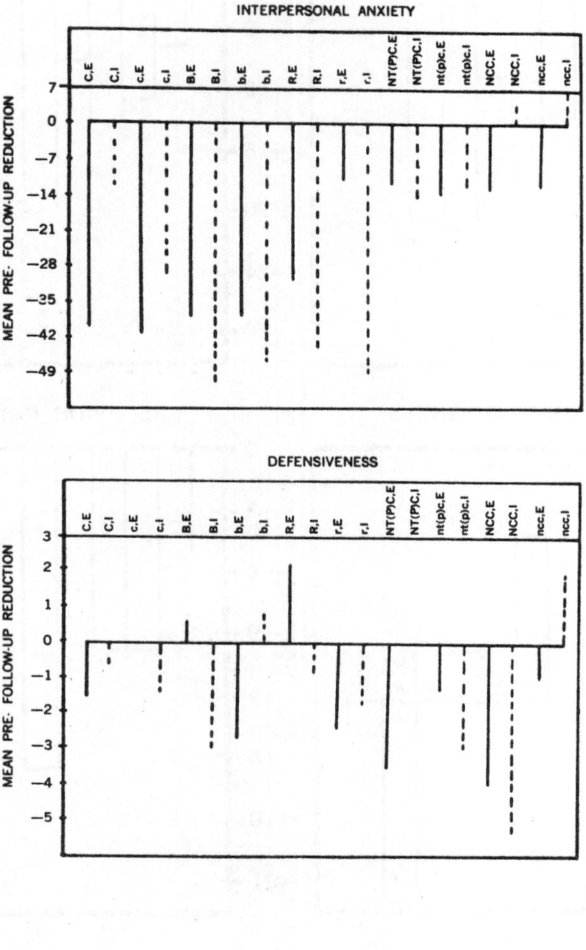

Figure 3.19 · *Mean pre-follow-up reduction in self-reports and behavior ratings of interpersonal anxiety, general anxiety, and defensiveness for each counselor and client personality type*

GENERAL ANXIETY

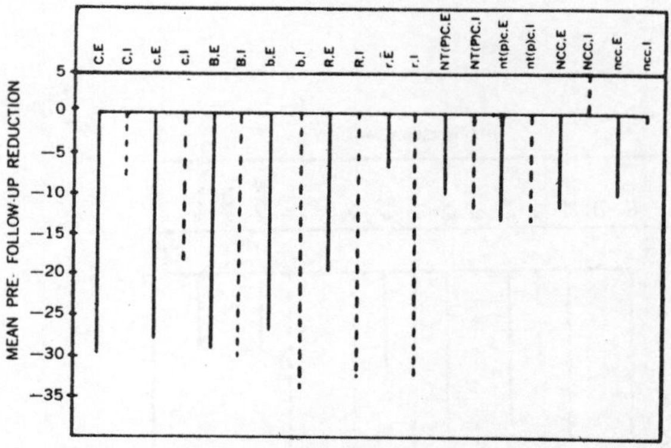

BEHAVIOR RATINGS

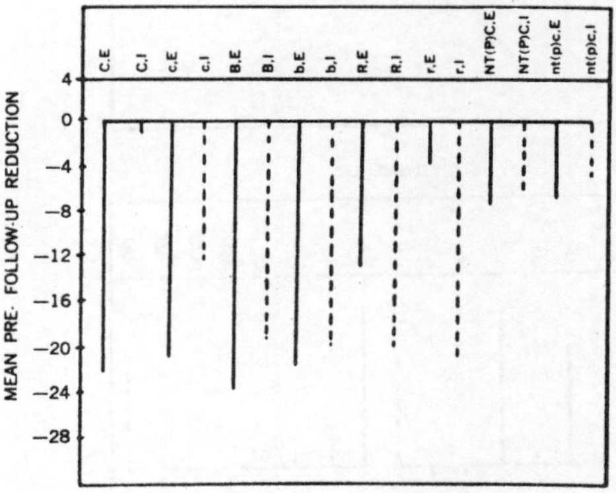

INTROVERSION-EXTROVERSION

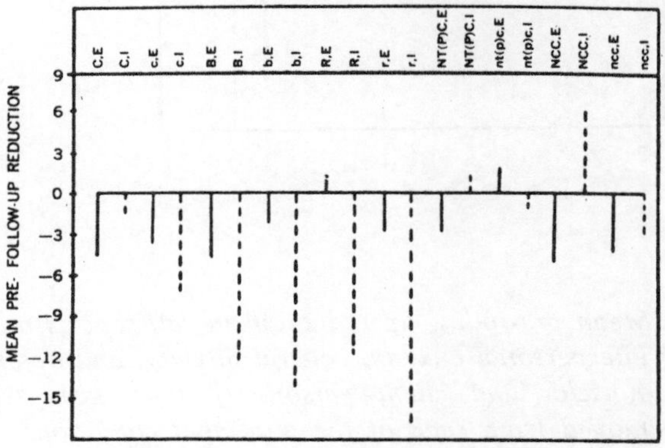

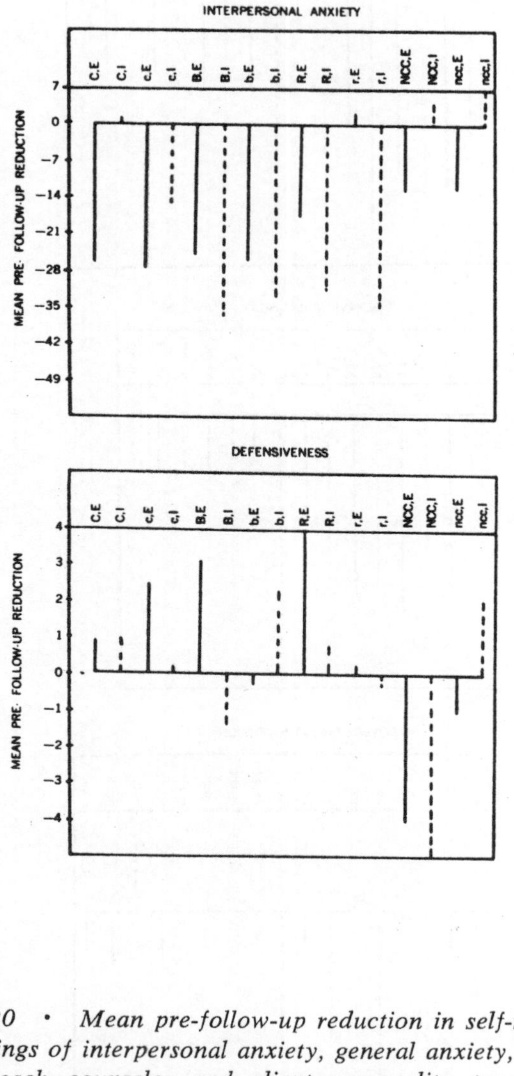

Figure 3.20 · Mean pre-follow-up reduction in self-reports and behavior ratings of interpersonal anxiety, general anxiety, and defensiveness for each counselor and client personality type with average placebo effects removed from each of the treatment conditions

GENERAL ANXIETY

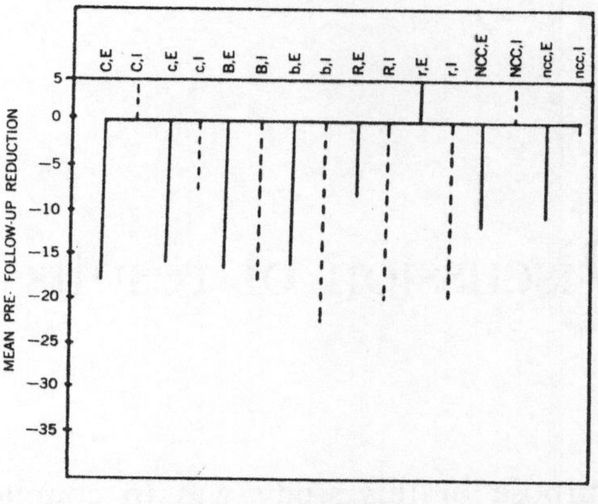

BEHAVIOR RATINGS

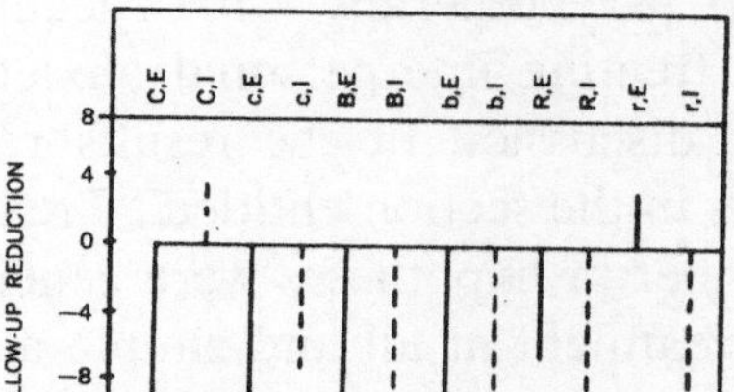

INTROVERSION-EXTROVERSION

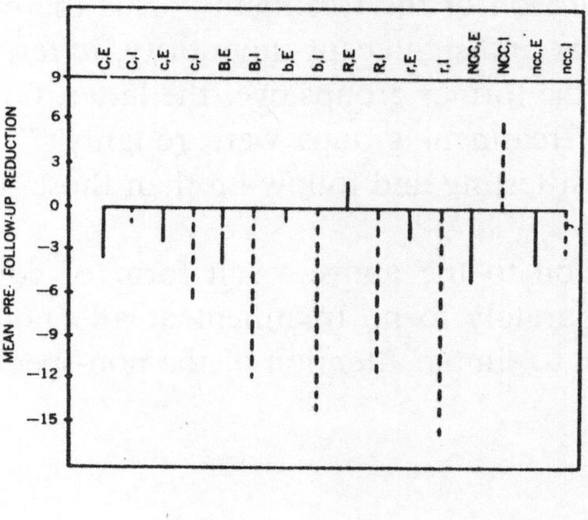

· 4 ·

Discussion of results

The main purpose of this study was to compare three approaches to group psychotherapy with specific reference to their outcomes in treating interpersonal anxiety in introverts and extroverts. A discussion of the results relative to these hypotheses appears in the section entitled "Treatment Effects." In addition, a number of hypotheses were generated regarding the effects of no treatment at all and simple attention. A discussion of these results appears below. Finally, a brief analysis of the role of the counselor, the generalization of treatment effects, and implications for future research is also presented.

• *Treatment-Control Hypotheses*

A comparison of the treatment versus the control *S*s revealed the clear and significant superiority, in terms of anxiety reduction, of the former groups over the latter. On the average the *S*s in the treatment groups were roughly 70 percent less anxious at post-testing and follow-up than those in the control groups.

In addition to the above, each form of counseling was compared separately to no treatment at all (no-contact control) and then to simple attention or the non-specific, ancillary benefits derived from personal contact, interviewing, and expectation of future treatment and relief (no-treatment, placebo control). The expectation, incorporated into hypotheses 5 and 6 (Chap. 1), that any of these forms of counseling would prove more anxiety reducing than either the no-contact or no-treatment (placebo) controls was upheld by both the outcome and follow-up results of this investigation. On the average, the *S*s in the treatment groups were about 60 percent less anxious than those in the no-treatment (placebo) control group and approximately 80 percent less anxious than those *S*s in the no-contact control group. Thus, the conclusion that psychotherapy does produce a greater measurable reduction in anxiety than either attention-placebo conditions or simply the passage of time seems warranted by these findings.

The prospect, incorporated into hypotheses 7 and 8, that simple attention-placebo conditions would be sufficient in and of themselves to bring about a significantly lowered level of anxiety over the simple passage of time was also upheld by the outcome and follow-up results of this study. On the average, the no-treatment (placebo) control condition was approximately 50 percent more effective in reducing interpersonal and general anxiety than no treatment at all.

A comparison of introvert-extrovert differences revealed further that the superiority of the no-treatment (placebo) control groups over the no-contact control groups was limited almost exclusively to the introverted *S*s. The extroverts in both groups showed about the same amount of anxiety reduction at both outcome and follow-up. One possible explanation for this finding is that the extroverts in both control groups were so much more active socially than the introverts (see Index of Interpersonal Activity) that they extinguished many of their own social fears, or at least, as many as were dissipated via the interaction provided by the no-treatment (placebo) control procedures. On the other hand, the no-contact control introverts by their very inactivity, that is, avoiding social situations failed to encounter the feared, conditioned stimulus. Furthermore, each time the latter evaded or avoided this testing of reality they were, in effect, consolidating the very behavior pattern which constituted their "neuroses" (Eysenck, 1967).

It is noteworthy that the introverts in the no-treatment (placebo) control group did show significantly more anxiety reduction than the no-contact control introverts. Paul (1966) has elucidated a number of factors which seem to account for the anxiety reduction noted in attention-placebo groups such as the one employed here. First, the implicit and explicit suggestion and reassurance offered by an "expert" that anxiety is not unique and it can be overcome, coupled with the promise of future treatment and relief, undoubtedly served to modify the *S*'s attitudes about themselves and their "crazy" behavior. This initial change very well may have served to break the maladaptive "vicious circle" of anxiety, lowered self-esteem, and heightened anxiety, replacing it with a more adaptive progression involving positive changes in self-attitudes, lessened anxiety, new hope and self-confidence, and further anxiety reduction. In addition, changes in expectancies due to increased attention may have further served to reinforce this more adaptive spiral progression by instilling intermittently increased hope, confidence, and feelings of self-worth and importance. Finally, the calm and confidence of the group leader, coupled with the rewards for pro-social behaviors which he encouraged with warmth, understanding, and interest, may have served to extinguish further a number of social fears among the *S*s and so sharpen the latter's social skills in interpersonal relationships.

• *Treatment Effects*

While no hypotheses were offered regarding the overall superiority of any one treatment approach independent of *S* personality type, there does seem to be sufficient evidence to warrant a *tentative* conclusion in this regard. When the problem to be treated is anxiety and the desired goal is a reduction in cognitive complaints and behavioral manifestations of anxiety, then SD appears to be the best choice of therapy. With the exception of the Index of Interpersonal Activity, both the CC and RT treatments were significantly less effective, resulting in approximately 30 percent less anxiety reduction than the SD approach.

As noted previously, the overwhelming success rate mentioned above was due to the fact that the SD treatment was equally effective with both introverted and extroverted *S*s. Because the findings involving SD ran somewhat contrary to the hypotheses stated in Chapter 1, a number of explanations regarding what seemed to be the differential effects of group and individual SD treatment with introverts and extroverts seem relevant here.

The evidence upon which hypotheses 1 through 4 were based suggested that introverts learn more rapidly and permanently than extroverts because of a higher level of cortical excitation (Eysenck, 1960), or as Gray (1967) has suggested, a higher level of arousal. Because of this higher level of cortical arousal, the introvert is more alert, more sensitive, and less dependent than the extrovert on external stimulation. It is partly for this reason that Eysenck (1967) maintains that SD is sufficiently stimulating, albeit quite "mechanical," for introverts while boring and repetitive for extroverts, According to Eysenck, the latter group requires for maximal learning efficiency considerable external stimulation, preferably in the form of interpersonal interaction.

Yet it is because of this difference in level of arousal that it has been suggested that group SD treatment favors extroverts rather than introverts (Weinstein, 1968). By placing introverts in a group setting, their already highly aroused state, which normally serves to facilitate learning, surpasses optimal level functioning and creates overstimulation and distraction due to the competing stimuli of other people. On the other hand, the extrovert's initially low arousal level is enhanced to facilitate focusing, concentration, and learning in the presence of others. Gray (1967) has found some support for this hypothesis in the fact that introverts perform more efficiently on a vigilance task undertaken in isolation, whereas extroverts perform at maximum efficiency in a group.

If the introvert performs most efficiently (Gray, 1967) and studies most effectively (Estabrook & Sommer, 1966) away from others, then it is not surprising that he will derive less than maximal benefit from group SD. Extroverts, on the other hand, work to advantage in the presence of others. Thus, since SD was conducted in groups, the extroverts received the additional stimulation necessary for their optimal level of functioning, while introverts were overstimulated and, consequently, distracted.

A second possible biasing factor which would favor extroverts relates to group treatment and the nature of the target behaviors presently under study. Cooke (1966) found that while both high and moderately anxious *S*s performed equally well with *in vivo* SD, high anxious *S*s showed significantly greater fear reduction than moderately anxious *S*s when an imaginal hierarchy was employed. Since the target behavior in the present study was interpersonal anxiety, and since *S*s were treated in *groups,* with one class of *S*s reporting more anxiety at pre-testing (introverts) than the other (extroverts), the present study seems somewhat analogous to the one reported by Cooke (1966). If this comparison is valid, then the ancillary effects derived from the "built in" *in vivo* components of the present study would indirectly favor the less anxious extroverts by maximizing the unanticipated *in vivo* benefits.

Finally, in a recent article, Davison (1968) discussed some practical limitations of the SD treatment. One such limitation, possibly affecting the outcome of group SD with introverts, was the level of relaxation achieved by the introverted *S*s. It is extremely likely that group SD exerts an inhibitory influence on introverts by preventing them from achieving the level of deep muscle relaxation commensurate with effective counter-conditioning. This seems even more likely in view of their initially heightened arousal state and high anxiety level, which is further exacerbated by the presence of the group. If relaxation were less complete with introverts, then the entire process of reciprocal inhibition may have been greatly retarded for them.

In view of the above considerations, it is not surprising that the introverts and extroverts treated by means of SD showed no significant differences. However, the fact that the SD treatment was significantly less effective than the RT treatment in increasing interpersonal activity outside of treatment (see Index of Interpersonal Activity) does seem somewhat of an enigma. Disregarding the crudeness of the Index of Interpersonal Activity (IIA) and the fact that required homework assignments may have "forced" the RT introverts to report spuriously high interpersonal activity levels, one hypothesis which also seems consistent with the aforementioned findings does seem to provide a partial explanation of this phenomena.

As Wolpe (1958) has suggested, the successful treatment of *S*s by SD results from an inhibition of avoidance behavior which is achieved by relaxation *before* approach or copying behaviors begin to emerge. If this is correct, along with the assumption that the introverts' excessive anxiety level and heightened arousal state in the group inhibited or retarded their process of deep muscle relaxation, then the fact that the SD introverts were slower and less successful than the RT introverts in developing approach behaviors outside of treatment is more understandable. The less deep the relaxation is, the less effectively each hierarchial item is desensitized, that is, the less reduction in avoidance behavior. The less reduction in avoidance behavior which occurs, the slower the emergence of approach or copying behaviors such as those assayed on the IIA. This, coupled with the fact that relaxation is not central to RT, seems to account for a good part of the discrepancy between the SD and RT introverts' scores on the IIA.

It should be noted that the entire aforementioned rationale is simply an attempt to explain the *obtained* results, not an endeavor to justify the maintenance of the original hypotheses concerning the effects of SD with introverts and extroverts. These findings are viewed as positive and should be considered a valuable aspect of the SD treatment. Whether or not the effects of individual versus group SD will actually emerge as salient will have to await further investigation.

In spite of the above findings, the results of the CC and RT treatments did conform to the expectations incorporated into Hypotheses 1 through 4. As anticipated, no significant differences were obtained between the CC and RT approaches on any of the self-reports or behavior ratings of anxiety, independent of *S* personality type. More specifically, the CC treatment resulted in the most anxiety reduction with extroverts, while the RT treatment was most effective with introverts. As a group, the CC introverts and the RT extroverts showed no greater anxiety reduction at outcome and follow-up than the comparable no-treatment (placebo) control.

Any explanation of the above findings must somehow incorporate the obvious co-variation between the level of client intrapersonal exploration during treatment and process, outcome, and follow-up measures of anxiety reduction. The findings here leave little doubt that the level of client self-exploration is a paramount factor in accounting for the ultimate outcome of traditional verbal counseling and psychotherapy. Those *S*s who explored their personal problems most and at the deepest levels showed the greatest amount of anxiety reduction both during and following treatment. In the case of introverted *S*s, deep levels of intrapersonal exploration were also associated with increased pro-social behaviors and "positive" personality changes, that is, increased extroversion. These findings have been numerously documented (Carkhuff & Berenson, 1967; Rogers et al., 1967; Truax & Carkhuff, 1967) and are well supported by the results of the present investigation.

The process measures incorporated into the present design suggest a number of promising, as well as a number of fruitless, leads in understanding what is involved in eliciting therapeutic levels of client self-exploration. There is no evidence here to suggest that counselor-client personality similarity is a salient factor, in and of itself, in eliciting therapeutic levels of client intrapersonal exploration. If nothing else, the higher overall success rate of counselors c and R over counselors C and r seems to clearly imply this fact. Similarly, the so-called "central therapeutic ingredients" of accurate empathy, non-passive warmth, genuineness, etc. do not seem to play a prominent role in this regard. However, an examination of the characteristics of CC and RT *per se,* as well as a consideration of the possible course of development of maladaptive anxiety with special reference to introversion-extroversion, does seem to offer a promising lead in understanding what causes some clients to engage in therapeutic levels of self-exploration.

Paul (1966) has summarized at least three forms of maladaptive anxiety which seems relevant here. First, anxiety may itself be a learned reaction in which previously neutral stimuli, for example, people, become associated with anxiety in a fashion analogous to the classical conditioning paradigm. With reference to interpersonal anxiety, such factors as deprivation, pain, punishment, negative reinforcement, loss of customary support, trauma, disconfirmation of expectancies, etc. may have served as the environmental events which led to the view of people as anxiety stimuli. The important point is that in cases such as these anxiety *is* the maladaptive behavior, occurring inappropriately in conjunction with real, that is, original or related, or imaginary stimuli. This seems to be the central feature in the symptom complex of interpersonal anxiety for extroverts. Second, behavioral deficits, or maladaptive behaviors (including ideas and attitudes as well as motor behaviors) resulting from inappropriate learning, may, in turn, produce anxiety as a reaction to ineffectual social gestures. In this instance, both the reactive anxiety and behavioral deficits are the maladaptive behaviors or presenting problem. Third, anxiety may be related to inappropriate learning, as in the case of maladaptive behaviors learned and maintained by anxiety reduction, for example, withdrawal. In instances such as these, the "defense mechanisms," learned via anxiety reduction, are the maladaptive behaviors or presenting problem. While all three forms of anxiety are undoubtedly present in *both* introverts and extroverts, the latter two examples seem more illustrative of the symptom complex of interpersonal anxiety for introverts.

With the foregoing as a theoretical base, the ability of the CC and RT counselors to elicit therapeutic levels of client self-exploration with extroverts and introverts, respectively, appears somewhat more comprehensible. Tables 3.8 and 3.10 indicate that the focus of the RT counselors was the *S*s maladaptive or irrational *cognitions* and *behaviors.* If the aforementioned analysis of anxiety development is correct, then it is precisely these maladaptive or irrational ideas, attitudes, or philosophies of living, (that is, behavioral deficits) and their concomitant social ineffectiveness which are the major source of the introverts interpersonal anxiety and which give rise to such defensive maneuvers as withdrawal and seclusiveness (see IIA), in an attempt to escape that anxiety.

Direct and forceful confrontations in the areas of these behavioral deficits may have directed the introverts toward exploring, examining, and revamping these "defective cognitions," replacing them with more adaptive or rational ones. While much of this "cognitive revamping" was done initially by the RT therapists, the process was soon imitated by the introverts (see Tables 3.9 and 3.10) via modeling and reinforcement. The implosive character of the RT treatment, while initially raising the introverts' anxiety level (see Figure 3.2), may well have been required to mobilize and direct the initial effort needed to engage these *S*s in self-exploration. As one of the introverts in the CC group so aptly put it, "Most of the time we just sat around and looked at each other. It just made me more anxious." Unlike the extroverts, the introverts did not volunteer to the counselors much material or data with which to work. By and large, they were quite inactive when left to their own devices.

In addition, required homework assignments undoubtedly encouraged a sharpening of social skills. Thus, the process of self-exploration, or discrimination learning, leading to attitudinal changes, coupled with the teaching of new and more effective pro-social behaviors might be expected to attenuate or limit the spiral progression of poor social skills, anxiety, lowered self-esteem due to ruminations, heightened anxiety. In addition, the uncovering and examining of irrational and maladaptive attitudinal complexes, with its attendent anxiety reduction, may have served to maintain and further encourage the continuation of the process of self-exploration, as might the counselor's direct and indirect reinforcements for emitting such behavior.

On the other hand, cognitive, attitudinal, or behavioral deficits, while undoubtedly present, do not seem to be the *central* problem in the symptom complex of interpersonal anxiety for extroverts; nor does withdrawal seem to be their means of controlling that anxiety. They are very active socially, in spite of their self-reported fear and anxiety, and quite skillful in interpersonal relationships (Eysenck, 1960). However, if their anxiety is a product of unfortunate or traumatic learning experiences, as indicated above, and if the extroverts "excessive" activity is an attempt to avoid or circumvent awareness of hurt or traumatized feeling (Fenichel, 1941), as their heightened pre-test defensiveness might suggest, then the effectiveness of CC with extroverts becomes somewhat more comprehensible. That is, the permissive atmosphere created by the CC counselor's attentive listening, non-critical acceptance and reflection, and self-disclosures undoubtedly led to considerable reassurance that their problems were not unique and that, in this group at least, every effort would be made to understand and accept the *S* and his view of the problem. Similarly, if traumatized (negatively reinforced) feelings are the major source of the extroverts' interpersonal anxiety, then an approach such as CC, which deals almost exclusively with feeling states (see Tables 3.8 and 3.10), may be the treatment of choice.

The sequential reduction of anxiety with the CC approach is viewed as similar to that resulting from the RT approach, with the exception of treatment technique and focus. The process of self-exploration, that is, discrimination learning and extinction, is viewed as the central therapeutic ingredient in both of these approaches, with the effectiveness of the techniques and treatment focus dependent on the *S*'s presenting problem and their pre-treatment personality make-up. In the case of the CC treatment, the counselor's and groups' non-critical acceptance and attentive listening might well lead to a sufficient reduction in anxiety to allow each *S* to feel secure enough to begin exploration of his formerly traumatized or negatively reinforced feelings. During the initial interviews, the appropriateness of the therapist's actions in relation to the *S*'s personality type and presenting problem seem to be the major impetus for eliciting or failing to elicit client self-exploration. The immediate reduction in anxiety resulting from this process, due to a reversal of incubation effects (White, 1956), may encourage further gestures at self-exploration. As the *S*'s attempts at intrapersonal exploration approximate the therapists "ideal," the latter may subtly and directly reinforce and so encourage the *S*'s efforts in this vein, shaping and directing the *S*'s behaviors as the therapist sees fit. Self-elimination of errors by *S*s may also be a salient factor, since theoretically these abortive or "incorrect" self-exploratory behaviors would lead to little or no anxiety reduction. The self-reinforcing, "error correcting" nature of this process may stimulate further client self-exploration at increasingly deeper levels, with only intermittent guidance and variably spaced reinforcements on the part of the therapist.

The effects of self-exploration, once initiated, seem to be somewhat universal (Paul, 1966; Dollard & Miller, 1950). Clients begin to *discriminate* aspects of their own feelings in relation to the realities of the current situation, halting the "vicious circle" created by the overgeneralization of anxiety responses and beginning a clearer realization of their feelings. While this can be done by a client by exploring the past and present feelings from his daily life, the interaction, expression, and self-analysis of feelings toward and about other group members and the therapist provide working data which is "more alive" from an affective standpoint and more easily extinguishable from the point of view of contiguity. Also, in addition to the "partitioning-off" or discrimination process, *extinction* of anxiety related to social or interpersonal situations might be expected to take place as the *S* talks and continues to explore anxiety producing material in greater quantity and at deeper levels in the presence of others and within the context of a relaxed, non-threatening therapeutic atmosphere.

While many of the effective therapeutic ingredients of traditional verbal counseling and psychotherapeutic approaches, such as CC and RT, are undoubtedly similar to those of the attention-placebo condition described earlier (Paul, 1966), the former interventions are applied in a more direct, controlled, and efficient manner, at least by effective therapists. Indeed, many of their differences may be analogous to the differences between experienced and inexperienced counselors, the latter producing only "average benefits" (Truax & Carkhuff, 1967) which in some instances are no more effective in reducing anxiety than simply the passage of time. More important, however, is the fact that under placebo conditions *S*s may feel much better but typically learn very little. With CC and RT, *S*s may learn what their problem areas are, how they got to be problems, how they are presently being maintained, etc. But what is even more important, they learn a process (e.g., self-exploration), a process which by its very nature prevents the incubation and overgeneralization of anxiety responses into "vicious circles" of neuroses.

Thus, the central therapeutic benefits of both CC and RT in reducing anxiety are believed to reside in their ability to teach and maintain the process of self-exploration. Their differential effectiveness with extroverts and introverts is believed to be due primarily to the characteristics of CC and RT *per se*, as well as to the differential nature of the symptom complex of interpersonal anxiety for introverts and extroverts. When the treatment techniques and therapeutic focus are not appropriate to the *S*'s presenting problem and personality type, self-exploration is superficial and essentially non-therapeutic, that is, little or no anxiety reduction results. This may well explain the nominal success of RT and CC with extroverts and introverts, respectively.

While much of the aforementioned rationale must, for the present, remain largely theoretical, this same notion of "matching" treatment and client personality type has recently been put forth by Kell and Burrow (1969). They classify clients into two categories: thinking types and feeling types. A client is classified as either a "thinker" or a "feeler" on the basis of his exclusive, or nearly exclusive, reliance on one or the other of these modes of responding to problem situations. In many respects this dichotomy is similar to the dimension of extroversion-introversion. In any case, Kell and Burrow maintain that successful treatment for the thinking-type client must center on his achieving trust in his own feelings, whereas successful therapy for the feeling-type client must center on his acquiring the ability to think and plan his life more carefully, so that he is not flooded or overwhelmed by unmodulated feelings provoked by a problem situation.

The results of this investigation seem to suggest that the above is a laudable approach to treatment planning. The underlying goal of this "matching" approach to treatment is to get the client functioning in a unified, wholistic manner, so that thoughts, feelings, and behavior "flow together" harmoniously, with no mode of response employed as a defense against the other.

If the foregoing analysis is correct, it would seem that the notion of one "ideal therapeutic relationship" (Truax & Carkhuff, 1967) independent of therapist and client, is just as much a myth as the assumption of homogeneity of treatment (Kiesler, 1966). What is suggested here is that the key to anxiety reduction in traditional verbal counseling and psychotherapy is the level of client self-exploration, and that different counselor behavoirs are required to elicit and maintain this process during, and hopefully following, the course of treatment. Thus, there are innumerable numbers of "ideal therapeutic relationships" dependent on the client's presenting problem and personality make-up.

• *Counselor Effects*

While no specific hypotheses were offered regarding the overall superiority of any one or two counselors, independent of treatment approach and *S* personality type, there seems little doubt that the counselor's role as an implementor of therapeutic techniques is paramount. Although the two SD therapists were about equally effective in reducing anxiety with both introverts and extroverts, counselors C, c, R, and r showed considerable variability. Both CC counselors were equally effective with extroverts, and both RT counselors were equally effective with introverts. However, counselor c was significantly more effective than counselor C with introverts, while therapist R was significantly more effective than therapist r with extroverts. Counselors c and R were approximately 25 percent more effective, across *S* personality type, than counselors C and r in reducing anxiety.

The process measures incorporated into the present design suggest that counselor personality type probably was not a salient factor. As noted previously, the assessed personality characteristics of the counselors in the present study were as similar as they were different. Furthermore, the obtained differences do not seem to coincide with the counselors' stated theoretical orientation. However, the number of years of therapy experience and the number of hours of personal therapy did seem to differentiate counselors C and r from counselors c and R. The latter group of therapists had nearly twice as much actual therapy experience as the former and anywhere from 25 to 40 hours more of personal analysis and/or therapy.

Although experience may well be the "great teacher," experience level *per se* should not be considered synonymous with expertness (Fey, 1958). As Kell (1968) has pointed out, there is a considerable difference between a therapist with ten years of experience and one who has repeated the same year's experience ten times. It is probably more accurate to conclude that *some* relatively inexperienced therapists are rather rigid and perservative in their therapeutic interventions, while *some* experienced therapists are sensitive and flexible and can change their counseling style depending on the client's presenting problem and personality make-up. It may well be that the amount of personal therapy and/or certain personality characteristics, not assessed here, allow some therapists to profit from their experiences, while others do not. Whatever experience level and amount of personal counseling mean operationally, they were certainly the hallmarks of the top-notch counselors in the present study.

• *Generalization of Effects and Symptom Substitution*

Although neither the personality nor the "general" anxiety scales employed here were concerned with the specific target behaviors of interpersonal anxiety, they were included to aid in identifying the sample and check on the generalization effects of treatment, or conversely, symptom substitution. According to learning theory principles, there should be no change in behaviors that are not specifically the focus of treatment, except in the case of behaviors that are altered by generalization to similar situations or behaviors that had previously been inhibited by the target behaviors being treated (Paul, 1966). Within the context of the present study, a successful reduction in interpersonal anxiety might be expected to lead to the *S*s becoming less anxious, generally, less introverted, etc.

The date presented earlier on changes in "general" anxiety and introversion-extroversion (see Tables 3.13 and 3.21) suggest that a substantial degree of generalization was contingent on the amount of anxiety reduction in the area of the target behaviors treated. For example, those introverts who achieved the most interpersonal anxiety reduction also showed the lowest levels of "general" anxiety, the largest increments in extroversion, and the most adaptive changes in interpersonal behavior outside of the therapy session. While the extroverts showed no changes in either extroversion or interpersonal behavior outside of treatment, the amount of reduction in "general" anxiety by these *S*s was commensurate with the amount of interpersonal anxiety reduction. Finally, none of the treatment or control *S*s showed significant changes in defensiveness, as measured by the *Edwards Social Desirability Scale.*

Thus, the familiar litany of symptom substitution, frequently leveled against such basically re-educational approaches to therapy as SD and RT (Bookbinder, 1962), seems unwarranted by the findings of the present investigation. Even at the time of the three month follow-up, no changes in client behaviors which would not be predicted on the basis of known learning principles were observed (Grossberg, 1964).

· 5 ·

Summary and conclusions

The present study was organized in an attempt to compare the outcome of three distinct forms of counseling with two distinct client personality types in the treatment of a specific, homogeneous problem. More succinctly, it was the purpose of this investigation to compare the *relative effectiveness* of Systematic Desensitization (SD), Rational-Emotive (RT), and Client-Centered (CC) group psychotherapy in the reduction of interpersonal anxiety in introverts and extroverts. The *direct* comparison of the SD, RT, and CC treatments, independent of *S* personality type, was not the major goal of this study. It was anticipated that each of these treatments would produce significantly more anxiety reduction than either of the control procedures. These expectations, incorporated into hypotheses 5 and 6, were upheld by the results of this study.

The decision to use these three particular treatments rested on a number of considerations. First and foremost was the fact that all three of these treatment approaches have dealt theoretically with the problem of interpersonal anxiety, and each claims to have treated it successfully with the techniques they respectively advocate. This comparative approach thus allowed for a test of each theory's constructs relative to the dependent variable of interpersonal anxiety. It also demonstrated each theory's actual effectiveness, all within the context of a single research design. Second, considerable speculation and some evidence has now accumulated regarding the relative efficacy of different forms of counseling and psychotherapy with clients of varying personality types. This procedure allowed for a direct test of at least one of these hypotheses. Finally, since these three approaches represent radically different forms of treatment, in terms of technique, treatment model, etc., this comparative procedure may well have provided a clearer understanding of what aspects of each treatment are, in fact, therapeutic.

The rationale underlying the employment of interpersonal anxiety as the treatment focus was further based on the presupposition that this dependent variable is delineated enough to allow for fairly rigorous experimental methodology; at the same time, it is a sufficiently significant emotional problem to allow generalization from the findings and to suggest implications for further study in the broader field of counseling and psychotherapy. In addition, anxiety reduction is a cogent aspect of most, if not all, existing theories of psychopathology and is seen as a salient therapeutic goal by most practitioners. Consequently, the area of interpersonal anxiety seemed fertile ground for research from both a theoretical and practical point of view.

The decision to use introversion-extroversion as the relatively stable client personality types further rested on the now widely held belief that these two bi-polar qualities account for the majority of variance on nearly all self-report personality questionnaires, are relatively easy to assess, and have a high construct validity. Also, introverts and extroverts have been found to differ on a number of characteristics which may be predictive of differential treatment outcome.

It was the author's belief that selecting, describing, and classifying clients, therapists, and treatments on the basis of pre-treatment individual differences, as indicated above, makes for better controlled, more easily interpretable, and thus more legitimately generalizable research findings. While the importance of this type of research, for purposes of unambiguously assessing treatment effects, has been noted by many investigators, research of this nature is conspicious by its absence. However, it is precisely this type of research which may someday allow researchers to circumvent the vague and misleading question, "Does psychotherapy work?" and attempt to answer the more specific and meaningful question, "What form of treatment, administered by whom, is most effective for this particular client with that specific problem and under what set of circumstances?"

A detailed analysis of the client, therapist, and treatment variables, briefly elucidated above, served as a basis for the research hypotheses that were developed and tested in the present study. These hypotheses were:

1. With regard to extroverts, the order of effectiveness of the three techniques in reducing interpersonal anxiety will be as follows (from most to least effective): Client-Centered, Rational-Emotive, and Systematic Desensitization treatment.

2. With regard to extroverts, the order of effectiveness of the three techniques in reducing "general anxiety" will be as follows (from most to least effective): Client-Centered, Rational-Emotive, and Systematic Desensitization treatment.

3. With regard to introverts, the order of effectiveness of the three techniques in reducing interpersonal anxiety will be as follows (from most to least effective): Systematic Desensitization, Rational-Emotive, and Client-Centered treatment.

4. With regard to introverts, the order of effectiveness of the three techniques in reducing "general anxiety" will be as follows (from most to least effective): Systematic Desensitization, Rational-Emotive, and Client-Centered treatment.

5. Each of the treatment conditions will produce a sig-

nificantly greater reduction in interpersonal anxiety than either of the control conditions.

6. Each of the treatment conditions will produce a significantly greater reduction in "general anxiety" than either of the control conditions.

7. The no-treatment (placebo) control condition will produce a significantly greater reduction in interpersonal anxiety than the no-contact control condition.

8. The no-treatment (placebo) control condition will produce a significantly greater reduction in "general anxiety" than the no-contact control condition.

Following a detailed explanation of the present research project as a program of help for students with interpersonal anxiety, 217 *S*s from an Introductory Psychology class of approximately 600 volunteered to take the pre-test battery. Of the 217 volunteers, 149 students met the selection criteria. Of these, 100 *S*s were then assigned randomly, within stratified blocks, to one of ten introvert and ten extrovert groups. Each of the 20 groups consisted of five *S*s. The modal composition of each group was two male and three female *S*s. Each of the ten introvert and ten extrovert groups were then assigned randomly to one of the three treatment or two control conditions and then to one of the counselors within treatment.

The 60 *S*s in the treatment groups received roughly 11 hours of RT, CC, or SD group counseling. The 20 students in the no-treatment (placebo) control group received approximately 11 hours of attention. Finally, the 20 *S*s in the no-contact control group met all the selection criteria but were never contacted and thus were unaware of their participation in the study. For the latter group, post-test and follow-up test batteries were secured by mail under the guise of a "random sampling" for test validation. All *S*s also filled out a number of miscellaneous questionnaires during the period of the ten weekly treatment interviews, in an effort to secure process measures on the course of anxiety reduction during treatment, changes in behavior outside of therapy, etc.

An analysis of variance, with Scheffe post hoc comparisons, was computed on the outcome and three month follow-up test data. The results of both analyses confirmed hypotheses 5 through 8. All treated *S*s had a lower post-test and follow-up anxiety level than any of the control *S*s. In addition, the no-treatment (placebo) controls had a lower post-test and follow-up level of anxiety than the no-contact controls. However, the placebo benefits were limited almost exclusively to introverts.

Hypotheses 1 through 4 were only partially supported. While both CC and RT exhibited significant introvert-extrovert differences in the predicted direction, the SD treatment was equally effective with introverts and extroverts. It was hypothesized that the former results were due to the differential effects of RT and CC in eliciting self-exploration in introverts and extroverts, respectively. The latter findings were attributed to the detrimental effects of *group* SD with introverts.

Finally, unpredicted but significant counselor differences were obtained independent of treatment and *S* personality type. RT counselor R was found to be significantly more effective with extroverts than counselor r, and CC counselor c was found to be significantly more effective with introverts than counselor C. The greater effectiveness of counselors c and R over counselors C and r was attributed to more years of therapy experience and more hours of personal therapy.

References

Anastasi, Anne. *Psychological Testing*. New York: Macmillan, 1954.

Arbuckle, D. S. Kinds of counseling: Meaningful or meaningless. *Journal of Counseling Psychology*, 1967, 14, 219–225.

Astin, A. W. The functional antonomy of psychotherapy. *American Psychologist*, 1961, 16, 75–78.

Bailey, P. B. The great psychiatric revolution. *American Journal of Psychiatry*, 1956, 113, 147–168.

Bandura, A. *Behavioristic psychotherapy*. New York: Holt, Rinehart and Winston, in press. Cited in A. Bandura & R. H. Walters, *Social learning and personality development*. New York: Holt, Rinehart and Winston, 1963.

———. On empirical disconfirmations of equivocal deductions with insufficient data. *Journal of Consulting and Clinical Psychology*, 1968, 32, 247–249.

———, & Walters, R. H. *Social learning and personality development*. New York: Holt, Rinehart and Winston, 1963.

Bartlett, M. R., and staff. Data on the personal adjustment counseling program for veterans. Personal Adjustment Counseling Division. Advisement and Guidance Service. Office of Vocational Rehabilitation and Education. Washington, D.C., 1949.

Battle, C. C., Imber, S. D., Hoehn-Saric, R., Stone, A. R., Nash, E. R., & Frank, J. D. Target complaints as criteria of improvement. *American Journal of Psychotherapy*, 1966, 20, 184–192.

Bergin, A. E. The effects of psychotherapy: Negative results revisited. *Journal of Counseling Psychology*, 1963, 10, 244–250.

Berne, E. *Transactional analysis in psychotherapy*. New York: Grove Press, 1961.

Betz, B. Experience in research in psychotherapy with schizophrenic patients. In H. H. Strupp and L. Luborsky (Eds.), *Research in psychotherapy*. Vol. 2., Washington, D.C.: American Psychological Association, 1962. Pp. 41–60.

Blocher, D. What counseling can offer clients: Implications for research on client selection. In J. M. Whiteley (Chm.), *Invitational Conference on Counseling: Reevaluation and Refocus*. Symposium presented at the Central Midwestern Regional Educational Laboratory, Conference Proceedings Series No. 2, Washington University, September, 1967.

Bookbinder, L. J. Simple conditioning vs. the dynamic approach to symptoms and symptom substitution: a reply to Yates. *Psychological Reports,* 1962, 10, 71–77.

Breger, L., & McGaugh, J. L. Critique and reformulation of "learning-theory" approaches to psychotherapy and neurosis. *Psychological Bulletin,* 1965, 63, 338–358.

Buss, A. H. Two anxiety factors in psychiatric patients. *Journal of Abnormal and Social Psychology,* 1962, 65, 426–427.

———. *Psychopathology*. New York: John Wiley & Sons, 1966.

Campbell, D. T., & Stanley, J. C. *Experimental and quasi-experimental designs for research*. Chicago: Rand McNally, 1963.

Carkhuff, R. R. & Berenson, B. B. *Beyond counseling and therapy*. New York: Holt, Rinehart and Winston, 1967.

Cattell, R. B. Anxiety and motivation: Theory and crucial experiments. In C. D. Spielberger (Ed.), *Anxiety and behavior*. New York: Academic Press, 1966. Pp. 23–62.

Colby, K. M. Psychotherapeutic processes. *Annual review of psychology,* 1964, 15, 347–370.

Cooke, G. The efficacy of two desensitization procedures: An analogue study. *Behavior Research and Therapy,* 1966, 4, 17–24.

Coons, W. H. Interaction and insight in group psychotherapy. *Canadian Journal of Psychology,* 1957, 11, 1–8.

Corsini, R. J., & Putzey, L. J. Bibliography of group psychotherapy research: 1906 through 1955. *Psychodrama and Group Psychotherapy Monographs*. No. 29. New York: Beacon House, 1957.

Cronback, L. J. *Essentials of psychological testing*. (2nd ed.). New York: Harper & Row, 1950.

Cross, H. J. The outcome of psychotherapy: A selected analysis of research findings. *Journal of Consulting Psychology,* 1964, 28, 413–417.

Davison, G. Systematic desensitization as a counterconditioning process. *Journal of Abnormal Psychology,* 1968, 73, 91–100.

Dittmann, A. T. Psychotherapeutic processes. *Annual review of psychology,* 1966, 17, 51–78.

Dollard, J., & Miller, N. E. *Personality and psychotherapy.* New York: McGraw-Hill, 1950.

Dymond, Rosalind F. Adjustment changes over therapy from thematic apperception test ratings. In C. R. Rogers and Rosalind F. Dymond (Eds.), *Psychotherapy and personality change.* Chicago: University of Chicago Press, 1954. Pp. 109–121.

Edgar, T. E. Wistful wish: Evaluation without values. *Personal & Guidance Journal,* 1966, 44, 1025–1029.

Edwards, A. L. *The social desirability variable in personality assessment and research.* New York: Dryden Press, 1957.

———. *The Edwards personal preference schedule.* New York: The Psychological Corp. (Revised Edition), 1959.

———, & Cronbach, L. J. Experimental design for research in psychotherapy. *Journal of Clinical Psychology,* 1952, 8, 51–59.

Ellis, A. Outcome of employing three techniques of psychotherapy. *Journal of Clinical Psychology,* 1957, 13, 334–350.

———. *Reason and emotion in psychotherapy.* New York: Lyle Stuart, 1962.

Endler, N. S., Hunt, J. McV., & Rosenstein, A. J. An S-R inventory of anxiousness. *Psychological Monographs,* 1962, 76, No. 536.

Estabrook, M., & Sommer, R. Study habits and introversion-extroversion. *Psychological Reports,* 1966, 19, 750–761.

Eysenck, H. J. The effects of psychotherapy: An evaluation. *Journal of Consulting Psychology,* 1952, 16, 319–324.

———. The effects of psychotherapy: A reply. *Journal of Abnormal & Social Psychology,* 1955, 50, 147–148.

———. The dynamic theory of anxiety and hysteria. *Journal of Mental Science,* 1955, 101, 28–49. (a)

———. Learning theory and behavior therapy. *Journal of Mental Science,* 1959, 105, 61–75.

———. *The structure of human personality.* New York: John Wiley & Sons, 1960.

———. (Ed.) *Behavior therapy and the neuroses.* New York: Pergamon Press, 1960. (a)

———. The effects of psychotherapy. In H. J. Eysenck (Ed.), *Handbook of abnormal psychology.* New York: Basic Books, 1961. Pp. 697–725.

———. The effects of psychotherapy. *International Journal of Psychiatry,* 1965, 1, 99–144.

———. New Ways in psychotherapy. *Psychology Today,* 1967, 1, 39–47.

———, and Rachman, S. *Causes and cures of neuroses.* San Diego: Robert R. Knapp, 1965.

Fenichel, O. *Problems of psychoanalytic technique.* New York: The Psychoanalytic Quarterly, Inc., 1941.

Festinger, L. *A theory of cognitive dissonance.* Evanston, Ill.: Row, Peterson, 1957.

Fey, W. F. Doctrine and experience: Their influence upon the psychotherapist. *Journal of Consulting Psychology,* 1958, 22, 403–409.

Frank, J. D. Problems of controls in psychotherapy as exemplified by the psychotherapy research project of the Phipps Psychiatric Clinic. In E. A. Rubinstein and M. B. Parloff (Eds.), *Research in psychotherapy.* Vol. 1. Washington, D.C.: American Psychological Association, 1959, Pp. 10–326.

———. The dynamics of the psychotherapeutic relationship: determinants and effects of the therapist's influence. *Psychiatry,* 1959, 22, 17–40. (a)

———. *Persuasion and healing.* Baltimore: Johns-Hopkins Press, 1961.

———. Does psychotherapy work? *International Journal of Psychiatry,* 1967, 3, 153–156.

Franks, C. Conditioning and abnormal behavior. In H. J. Eysenck (Ed.), *Handbook of abnormal psychology.* New York: Basic Books, 1961. Pp. 411–421.

Garfield, S. L, & Affleck, D. C. Therapists' judgements concerning patients considered for psychotherapy. *Journal of Consulting Psychology,* 1961, 25, 505–509.

Gelder, M., & Wolff, H. Desensitization and psychotherapy in the treatment of phobic states: A controlled inquiry. *British Journal of Psychiatry,* 1967, 113, 53–78.

Gelfand, Donna M., & Hartmann, D. P. Behavior therapy with children: A review and evaluation of research methodology. *Psychological Bulletin,* 1968, 69, 204–215.

Gendlin, E. T. The social significance of the research. In C. R. Rogers, E. T. Gendlin, D. J. Kiesler, and C. B. Traux, (Eds.), *The therapeutic relationship and its impact: A study of psychotherapy with schizophrenics.* Madison: University of Wisconsin Press, 1967. Pp. 523–542.

Gilbert, W. Counseling: Therapy and diagnosis. *Annual Review of Psychology,* 1952, 3, 351–380.

Goldstein, A. P. Patient's expectancies and non-specific therapy as a basis for (un)spontaneous remission. *Journal of Clinical Psychology,* 1960, 16, 399–403.

———, Heller, K., & Sechrest, L. B. *Psychotherapy and the psychology of behavior change.* New York: John Wiley & Sons, 1966.

Good, C. V., & Scates, D. E. *Methods of research.* New York: Appleton-Century-Crofts, 1954.

Gray, J. Strength of the nervous system, introversion-extraversion, conditionability and arousal. *Behavior Research and Therapy,* 1967, 5, 151–170.

Greenhouse, S. W. Principles in the evaluation of therapies for mental disorders. In P. H. Hock and J. Zubin (Eds.), *The evaluation of psychiatric treatment.* New York: Grune & Stratton, 1964. Pp. 94–105.

Grinker, R. R. The psychosomatic aspects of anxiety. In C. D. Spielberger (Ed.), *Anxiety and behavior.* New York: Academic Press, 1966. Pp. 129–142.

Grossberg, J. M. Behavior therapy: A review. *Psychological Bulletin,* 1964, 62, 73–88.

Grummon, D. L. Client-centered theory. In B. Stefflre (Ed.), *Theories of counseling.* New York: McGraw-Hill, 1965, Pp. 30–90.

———, & John, Eve S. Changes over client-centered therapy evaluated in psychoanalytically based TAT scales. In C. R. Rogers and Rosalind F. Dymond (Eds.), *Psychotherapy and personality change.* Chicago: University of Chicago Press, 1954. Pp. 121–144.

Guilford, J. P. *Personality.* New York: McGraw-Hill, 1959.

Hamilton, M. The assessment of anxiety states by rating. *British Journal of Medical Psychology,* 1959, 32, 50–59.

Harris, C. W. (Ed.) *Problems in measuring change.* Madison: University of Wisconsin Press, 1963.

Hayes, W. L. *Statistics for psychologists.* New York: Holt, Rinehart and Winston, 1963.

Hobbs, N. Sources of gain in psychotherapy. *American Psychologist,* 1962, 17, 741–747.

Hoppock, R. What is the real problem? *American Psychologist,* 1953, 8, 124–130.

Hoskisson, J. B. *Loneliness.* New York: The Citadel Press, 1965.

Hunt, W. A. *The clinical psychologist.* Springfield, Ill.: Charles C Thomas, 1956.

Hyman, R., & Berger, L. Discussion of H. J. Eysenck's "The effects of psychotherapy." *International Journal of Psychiatry,* 1965, 1, 317–322.

Kell, B. L., & Burrow, Josephine M. *Human development therapy: theory, practice, and supervision.* New York: McGraw-Hill, 1969 (in press).

Kiesler, D. J. Some myths of psychotherapy research and the search for a paradigm. *Psychological Bulletin,* 1966, 65, 110–136.

Lang, P., Lazovik, A., & Reynolds, D. Desensitization, suggestibility and pseudo-therapy. *Journal of Abnormal Psychology,* 1965, 70, 395–402.

Lazarus, A. A. New group techniques in the treatment of phobic conditions. Unpublished doctoral dissertation, University of Witwatersrand, Johannesburg, South Africa, 1960.

———. Group therapy of phobic disorders by systematic desensitization. *Journal of Abnormal and Social Psychology,* 1961, 63, 504–510.

———. The results of behavior therapy in 126 cases of severe neurosis. *Behavior Research & Therapy,* 1963, 1, 69–79.

———. Behavior rehearsal vs. non-directive therapy vs. advice in effecting behavior change. *Behavior Research & Therapy,* 1966, 4, 209–212.

———, & Rachman, S. The use of systematic desensitization in psychotherapy. *South African Medical Journal,* 1957, 31, 934–937.

Leary, T. *Multilevel measurement of interpersonal behavior.* Berkeley, Calif.: Psychological Consultation Services, 1956.

Levinson, D. J. The psychotherapist's contribution to the patient's treatment career. In H. H. Strupp and L. Luborsky (Eds.), *Research in psychotherapy.* Vol. 2. Washington, D.C.: American Psychological Association, 1962. Pp. 13–24.

Levitt, E. E. The results of psychotherapy with children: An evaluation. *Journal of Consulting Psychology,* 1957, 21, 189–196.

———. *The problem of anxiety.* New York: Bobbs-Merrill, 1967.

London, P. *The modes and morals of psychotherapy.* New York: Holt, Rinehart and Winston, 1964.

Lorr, M., Katz, M., & Rubenstein, E. The prediction of length of stay in psychotherapy. *Journal of Counseling Psychology,* 1958, 22, 321–327.

Lubin, B., & Lubin, Alice W. *Group psychotherapy: a bibliography of the literature from 1956 through 1964.* East Lansing: Michigan State University Press, 1966.

Luborsky, L. The patient's personality and psychotherapeutic change. In H. H. Strupp and L. Luborsky (Eds.), *Research in psychotherapy.* Vol. 2. Washington D.C.: American Psychological Association, 1962. Pp. 115–133.

———, & Strupp, H. H. Research problems in psychotherapy: A three year follow-up. In H. H. Strupp and L. Luborsky (Eds.), *Research in psychotherapy*. Vol. 2. Washington, D.C.: American

Luria, A. R. *The nature of human conflict*. New York: Liveright, 1932.

Malmo, R. B. Studies of anxiety: Some clinical origins of the activation concept. In C. D. Spielberger (Ed.), *Anxiety and behavior*. New York: Academic Press, 1966. Pp. 157–177.

———, & Shagass, C. Physiologic studies of reaction to stress in anxiety and early schizophrenia. *Psychosomatic Medicine*, 1949, 11, 9–24.

Martin, Irene. A note on reflex sensitivity and formation of conditioned responses. *Behavior Research & Therapy*, 1963, 1, 185–190.

Matarazzo, J. D. Psychotherapeutic processes. *Annual Review of Psychology*, 1965, 16, 181–224.

Mowrer, O. Abnormal reactions or actions? (An autobiographical answer). *Introduction to general psychology: A self selection textbook*. Dubuque, Iowa: William C. Brown, 1966.

Myers, Isabel B. *The Myers-Briggs type indicator*. Princeton, N. J.: Educational Testing Service (2nd ed.), 1962.

Neuman, D. R. Professional and subprofessional counselors using group desensitization and insight procedures to reduce examination anxiety. Unpublished doctoral dissertation, Michigan State University, 1968.

Patterson, C. H. Counseling. *Annual Reveiw of Psychology*, 1966, 17, 79–110.

———. *Theories of counseling and psychotherapy*. New York: Harper & Row, 1966. (a)

Paul, G. L. *Insight vs. desensitization in psychotherapy*. Stanford, Calif.: Stanford University Press, 1966.

———. The specific control of anxiety: "Hypnosis and conditioning." Paper read at APA symposium on innovations in therapeutic interactions, 1966. (a)

———. Strategy of outcome research in psychotherapy. *Journal of Consulting Psychology*, 1967, 31, 109–118.

———. Insight vs. desensitization in psychotherapy two years after termination. *Journal of Consulting Psychology*, 1967, 31, 333–348. (a)

———. Systematic desensitization in groups: Reducing examination anxiety. Discussant paper presented at symposium: Systematic desensitization in groups, American Educational Research Association, Chicago, 1968.

———, & Shannon, D. Treatment of anxiety through systematic desensitization in therapy groups. *Journal of Abnormal Psychology*, 1966, 71, 124–135.

Pavlov, I. *Experimental psychology and other essays.* New York: Philosophical Library, 1957.

Perry, Helen S., & Garvel, M. L. *The collected works of Harry Stack Sullivan.* New York: W. W. Norton, 1953. 2 vols.

Phillips, E. L. *Psychotherapy: A modern theory and practice.* Englewood Cliffs, N. J.: Prentice-Hall, 1956.

Raimy, V. C. (Ed.) *Training in clinical psychology.* Englewood Cliffs, N. J.: Prentice-Hall, 1950.

Reyna, L. J. Conditioning therapies, learning theory and research. In J. Wolpe, A. Salter, and L. J. Reyna (Eds.), *The conditioning therapies.* New York: Holt, Rinehart and Winston, 1964. Pp. 169–179.

Rickard, H. C. Tailored criteria of change in psychotherapy. *Journal of General Psychology,* 1965, 72, 63–68.

Rogers, C. R. *Client-centered therapy: Its current practice, implications and theory.* Boston: Houghton Mifflin, 1951.

———. Changes in the maturity of behavior as related to therapy. In C. R. Rogers and Rosalind F. Dymond (Eds.), *Psychotherapy and personality change.* Chicago: University of Chicago Press, 1954. Pp. 215–237.

———. Persons or science? A philosophical question. *American Psychologist,* 1955, 10, 267–278.

———. A theory of therapy, personality and interpersonal relationships, as developed in the client-centered framework. In S. Koch (Ed.), *Psychology: A study of a science.* Vol. 3. Formulations of the person and the social context. New York: McGraw-Hill, 1959. Pp. 184–258.

———. The essence of psychotherapy: A client-centered view. *Annals of Psychotherapy,* 1959, 1, 51–57. (a)

———. The interpersonal relationship: The core of guidance. *Harvard Educational Review,* 1962, 32, 416–429.

———. Psychotherapy today or where do we go from here? *American Journal of Psychotherapy,* 1963, 17, 5–16.

———. (Ed.). *The therapeutic relationship and its impact: A study of psychotherapy with schizophrenics.* Madison: The University of Wisconsin Press, 1967.

———, and Dymond, Rosalind F. (Eds.) *Psychotherapy and personality change.* Chicago: University of Chicago Press, 1954.

Rubinstein, E. A., & Parloff, M. B. (Eds.) *Research in psychotherapy.* Vol. 1. Washington, D.C.: American Psychological Association, 1959.

Salter, A. *Conditioned reflex therapy.* New York: Capricorn Books, 1961.

Saltz, E., & Di Loreto, A. 'Defense' against traumatic concepts. *Journal of Abnormal Psychology,* 1965, 70, 281–284.

Sanford, N. Clinical methods: Psychotherapy. *Annual Reveiw of Psychology,* 1953, 4, 317–342.

Sargent, Helen D. Methodological problems of follow-up studies in psychotherapy research. *American Journal of Orthopsychiatry,* 1960, 30, 495–506.

———. Intropsychic change: Methodological problems in psychotherapy research. *Psychiatry,* 1961, 24, 93–108.

Shlien, J. M. Time-limited psychotherapy: an experimental investigation of practical values and theoretical implications. *Journal of Counseling Psychology,* 1957, 4, 318–324.

———. Comparison of results with different forms of psychotherapy. *American Journal of Psychotherapy,* 1964, 18 (Monogr. Suppl. 1), 15–22.

———. Cross-theoretical criteria for the evaluation of psychotherapy. *American Journal of Psychotherapy,* 1966, 1, 125–134.

———. (Ed.) *Research in psychotherapy.* Vol. 3. Washington, D.C.: American Psychological Association, 1968.

———, Mosak, H. H., & Dreikurs, R. Effects of time limits: A comparison of client-centered and adlerian psychotherapy. *Journal of Counseling Psychology,* 1962, 9, 318–324.

Singer, J. L. The importance of daydreaming. *Psychology Today,* 1968, 1, 18–27.

Spielberger, C. D. Theory and research on anxiety. In C. D. Spielberger (Ed.), *Anxiety and behavior.* New York: Academic Press, 1966. Pp. 3–19

———, & Gorsuch, R. L. Mediating processes in verbal conditioning. Educational Publishing Service, Department of Psychology, Vanderbilt University, 1966.

Sprinthall, N. Selecting clients for counseling: Are prior conditions limiting or illusions? In J. M. Whiteley (Chm.), Invitational Conference on Counseling: Reevaluation and Refocus. Symposium presented at the Central Midwestern Regional Educational Laboratory, Conference Proceedings Series No. 2, Washington University, September, 1967.

Stampfl, T. G., & Levis, D. J. The essentials of implosive therapy: A learning theory based psychodynamic behavioral therapy. Unpublished manuscript, John Carroll University, 1967.

Strupp, H. H. *Psychotherapists in action.* New York: Grune & Stratton, 1960.

———. Psychotherapy. *Annual Review of Psychology,* 1962, 13, 445–478.

———. The outcome problem in psychotherapy revisited. *Psychotherapy,* 1963, 1, 1–13.

———. A bibliography of research in psychotherapy. Psychotherapy Research Project. Department of Psychiatry, University of North Carolina School of Medicine. Chapel Hill, N. C., July, 1964.

———. What is psychotherapy? *Contemporary Psychology,* 1967, 12, 41–42.

———. Psychoanalytic therapy of the individual. In J. Marmor (Ed.), *Modern psychoanalysis.* New York: Basic Books, 1968. Pp. 293–342.

———, & Luborsky, L. (Eds.) *Research in psychotherapy.* Vol. 2. Washington, D.C.: American Psychological Association, 1962.

Snyder, W. U. Summary report: Therapist's contribution. In H. H. Strupp and L. Luborsky (Eds.), *Research in psychotherapy.* Vol. 2. Washington, D.C.: American Psychological Association, 1962. Pp. 259–262.

Sundland, D. M., & Barker, E. N. The orientation of psychotherapists. *Journal of Consulting Psychology,* 1962, 26, 201–212.

Szasz, T. S. *The myth of mental illness.* New York: Hoeber-Harper, 1961.

Truax, C. B., & Carkhuff, R. R. Client and therapist transparency in the psychotherapeutic encounter. *Journal of Counseling Psychology,* 1965, 12, 3–9.

———. *Toward effective counseling and psychotherapy: Training and practice.* Chicago: Aldine · Atherton, 1967.

Underwood, B. J. *Psychological research.* New York: Appleton-Century-Crofts, 1957.

Urban, H. B., & Ford, D. H. *Systems of psychotherapy: A comparative study.* John Wiley & Sons, 1963.

Weinstein, Francine T. The effect of personality type on systematic desensitization and structured group interaction in reducing examination anxiety. Unpublished doctoral dissertation, Michigan State University, 1968.

White, R. W. *The abnormal personality.* New York: Ronald Press Company, 1956.

Wolpe, J. *Psychotherapy by reciprocal inhibition.* Stanford, Calif: Stanford University Press, 1958.

———. The systematic desensitization treatment of neurosis. *Journal of Nervous and Mental Disorders,* 1961, 112, 189–203.

———. Psychotherapy: The non-scientific heritage and the new science. *Behavior Research and Therapy,* 1963, 1, 23–28.

———. The conditioning and deconditioning of neurotic anxiety. In C. D. Spielberger (Ed.), *Anxiety and behavior.* New York: Academic Press, 1966. Pp. 179–191.

———, Salter, A., & Reyna, L. J. (Eds.) *The conditioning therapies.* New York: Holt, Rinehart and Winston, 1964.

———, & Lazarus, A. A. *Behavior therapy techniques: A guide to the treatment of neurosis.* New York: Pergamon Press, 1966.

Wolpin, M., & Raines, J. Visual imagery, expected roles and extinction as possible factors in reducing fear and avoidance behavior. *Behavior Research and Therapy,* 1966, 4, 25–37.

Zax, M., & Klein, A. Measurement of personality and behavior change following psychotherapy. *Psychological Bulletin,* 1960, 57, 435–448.

Zubin, J. Technical issues: Discussion. In P. H. Hock and J. Zubin (Eds.), *The evaluation of psychotherapy.* New York: Grune & Stratton, 1964. Pp. 122–128.

Critiques

A critique by Albert Ellis*

Dr. Di Loreto's excellent study ably demonstrates that the effectiveness of different types of psychotherapy can to some degree be measured, and I certainly hope that more studies of this kind become prevalent in the psychological literature. However, since his investigation included a limited number of clients (twenty) in each of three therapeutic groups and only two counselors from each approach or "school," it would be interesting to see it duplicated with more clients and counselors. Otherwise, conclusions from the study (as is true of most psychological experiments) are of dubious generality.

What of the effectiveness of Rational-Emotive psychotherapy, as indicated by Dr. Di Loreto's thesis? Naturally, I am gratified to note that in only ten group therapy sessions, led by young counselors who were hardly intensively trained in Rational-Emotive methods, this technique which I originated came off so well, particularly in regard to introverted clients—who not only reduced their interpersonal anxiety as much as they did with systematic desensitization but who also showed a significantly greater increase in interpersonal activity. As Dr.

*Executive Director of the Institute for Advanced Study in Rational Psychotherapy, New York, New York.

Di Loreto notes, "The benefits which accrued from the RT treatment approach did appear to be more quickly implemented into activity outside of treatment than those resulting from SD."

Several other favorite Rational-Emotive hypotheses seem to be supported by the data of this study; namely, that Client-Centered counselors proved to be less active verbally than RT counselors: that "cognitive revamping" did prove to be an effective therapeutic method: that introverted clients definitely need prodding and were "quite inactive when left to their own devices": that activity oriented homework assignments, to be done by the client in between the therapeutic sessions, proved to be highly workable and efficient: and that Rational-Emotive therapy actively teaches self-exploration, which was found to be most helpful in this study.

Although RT did not prove to be terribly effective in regard to extroverted clients, this is hardly the handicap it might at first appear. For one, most experienced therapists seem to acknowledge that introverts are much more common in actual therapeutic practice than are extroverts. A study by Mendelsohn and Kirk (1962), for example, shows that "compared to the nonclient subjects, the students who seek counseling score less toward the judging side, more toward the intuitive side, less toward the feeling side, and more toward the introversion side of the respective dimensions." These investigators employed the *Myers-Briggs Type Indicator* to measure introversion-extroversion—the very same test that Dr. Di Loreto used in the present study. Similarly, Hammer (1968) states that, "While the extrovertive patient may look for therapy to supply little more than symptom removal, the more introspective individual hopes for more including the possibility of an inward vision."

Even more significant to me than the fairly good results obtained with the Rational-Emotive approach used in this study is the fact that the specific technique employed was an exceptionally watered-down version of RT that is undoubtedly based on my own theory but that only modestly resembles much of the clinical practice that we teach at the Institute for Advanced Study in Rational Psychotherapy. The method that Dr. Di Loreto's RT counselors used, as he indicates in the appendix, (1) is much too *generally* didactic and lecturing and does not seem to make much use of the specific clinical examples that are constantly employed in actual RT: (2) wrongly tells the client that the irrational ideas he keeps telling himself are learned when actually [as I indicate in *Reason and Emotion in Psychotherapy* (Ellis, 1962)], the tendency to believe them is probably inborn: (3) never seems to stress the great difficulty and the enormous amount of everyday *practice* that the client will probably have to undergo to overcome his severe tendencies toward irrational thinking: (4) emphasizes a warm, interested, and helpful, rather than a hard-headed, no-nonsense-about-facing-reality attitude on the part of the therapist: (5) does not, as far as I can see, specifically show the client why his basic philosophical assumptions are untenable and what he can do about constantly challenging them: (6) does not particularly stress the highly-important non-blaming aspects of RT, nor the corollary point that human beings cannot be legitimately rated and that even "ego-bolstering" or "self-esteem" are inappropriate and irrational constructs: and (7) makes relatively little use of the therapist's active-directive, Socratic dialoguing approach.

At the same time that Dr. Di Loreto's RT counselors kept employing a highly pale and wan Rational-Emotive approach, his Systematic Desensitization and Client-Centered counselors (ironically enough!) kept using what I would consider to be some highly effective RT-flavored methods. Thus, his SD treatment group was told, "The more you avoid people and interpersonal situations, the more anxious you get." They were also given some time each session for verbal interchanges among clients and between clients and counselor, which "was not limited exclusively to treatment related material," and "during the last few minutes of each session following the *successful com-*

pletion of an item, the *S*s were aroused and reactions to images, etc. were discussed." Also, in a typically Client-Centered manner, each SD "counselor was instructed to maintain a warm, interested, and helpful attitude."

As for the Client-Centered counselors, instead of merely giving their own feelings about their clients, confronting him, and reflecting his feelings about himself, they were instructed to use highly didactic methods that have an exceptionally strong RT quality. Thus, they were told that an individual "doesn't have to feel guilty and thus pretend he is interested or blame himself or his friend for *making him bored.* He simply uncritically accepts his feeling of boredom. He is being honest with both himself and his friend by conveying his boredom to his friend, not with the intent of blaming, but with the idea of 'Let's make this unboring! ' " And again: "But this is how you learn to listen uncritically, you focus on what, *in fact,* is coming across to you, not on classifying it as good or bad, right or wrong, etc. This holds even for feelings of anger. If they are there, then trying to decide if they are important, bad, etc. makes no sense. They're just there. . . .If you are less blaming and less condemning, people are going to feel freer and more at ease in communicating with you about their feelings." These so-called "Client-Centered" methods mirror, in fact almost ape, much of the material I included in *Reason and Emotion in Psychotherapy* and which I actively demonstrate to individual and group clients, to workshop and marathon participants, and to other RT-sponsored therapy gatherings all over the country.

It is not exactly remarkable that the philosophic cores of Rational-Emotive and Client-Centered therapy significantly overlap, in that both teach individuals how to unconditionally accept themselves and others. In fact, Harry Bone (1968) has clearly noted this overlap in an important paper on interpretation in psychotherapy. However, one of the main differences between the two systems is that RT counselors directly, actively, and concretely teach their clients non-damning philosophies of life, while CC counselors presumably do so by existential encounters and by highlighting their own personal feelings. Dr. Di Loreto's CC counselors, however, seem to be almost as didactic and argumentative, at least in their first instructions to their clients, as are his RT counselors: and his SD counselors are not too far behind in these respects, either.

I might well contend, in other words, that while the SD and CC counselors in this study tended not to stick to their own lasts, but to use explanatory, challenging, and other approaches that are more traditionally allied with the Rational-Emotive approach, Dr. Di Loreto's RT counselors stuck much too closely to a very narrow definition of RT and omitted some of its most powerful philosophical and confronting methods. This does not mean that the basic RT methodology was badly neglected or violated, nor that some of the results favoring the SD and CC systems would have been quite different had the counselors in each school more rigorously stuck to their own last. But, of course, one wonders.

Assuming that the results of Dr. Di Loreto's study prove to be more broadly duplicated and hence valid, the question arises: Why did RT do relatively badly with the extroverts? Some hypotheses I might set forth here include the following: (1) The extroverts were more defensive, more complusively acting out, more disturbed, and less inclined to listen to reason than were the introverts. Consequently, they resented therapists who were more actively trying to teach them, or talk them out of, their upsetness and preferred to "listen" to therapists who were warmer to them (the CC counselors) or who didn't bother to talk to them too much at all (the SD counselors). (2) Because of their severe disturbances and their basic unwillingness to *work* at changing themselves, the extroverts preferred types of therapy which helped them *feel* rather than *get* better, as Hammer (1968) intimates. They preferred to have their dire love needs catered to rather than to look at and uproot their symptom-creating, basic philosophies. (3) In order to change their basic attitudes to a significant degree, the extroverts (who tend to be more difficult clients) would have required Rational-Emotive counselors who were distinctly more effective than those who were employed in Dr. Di Loreto's study. Actually, they had one counselor, r, who was inexperienced, and who turned out to be no more effective in reducing self-reports and behavior ratings of anxiety with extroverts than the group receiving simple attention or no treatment at all, and counselor R, who was considerably more effective. If they had had two counselors as effective (or even more effective) as counselor R, the results of Dr. Di Loreto's study would have presumably been much different.

Assuming, again, that the results of Dr. Di Loreto's study turn out to be duplicatable and valid, the question arises: Why was the RT approach that was used in this study so effective that "in terms of changes in target behaviors outside of the treatment setting (it) appears to have produced a *greater* increase in interpersonal activity" than the SD and CC approaches, while at the same time it was not similarly as effective in producing the greatest amount of anxiety reduction except in introverted clients? Aside from the reasons given in the preceding paragraph, another important possibility exists; namely, that for the length of time this study continued, increase in interpersonal activity and anxiety reduction were to some extent incompatible. That is to say, some individuals who are induced by the therapeutic process to do their homework assignments and to increase their interpersonal activity in areas where they are notably anxious (e.g., to order a cup of coffe in a restaurant and to tell the waitress they have changed their mind and now want a coke) will *at first* be expected to feel *more* anxious than if they do not carry out this assignment, although ultimately they may become less anxious about these assignments and about similar activities. Consequently, the fact that Dr. Di Loreto's RT clients did so well in their interpersonal activity but not as concomitantly well in their anxiety reduction may be the result of their not acting in a risk-taking manner for a sufficiently long enough time to prove to themselves that it is *not* terrible for them to make mistakes or to be criticized. In actual Rational-Emotive therapy, it is frequently found that clients at first become more anxious as they think about taking or actually take outside risks. However, the more they actually do what they are afraid of, the more their anxiety decreases. To some degree, time is the essence of personality change in these particular clients, and Dr. Di Loreto's study was, of course, deliberately time-limited.

In this respect, it is easy to draw an essentially false conclusion from the present study: namely, that individual clients tend to be so different that one type of therapy may well work best for a given client but not work at all well for another, and that, therefore, a therapist would better be trained to be fairly eclectic, or to employ a large variety of techniques within the framework of his fairly consistent theoretical system, so that he is able to work well with many different types of clients. I am reasonably sure, from my own quarter of a century of therapeutic practice, in the course of which I have used several different basic approaches (including Freudian, Ferenczi warmth-giving, and Rational-Emotive techniques), that there is *some* validity to this idea. Consequently, I have incorporated into the Rational-Emotive methodology a wide range of perceptive-cognitive, experimental-emotive, and activity-behavioristic techniques (Ellis, 1969a, 1969b). I have also pointed out (Ellis, 1968) that practically all existing schools of psychotherapy, including the Client-Centered and the Behavior Therapy schools, are really somewhat comprehensive systems, in that they include cognitive-emotive-behavioristic elements. This does not mean that they (or Rational-Emotive therapy) are eclectic, for most schools have a somewhat consistent theory of personality and of treatment, and the varied approaches they employ stem somewhat from their system, rather than from purely pragmatic considerations.

Thus, RT (in its full form, though not in the truncated manner in which Dr. Di Loreto's counselors employed it) deliberately uses dramatic-emotive methods (such as down-to-earth language and direct and sometimes humorous assaults on a client's irrational ideas) and uses Behavior Therapy methods [such as homework assignments and teaching the client to reinforce himself by employing Premack's (1965) principle] in order to help him change his ideas, and it is consistently *ideologically* or *philosophically* oriented in virtually every technique that it utilizes.

The main point I would like to make here is that although clients are individually different and can sometimes be categorized (as Dr. Di Loreto categorizes them) into distinct personality types, and although one specific technique (such as persuasive discussion) may seem to work better with a certain client than another technique (such as the therapist's revealing his own true feelings), it is still quite probable that (1) one technique will be more effective *most of the time* with *more* clients than will another, that (2) this same technique will usually help bring about more elegant or "deeper" solutions than will an alternative method, and that (3) this same technique, if practiced by competent therapists for a sufficiently long period of time, will achieve better results than an alternative method which over a shorter period *seems* to work better.

It will be noted, for example, that proponents of classical psychoanalysis have tended to uphold the last two of these hypotheses, and sometimes even the first, in regard to the value of their own methodology. I do not think that there is any empirical evidence to sustain their views; but as yet there isn't very much evidence to refute them either. What I am suggesting is that after a number of studies such as Dr. Di Loreto's pioneering experiment have been done—and the more the better, in my estimation—a group of further studies be instituted to test the above hypotheses. Meanwhile, we can only be grateful for Dr. Di Loreto's investigation and for some of the most interesting data, conclusions, and hypotheses for future testing that it presents.

REFERENCES

Bone, H. Two proposed alternatives to psychoanalytic interpreting. In Hammer, E. F. (Ed.), *Use of interpretation in treatment.* New York: Grune & Stratton, 1968, 169–196.

Ellis, A. *Reason and emotion in psychotherapy.* New York: Lyle Stuart, 1962.

Ellis, A. What *really* causes psychotherapeutic change? *Voices,* 1968, 4, No. 2, 90–97.

Ellis, A. A weekend of rational encounter. In Burton, A. (Ed.), *Encounter.* San Francisco: Jossey-Bass, 1969a, 112–127.

Ellis, A. Rational-emotive therapy. *Journal of Contemporary Psychotherapy,* 1969b, 1, 82–90.

Hammer, E. F. Interpretation: What is it? In Hammer, E. F. (Ed.), *Use of interpretation in treatment.* New York: Grune & Stratton, 1968, 1–5.

Mendelsohn, G. A., and Kirk, B. A. Personality differences between students who do and do not use a counseling facility. *Journal of Counseling Psychology,* 1962, 9, 341–346.

Premack, D. Reinforcement theory. In Levine, D. (Ed.), *Nebraska symposium on motivation.* Lincoln: University of Nebraska Press, 1965.

A critique by Alan Goldstein and Joseph Wolpe*

Dr. Di Loreto's efforts have produced one of the few studies in the area of psychotherapy which can be called well designed, well executed, and meaningful. Particularly impressive, in terms of design, is the fact that the input variables (forms of therapy) across groups are definably different. There was a very adequate check to determine that each therapist was performing essentially within the guidelines of his theoretical approach. The pertinent variables under consideration were well delineated and defined. As to execution, apparently the problems often encountered, such as dropout rate leading to uneven and unmatched groups, variability of number of sessions across groups, etc., were anticipated and avoided. This study is particularly meaningful in that it deals with a target, maladaptive behavior (interpersonal anxiety) which is central to most theoretical models of neurosis and more importantly is the *most salient presenting complaint of the large majority of people presenting themselves for treatment*. The ubiquity

*Temple University School of Medicine, Department of Behavioral Science, Philadelphia, Pennsylvania.

of this problem is dramatically demonstrated by the fact that approximately 35 percent of the college freshman class in this study reported interpersonal anxiety to a degree sufficient to motivate them to be treated for it.

I find no serious flaws in the study; however, the method of S selection renders the research less than ideal. While it may be so that procurement of a sufficient number of *S*s from the population at hand required solicitation, it has yet to be demonstrated that solicited *S*s do not differ significantly from those who decide on their own to present themselves for treatment. Ideally, the *S*s would be selected from the population of people seeking therapy on their own, as this is the population to which the results must be generalized. A further limitation to generalization is a result of the fact that almost 25 percent (51 out of 217) of the *S*s volunteering were eliminated on the basis of falling into the midrange on the introversion-extraversion continuum. This leaves open the question of the treatment-outcome relationship for a significant proportion of prospective clients, particularly for CC and RT treatments, since their effectiveness is shown to be related to extraversion and introversion, respectively. The outcome of SD treatment appears to be unrelated to the introversion-extraversion variable, so that it is highly probably that SD would prove to be as effective with midrange *S*s as with the included extremes. However, it would be a comfort to have this empirically confirmed.

While it cannot be considered a criticism of the present study, it is important to note that *systematic desensitization is not equal to behavior therapy*. The CC and RT therapists were given an opportunity to operate within the full range dictated by their theoretical positions, but the SD groups were limited to systematic desensitization only. It appears that the SD technique was misunderstood to be typical of the course that behavior therapists take with all their patients. Unfortunately, this sort of misconception is widespread and is probably due to several causes. Since classically oriented behaviorists conceptualize most neuroses as maladaptive behaviors (including thoughts and feelings as well as overt motor behavior) driven by anxiety and or the avoidance of anxiety, then they tend to focus upon communicating about ways in which "desensitization" may be accomplished. Again, desensitization is not equal to systematic desensitization, but systematic desensitization is the most publicized technique by which desensitization may be brought about and has apparently become the shorthand connotation of behavior therapy to many who have only passing knowledge of the field.

This oversimplification error is compounded by the fact that the overwhelming number of behavioral studies in the literature deal with systematic desensitization. Of course, these studies represent simplification of the therapy regime, as they *must,* in order to be useful in delineating and sharpening effective treatment techniques as well as disqualifying ineffective ones. Scientific rigor dictates isolation of some variable so that it may be tested with as little contamination as possible. Undoubtedly, it would be naive not to consider that the interaction of variables is important, but it is essential to start with the delineation of the effects of each variable separately before attempting to determine interaction effects. While this procedure is the appropriate one for a scientific inquiry, therapists attempting to deal with problems that need immediate solution cannot afford such investigative rigor. The usual approach is one in which a number of interventions are employed simultaneously. In the case of interpersonal anxiety, behavior therapists might be giving instruction in assertive training, employing systematic desensitization, advising, giving "homework," correcting misconceptions, all in the context of a warm and accepting atmosphere.

In order to decide upon what is appropriate the therapist must make as detailed a behavioral analysis as possible. It is important to get the particulars of the stimuli that elicit anxiety. The variety of classes of people and circumstances that may elicit anxiety leads to large variation between patients as to disturbing stimuli. While one person may respond with anxiety to authority figures and situations that require the assumption of responsibility, another may do quite well with such persons and situations, but become anxious when in the company of peers and respond with anxiety when feeling that he is in any way being compared to others. If, after a thorough behavioral analysis, systematic desensitization is indicated, of course the most effective hierarchy will take into account the specifics of the individual case. The most commonly included technique when treating interpersonal anxiety is "assertive training" (Wolpe 1958) which refers not only to appropriate aggressive behavior but also to the outward expression of friendly, affectionate, and other non-anxious feelings. This is particularly appropriate to interpersonal anxiety, as such anxiety is often the result of interpersonal inadequacy. Training in appropriate assertive responsiveness serves two ends. It offers responses antagonistic to anxiety which when used cause reduction of anxiety in subsequent encounters. Secondly, it serves the purpose of teaching the patient effective coping mechanisms so that his ability to handle people and situations is increased.

• *Illustrative Case History*

Mrs. S., a married mother of three children in her early thirties, sought treatment, complaining of chronic depression marked by feelings of being totally inadequate. She reported that she was unable to deal with people without feeling anxious, and that even her husband or children's presence was anxiety provoking. Inquiry into the onset of these difficulties revealed that she had "always" been somewhat uncomfortable with people, but that things had become worse for her since her marriage 10 years before to a rather demanding, critical man. Further investigation of particulars revealed that she responded to anxiety in the following circumstances: (1) *Criticism*—She was anxious when performing in any way that might be criticized by her husband—this included cleaning the house, choice of clothes, budgeting of money, etc. She was also anxious in the presence of anyone else who might make remarks that could be construed as critical. For example, she became anxious in the grocery store when selecting a cereal for fear that another shopper might make a critical remark about that brand. (2) *People who behave peculiarly*—Although she was unable to clarify this very well, it turned out that each example she gave involved drunkenness or the possibility of another having consumed alcohol. For example, parties were anxiety producing, and the more certain she was that they would be drinking, the more anxious she was. If her husband began to drink, she would become so disturbed that she would have to leave. She was even disturbed by movie scenes in which people were drinking. (3) *Sick people*—Again it was difficult for her to isolate the details, but with the examples given, it became apparent that wheezing and difficulty with breathing was the particular anxiety provoking component. Examples included hearing the children breathing heavily while sleeping, people coughing, and contact with, or knowledge of, people with respiratory infections.

In addition to the above, information about her general assertiveness in life was ascertained. She was asked questions such as, "When someone gets in front of you in the grocery store checkout line, what do you do?"; "If you should find that you have been shortchanged after leaving a store, what would you do?"; "Do you make it a point to tell your husband about the things that he does that make you feel good?"; "Do you give honest compliments to your friends?" Answers to these questions and others revealed a general lack of ability in appropriate interpersonal behavior. She indicated that to be appropriately assertive in these circumstances might be perceived as "pushy".

Her history revealed that she had been quite attached to her father, and that his disapproval was the worst thing that could have happened. She recalled instances of being frightened many times when he would come home smelling of alcohol and with slurred speech. He became ill about two years after Mrs. S. was married, and the disorder was diagnosed as emphezema. She recalled with great distress the five year course of the illness terminating in his death. These facts were embedded in a complete history, of course, and she seemed unaware of any connection between the father and the present difficulties for which she largely blamed her husband's inconsiderateness.

The treatment plan consisted, primarily, of assertive training and systematic desensitization. She was urged to see it as standing up for her rights when asking people to please take their place in the back of the line, to return for her change, and feeling free to comment to others about things she liked about them. We practiced such interchanges in the office, and she was given assignments each week which included speaking to any casual acquaintance she might see, asking for change at stores without buying anything, and informing her husband in a non-threatening way of her sexual frustration when left unsatisfied. She was instructed in ways of engaging others in conversation and the art of being a good listener, for which she got almost immediate positive feedback from friends and family. These endeavors resulted in a considerable boost in her self-concept and self-confidence and led to concrete satisfactions such as a very mutually satisfactory sexual relationship with her husband that had never existed before. He revealed that he had been feeling inadequate about his performance, sensing that she was not satisfied, but did not know what she needed. This apparently accounted for a good deal of his hostilities toward her. Areas isolated for desensitization were: (1) criticism, (2) others' drunkenness, (3) heavy breathing and wheezing. The last two hierarchies led back to memories of her father, and the top of both included such memories. Particularly potent eliciters of anxiety were memories of her father just before death, as he struggled to breath.

Throughout the treatment regime (22 sessions over the course of 6 months), Mrs. S's husband was in touch with the therapist, and after discussing his own difficulties in relation to his wife, he was given reassurance and urged to encourage the changes taking place which at first were quite threatening to him. A one year follow-up showed continued increase in self-assurance and no areas of unadaptive anxiety.

While it may be hypothesized that a straightforward systematic desensitization to interpersonal situations seemingly responsible for anxiety would have reduced Mrs. S's interpersonal anxiety, it is highly unlikely that it would have resulted in either sufficient or lasting benefit. I cannot stress this point too much. To be deceived as to the simplicity of an appropriate behavior therapy technique is to be led into a therapy regime producing disappointing results or a return of maladaptive behaviors upon subsequent stress.

How then can the progress of the SD groups in the present study be perceived? In most cases in which SD is employed, the beginning hierarchy items are anchored in present situations eliciting anxiety. However, the items employed in this study are grouped into central themes, each of which is exhausted through an organized presentation of scenes along a gradient from least to most disturbing. The present study employed a shotgun approach, apparently hitting most of the present day anxiety provoking situations without an attempt at organizing them into themes. Actually, the SD therapists have presented the least disturbing items of several potential hierarchies. For example, counselor B's introverts were presented 24 items, some of which can be broken down into themes. For instance, it can be seen that items 1, 5, 6, and 16 through 19 all probably relate to sensitivity to rejection, while items 2, 23, and 24 could all relate to sensitivity to being seen making mistakes. Of course, the central themes would have to be determined with each individual because the meaning of the situation will vary from one person to another. For instance, item 15, "you are asking for a refund on bad merchandise" might elicit anxiety in one person because he responds anxiously to anger in others, but to another person this may be anxiety provoking because he responds with anxiety whenever he feels taken advantage of. Since the scenes presented to the *S*s in the present study are very likely the beginning items of many potential hierarchies, we expected that a reduction in anxiety corresponding to the progress of systematic desensitation would occur. The diversity of items undoubtedly is due to the attempts by the experimenter to make as many items meaningful to as many of the five *S*s in the group as possible, but at some sacrifice in meaningfulness to any given *S*.

A part of the reduction in anxiety of the SD subjects may be attributed to the relaxation training which took place within the mixed group. To whatever degree same sex and opposite sex peers and the therapist were anxiety provoking to these *S*s, simply repetitively practicing relaxation in the group resulted in an in vivo interpersonal desensitization which we would expect to generalize to other people and situations outside the group.

The results of the present study lead to interesting hypotheses in the area defined by Kiesler (1966) as the "Patient Uniformity Myths." Dr. Di Loreto has apparently chosen a patient personality variable (introversion-extroversion) which is meaningfully related to outcome with both Rogerian and Rationally-Emotive therapies. For SD, however, this appears to be an irrelevant variable. Possible assumptions concerning this finding include the following: (1) the very direct attack upon the mechanism of anxiety vitiates the importance of individual patient differences, since the core mechanism for the learning and unlearning of anxiety is approximately the same for all physically intact persons. Since interaction between therapist and patient is minimized during the use of a particular technique, personality variables of both become less important. In support of the irrelevance of the therapist's personality, it has been demonstrated that systematic desensitization hierarchies presented by automated devices are as effective as those presented by a therapist (Donner & Guerney, 1969; Migler & Wolpe, 1967). (2) While introversion-extroversion is apparently not related to outcome of SD treatment, there are still other patient personality variables that probably are.

While there is a seed of truth in the first possibility, it is certain that the present state of development of behavior therapy leaves us far short of having enough purely technical interventions of sufficient power for the successful treatment of neurotic disorders without regard to individual differences among patients. We certainly do fail with some neurotic patients. My own experience as a therapist suggests that there are predictor variables concerning the use of behavior therapy techniques presently at hand. Research directed at determining the relationship between the outcome of behavioral therapy and the patient variables of need to control and/or degree of hostility directed toward helping others will probably result in a negative correlation.

It would not be surprising if this study should be criticized on the basis of criterion used for evaluating outcome. Kiesler (1966) raises this issue as a problem.

> Here the Patient Uniformity Myth has dictated the search for the one patient "process" dimension along which beneficial patient change occurs. For analytic therapy, this dimension has resided somewhere among such variables as insight,—working through, reduction in anxiety and resistance, etc. For Rogers it is found somewhere among the 7 strands of the process of Experiencing. For behavior therapy it seems to reside somewhere in the process of anxiety reduction and symptom removal. (Kiesler, 1966, p.129)

Rogers (1963) agrees that:

> An experience which is seen by one therapist as healing, growth promoting, helpful, is seen by another as none of these things. And the experience which to the second therapist is seen as possessing these qualities is not so perceived by the first. Some people may feel that though we differ regarding specific incidents —nevertheless, there is much agreement and unity. I think not. To me it seems that therapists are equally divergent in these realms. [See the first page of this study.]

I agree that these differences are real. I do not, however, believe that it is an issue relevant to this study or any other. Eysenck (in press) outlines the futility of attempts at resolution of these differences. Speaking of the differences between the dynamic school and the behavioral school he states:

> We must now turn to one last criticism, namely that the two types of therapy attempt to do different and incommensurate things; if this were true, then no proper comparison would be possible between their achievements. As Kuhn (1962) has pointed out, this often happens when a revolution occurs in science, and a new paradigm (as he calls it) takes the place of the old. When this happens, there is a failure of comprehension; the representatives of the old do not understand what the representatives of the new are trying to do, and continue to evaluate their achievements in terms of inappropriate criteria. Similarly, the advocates of the new paradigm dismiss the old criteria as inappropriate and irrelevant. Clearly something of this kind had taken place in connection with the rejection of psychotherapy and the substitution for it of behavior therapy; there is no meeting of minds but rather a change of emphasis which carries the protagonists further and further away from each other. Max Planch, in his Autobiography, put the matter very well: "A new scientific truth does not triumph by convincing its opponents and making them see the light, but rather because its opponents eventually die, and a new generation grows up that is familiar with it." Psychotherapists often have genuine difficulties in seeing that to the behaviorist not only do "symptom" and "illness" coincide, but to him the elimation of the "symptom" is all important. What they seem to be concerned with is not the symptom the patient complains about, but rather some suppositious "inner state" which they wish to change; their regard for the "symptom" is minimal. Such differences in outlook may easily lead to differences in criteria for therapeutic outcome (Malan *et al.,* 1968). It is not easy to see how this difference can be overcome, and to the behavior therapist it probably does not seem important; within his framework the concerns of many psychotherapists can find no resting place. As the therapist, concerned with cures, the ultimate state of the soul of his patients is not his concern, nor are immeasurable and probably unspecifiable "inner states" which may be a part of the patient's personality but do form part of the "symptom" he complains about. There is no obvious empirical way of reconciling these views or testing their values; society will have to cut the Gordian knot and decide which of these incommensurable criteria it is willing to adopt. [Eysenck, in press]

In the meanwhile, for those who find it meaningful to ask the question, "What is the most efficient and effective means of contributing to the reduction of interpersonal anxiety through therapeutic intervention?" this study is extremely helpful.

References

Donner, L. and Guerney, B. G. Automated group desensitization for test anxiety. *Behavior Research and Therapy,* 1969, 7, 1–14.

Eysenck, H. J. In press. *Journal of Behavior Therapy and Experimental Psychiatry.*

Kiesler, D. J. Some myths of psychotherapy research and the search for a paradigm. *Psychological Bulletin,* 1966, 64, 110–136.

Kuhn, T. S. *The structure of scientific revolution.* Chicago: University of Chicago Press, 1962.

Malan, D. H., Bacal, H. A., Heath, E. S., and Balfour, F. H. G. A study of psychodynamic changes in untreated neurotic patients. *British Journal of Psychiatry,* 1968, 114, 525–552.

Migler, B. and Wolpe, J. Automated desensitization: A case report. *Behavior Research and Therapy,* 1967, 5, 133.

Rogers, C. R. Psychotherapy today or where do we go from here. *American Journal of Psychotherapy,* 1963, 17, 5–16.

Wolpe, J. *Psychotherapy by reciprocal inhibition.* Stanford: Stanford University Press, 1958.

A critique by Angelo V. Boy*

• *Introduction*

Since Dr. Di Loreto's study is massive in scope, detailed in research design and methodology, and broadly impactful in its outcomes, I shall organize my critique into three sections: (1) strengths, (2) observations, and (3) limitations.

Dr. Di Loreto's study is scholarly and, therefore, impressive. It indicates an awareness of the past deficiencies of both psychotherapy and its research, and it is a professionally sophisticated response. I consider it a privilege to have been invited to render a critique.

• *Strengths*

1. Dr. Di Loreto scores psychotherapy for its academic tribalism (Chapter 1). As professionals we purport to possess scientific objectivity but in our observable behavior we often defend our approach to counseling as if it were a secular re-

*Professor of Education, University of New Hampshire, Durham, New Hampshire.

ligion, complete with a messianically inspired set of beliefs and rituals. This study is a necessary antidote for those who simply feel euphoric about their "school" of counseling and don't temper their enthusiasm with evidence beyond their viscera.

2. This study indicates that research in counseling should be done with "target behaviors" and addresses itself to "interpersonal anxiety" as the target behavior to be studied. Dr. Di Loreto may have identified a target behavior which could whet the appetite of researchers in counseling, since all approaches to counseling have a crucial concern with reducing interpersonal anxiety. As a target behavior, it provides ground from which a variety of research projects could be launched by the various specialists within the behavioral sciences. For example, an urbanologist might engage in research concerned with the degree to which different housing patterns and arrangements could decrease the interpersonal anxiety of those who reside in the inner city.

All too often research in the outcomes of counseling has addressed itself to measuring the size of a man's suit rather than looking at the man inside the suit.

3. This study indicates the importance of identifying behavioral criteria which are external to the treatment setting (Chapter 1). Much of the process research in counseling has addressed itself to identifying in-treatment behaviors which indicate psychological change. It has always been easier to study behavior in a controlled situation (the therapy session) while neglecting to study that behavior in the uncontrolled realities of daily existence. Whatever delusions we have developed in our academic tribalism have been largely due to our enchantment with in-process behavioral change without the buttressing evidence furnished by the behavior which occurs outside of the treatment setting.

4. This study indicates the importance of reducing the pre-treatment variability for both the counselors and the cli-

ents (Chapter 1). All too often research in counseling succeeds in accomplishing one of the reductions but not the others. The credibility of any research in counseling is enhanced when the variability between and among the participating groups is reduced to its lowest possible level, and there is an equalizing of the variability between and among the participating groups. This study devotes much effort toward accomplishing this needed base for conducting any bona fide research.

5. This study justifiably declares that researchers in counseling must discard the notion that one counselor is expert enough to objectively use different approaches to counseling with equal quality and efficiency (Chapter 1). In our research, we must realize that when one counselor attempts to use distinctly different models in the process of counseling, he still possesses an intuitive and operational bias, and this bias will skew the research in the direction of that bias. Each counselor involved in this study used one particular theoretical and operational approach to counseling, and this enhances the design of the study and makes its outcomes more credible.

6. This study indicates that there is only one legitimate criteria for measuring the outcomes of counseling: evidence that the behavior of the client has improved outside of, and because of, the counseling experience. Therefore, process research becomes a legitimate area of study only when it is linked to outcome research (Chapter 1). As a profession, we could devote much time and energy researching and quantifying the process of counseling without knowing whether or not the process we've developed leads to any observable post-counseling behavioral change. Ultimately, we would render a greater contribution to man and our profession if we expanded our process research in qualitative directions and did a better job in quantifying our outcome research.

7. This study indicates that in the final stages of counseling the clients began to do for themselves what initially the

counselors had been doing to or for them (Chapter 1). This is an interesting phenomenon, and this study adds to our knowledge regarding the extent to which clients move toward the counselor's behavioral model in their in-process behavior. It also reinforces the importance of developing appropriate in-process behavioral models of the counselor which are consistent with personal, professional, and societal values.

8. This study indicates that the variables of accurate empathy, nonpossessive warmth, genuineness, etc. are, at best, necessary but not sufficient conditions of therapeutic change (Chapter 3). For too long some counselors, expecially those new to the profession, have relied on these conditions as the only catalysts which would induce behavioral change in a clientele. For a counselor to rely solely on these conditions as the totality of his counseling relationship is somewhat naive; to represent these conditions as the exclusive preserve of a particular approach to counseling is myopic. However, it is still important for counselors to realize that these conditions are a necessary *part* of an effective counseling relationship.

9. This study indicates that Client-Centered counseling utilizes the process of encouragement through reflection of feelings (Chapter 2), and that it can also be classified as a reinforcing technique (Chapter 4). Client-Centered counselors who engage in academic tribalism might shudder when these two points are made. A more enlightened reaction would be to admit that *all* approaches to counseling are inherently both encouraging and reinforcing; and the differences among the "schools" of counseling, on these two conditions, are differences of degree. The fact that encouragement and reinforcement are *also* characteristics of Client-Centered counseling is an important contribution on the part of this study.

10. Although this study concerned itself with measuring the relative effectiveness of affective, behavioral, and cognitive group counseling in diminishing the interpersonal anxiety of extroverts and introverts, the statement which, to me, augers

the direction in which future process and outcome research should go, is as follows: successful treatment for the thinking type client must focus on his achieving trust in his own feelings, whereas successful therapy for the feeling type client must center on his acquiring the ability to think and plan his life more carefully, so that he is not flooded or overwhelmed by unmodulated feelings provoked by a problem situation (Chapter 4).

Building a process model based upon the above, and more adequate than those we currently possess, is a goal which should engage the serious attention of those representing different "schools" of counseling.

• *Observations*

1. This study indicates that, in terms of interpersonal anxiety, affective group counseling is *generally* more effective with extroverts; cognitive group counseling is *generally* more effective with introverts; and behavioral group counseling is *generally* more effective with both extroverts and introverts.

Therefore, if we could reduce all of man's problems to interpersonal anxiety, and if all men could be defined as being either extrovertic or introvertic, then the utilization of a behavioral approach to counseling would be the only logical conclusion; and such a conclusion would be considered logical only if the two propositions upon which it is based are legitimate.

2. This is an important study and should be replicated with extroverts and introverts who experience interpersonal anxiety but who differ from the population included in this study in terms of age, socioeconomic status, and institutional or community environment. Generalizing the results of this study would determine the degree to which it has further application. If a broadened base of evidence served to reinforce the findings of this study, then growing numbers of group

counselors would be inclined to include behavioral techniques in their repertoire of procedures.

3. It appears unlikely that those clients in the behavioral and cognitive groups were not exposed to some degree of affect which could have influenced outcomes. It also appears unlikely that those clients in the affective groups were not, to some degree, exposed to cognition and conditioning procedures.

That is, group members interact with each other and in that interaction can transmit behaviors to each other that are different from the counselor's behavior, thus introducing an element of contamination into groups which are described as being exclusively affective, behavioral, or cognitive.

It seems that, unless the leader exercises extreme control over a group, no group can be exclusively affective, behavioral, or cognitive. In fact, in this study, there is no clear *in-process evidence* which indicates that the three counseling approaches were distinctly different from each other. I am still left with: (1) what were the affective elements of the SD and RT interactive processes which could have contributed to the effectiveness of these approaches? and conversely, (2) what were the cognitive and conditioning elements of the CC interactive process which could have contributed to its effectiveness?

The affective and cognitive dichotomy is a historical shibboleth promulgated, it seems, only in the counseling profession. It appears that everyone except professional counselors know that, (1) man is an amalgamation of affect and cognition, (2) the unclogging of one's emotions enables the intellect to function with greater clarity, and (3) a clear mind serves to temper one's emotionality.

4. This study indicates that we must include process and outcome measures and assess input variables so that we know what form of treatment is the most effective for this particular

client with that specific problem and under what set of circumstances (Chapter 1).

I observe that this study paid only passing attention to those input variables which affected process, which, in turn, affected outcomes. Therefore, it seems that *any* study which examines the outcomes of counseling must also make an equivalent examination of those input variables which, in the actual process of counseling, can and do affect outcomes. These process variables go far beyond matching the counselors and determining their allegiance to a particular "school" of counseling.

It appears difficult to have either a commendable study of process or a commendable study of outcomes, but a study improves its credibility only when it devotes itself to examining *both* process and outcomes and their interrelationship.

5. The tenth meetings of the groups involved in this study are only given cursory attention. These tenth meetings are described as being "active group discussions" which occurred without the same peers or counselor with whom the client participated during the previous nine meetings (Chapter 2).

This study assumes that the nine meetings were the ones which influenced the behavior of participants. I observe that the tenth meeting, because it was an "active group discussion," with a different set of peers and a different counselor, could have been even more of an influence upon behavior than the previous nine meetings! It seems more spontaneous, the self could have been risked more because strangers were present, and an "active group discussion" may have had more of an influence upon behavior than the neatly packaged affective, behavioral, and cognitive approaches to which the participants were previously exposed.

6. This study indicates that the extroverts in the no-treatment (placebo) and no-contact control groups reduced their

interpersonal anxiety during the period of the study more than the introverts in the no-treatment (placebo) and no-contact control groups (Chapter 4).

If extroverts, by the nature of their functional existence can reduce their interpersonal anxiety more than introverts then perhaps the various institutions which affect behavior can be induced to value extrovertism more than introvertism in the experiences which they make available to our society.

7. To what extent did the personal charisma of each of the counselors affect the behavioral outcomes achieved by group members? That is, were the participants responding to the scientific application of the affective, behavioral, and cognitive approaches; or were they responding more to the counselor as a *person,* a *person* with whom they felt psychologically comfortable and to whom they could personally relate?

8. Research in counseling has generally been concerned with indicating the effectiveness of counseling when compared to no counseling. This study takes us to a higher level of examination when it enables us to compare three different approaches to counseling with each other and with a placebo group.

Perhaps the next level of research should address itself to a comparison of various approaches to counseling with other types of non-counseling experiences which also possess the potential to be therapeutic. These other types of therapeutic experiences might be generally classified as human, vocational, recreational, and religious. Perhaps interpersonal anxiety can be reduced by exposing people to experiences which are different from the traditional verbal transactions perpetuated by our profession.

• *Limitations*

1. The model of Client-Centered Counseling reported in Appendix G is classical, traditional, wooden, and outmoded in

terms of the more current Rogerian model. It is also outmoded in terms of other current affective concepts of group work as promulgated by Esalen Institute, National Training Laboratories, and the Center for Studies of the Person.

There is evidence that the affective counselors involved in this study *even* violated the traditional model of Client-Centered Counseling. For example, they concluded their first group counseling sessions with "an explanation of the construction and use of the Index of Interpersonal Activity" (Chapter 2) and a six page (Appendix G) "Explanation of Interpersonal Anxiety." Furthermore, "all counselors employed questioning, interpretation, and reinforcement with about equal frequency." (Chapter 3).

Therefore, the affective counselors involved in this study cannot be accurately classified as Client-Centered, because the above behaviors run contrary to the behavior of a Client-Centered Counselor as contained in the older and more recent contributions of Carl R. Rogers and his colleagues.

2. Thirteen weeks after the conclusion of the group counseling phase of this study, a follow-up was conducted in order to determine the staying power of the behavioral changes which did occur. The justification for the follow-up occurring in the relatively short period of 13 weeks is the assertion that: "a six week follow-up is as good as a two year one." (Chapter 1).

Further *research evidence* will be needed in order to determine at what point in time a follow-up (or follow-ups) is scientifically accurate enough to improve the credibility of studies dealing with behavioral change. At this moment, however, it seems reasonable to conclude that any behavioral change must be examined over a longer time span than 13 weeks, if we are to make any definitive judgment regarding the permanency of the behavioral change. Further, we need evidence which indicates the number of follow-ups that are necessary in order to indicate that a particular behavioral change has staying power. If someone has stopped smokin cigarettes for 13 weeks, can we justifiably conclude that he i indeed a non-smoker? Or must we monitor the smoking habit of that individual one to five years later in order to ascertai the permanency of his non-smoking behavior? If a follow-u of the participants in this study were *now* conducted, woul the findings correlate with and support the 13 week follow-up

My comments here not only apply to this study but to an study, past and future, which attempts to measure behavior change.

3. Two raters were trained for ten hours and were ut lized in the detection and reporting of behavior indicative c anxiety among participants. One is identified as an advance graduate student and the other as a secretary. Although, a different monitoring points, the inter-rater reliability is re ported to be .825 (Chap. 2) and .889 (Chap. 2), there is n evidence of the raters' reliability in accurately detecting th components of behavior which are indicative of anxiety. Tha is, although the raters agree with each other, they could bot be "wrong" in their ability to "read" anxious behavior.

This problem is compounded when "new" raters wer used in the follow-up phase of the study; these "new" rater were trained by the "old" raters. Further, the "old" raters onl observed in-process behavior (while counseling was occu ring) while the "new" raters only measured outcome behavior.

4. A total of twelve groups were exposed to affective, be havioral, and cognitive counseling. In each group there wer five participants, three female and two male.

Although there is no definitive research which indicate what the ideal size of a counseled group should be, there i *clinical agreement* that the *minimum* size group for affectiv counseling should be six to eight clients; when an affectiv group size slips below this range, then effective interpersona exploration becomes hampered because of the limited numbe of feedback systems (clients) available. The outcomes of thi study may have been influenced by the size of the groups, with group sizes of five lending themselves more to behavioral or cognitive process models.

5. The index of Interpersonal Activity (Appendix D) is used as a basic instrument to measure the number of interpersonal activities ("dates") engaged in by subjects as a result of their exposure to affective, behavioral, and cognitive group counseling.

Dr. Di Loreto indicates that the IIA is a crude instrument, and I fully concur. He doesn't elaborate on why he considers the instrument to be crude, but an examination of the IIA clearly shows that no provision is made for assessing the *quality* of the interpersonal activities in which the subjects engaged; the instrument only allows a recording of the number of interpersonal activities in which a subject engaged. That is, a participant may have listed one such activity but an examination of the quality of that activity could reveal that it was a personally meaningful experience that could have positively impacted upon behavior. Another participant may have listed six interpersonal activities, none of which were qualitative.

Further, the IIA doesn't provide the subject with an opportunity to record the re-establishment of an interpersonal relationship with someone with whom he has regular contact and from whom he has been estranged.

6. In the "Manual Employed in Classifying Each Therapist's In-Treatment Verbal Behavior" (Appendix I), there is much ambiguity. The raters were asked to identify the degree to which each of the therapists utilized each of the following ten possible responses in their group counseling: reflection and clarification, questioning, interpretation, direct confrontation, suggestion, information and advice giving, redirecting questions, self-disclosure, free association, and reinforcement. Although there is an inter-rater reliability here of .831, perhaps the raters agreed that they were both confused.

It was necessary for the raters to *clearly* know the differences among the ten responses; such discriminatory ability is severely hampered, when we examine some of the samples used within each counselor response category. Instead of the responses being clearly distinguishable from each other, they are very similar to each other. Therefore, although the raters agreed with each other in what they observed, there is a strong possibility that they agreed with and reinforced each other's confusion. The fact that some counselor response categories were more alike than unlike is demonstrated in the following examples of therapist responses and the classifications of these responses taken from Appendix I.

Cl: "I can't do that, I just can't!"
Th: "Can't?" (*Clarification*)

and

Cl: "I just get upset when I'm around him."
Th: "What do you mean, upset? Do you get angry, depressed, disgusted or what?" (*Questioning*)

Cl: "I just feel like there's nothing I can do to please her."
Th: "You've had that feeling before, haven't you? Remember what you said about your parents?" (*Interpretation*)

and

Cl: "That really hurt my feelings."
Th: "How can he hurt your feelings? What you mean is that you took what he said and hurt your own feelings with it." (*Direct Confrontation*)

and

Cl: "I don't really know what to do. I do need the money."
Th: "Well, if it were I, I probably wouldn't take it, because I think you're right. There are too many strings attached." (*Suggestion*)

Cl: "I don't think it helps much to talk about them."
Th: "No, neither do I." (*Information and Advice Giving*)

and

Cl: "Yes, but . . ."
Th: "No, just shut up, God damn it, and *listen* to me for a change . . ." (*Self-Disclosure*)

Cl: (*S* speaking and acting like a "little girl.")
Th: "I'm sure that half the reason why people don't want to be around you is because you act like a damn 9-year old spoiled brat." (*Direct Confrontation*)

and

Cl: "He says he doesn't trust me."
Th: "I wouldn't either. I think what you do is so far removed from your inner feelings that I just wouldn't trust you with what I think are the important parts of me." (*Self-Disclosure*)

and

Cl: "I really think I could do better at another university."
Th: "I think you're like a bar of Ivory soap. 99 and 44/100 percent gas and hot air." (*Reinforcement, via disapproval*)

7. The Interpersonal Anxiety Scales, Forms A and B (Appendix C) are basic instruments used in this study, and their validity and reliability is questionable. Of the various psychometric instuments available to human behavior researchers, personality inventories, especially paper and pencil, possess the least degree of validity and reliability. The fact that the mode of response to the items included on the scales is "True" or "False" further decreases their validity and reliability; and the fact that there is not a third neutral response category available beyond "True" or "False" further diminshes the credibility of these scales in accurately representing the interpersonal anxiety of the subjects.

Appendixes

Appendix A • Behavior Checklist of Interpersonal Anxiety

	30-Second Time Periods										
Behavior Observed	1	2	3	4	5	6	7	8	9	10	Σ
HEAD AND FACE											
Plays with hair											
Brushes hair from eyes/face											
Rubs forehead											
Rubs eyes											
Stares blankly/blinks eyes rapidly											
No eye contact											
Scratches nose											
Grimaces/makes faces/face strained											
Bites lips											
Moistens lips											
Purses lips											
Swallows											
Cough/clears throat											
Voice quivers											
Speech blocks											
Fingers in mouth/ears/nose											
Chews on nails/pencil											
Breathing heavy/fast/uneven											
Blushing or redness of face/neck											
SHOULDERS, ARMS AND HANDS											
Extraneous, jerky arms/hands/head movements											
Arms rigid/folded/crossed											
Shoulders shrugged											

Rubs neck
"Scratching" arms/legs/head/hands
Wringing hands
Hands restrained/pockets/behind back/clasped
Manipulation of pen/object/necklace /watch, etc.
Hand tremors
Perspires/face/hands/armpits
"Cracking" knuckles
Drums fingers on desk/table/chair
TRUNK AND LEGS
Moves about in chair
Shuffles/taps feet/shakes foot
Crosses/re-crosses legs/kicks leg

ΣΣ

IMPORTANT: Do not "guess" or make "judgments" of anxiety. Simply indicate the presence or absence of the above listed behaviors.

Appendix B • Pre-test, Post-test, and Follow-up Test Data Sheets

PRE-TEST

PERSONAL DATA SHEET

Name ______________________________ Age____ Sex M F
College Major ____________________ Student Number ____
Local Address ____________________ Local Phone No. ____
Academic Standing: Freshman Sophomore Junior Senior

Please indicate below the times which you are *free* (i.e., the times when you *do not* have classes or other meetings scheduled).

	8:00	9:10	10:20	11:30	12:40	1:50	3:00	4:10	
M									M
T									T
W									W
T									T
F									F

Please underline below the description which best depicts your interest in the project just discussed with you:

Extremely interested Want to know more

Extremely disinterested

REMEMBER: If you wish to participate in this project, you will be required to attend all ten of the counseling sessions.

POST-TEST
PERSONAL DATA SHEET

Name ______________________________ Age ____ Sex M F
Current Academic Standing (in terms of the number of terms you have attended college): Freshman Sophomore Junior Senior

Other than your weekly groups, have you had any other counseling or therapy since the beginning of this term: YES NO

If yes, briefly explain: ______________________________
____
____

Approximately how many sessions did you have? __________

Have you *ever* had counseling or therapy for personal or vocational problems prior to the beginning of this semester: YES NO

If yes, briefly explain: ______________________________
____
____

Approximately how many sessions did you have? __________

If you have filled out your name and age on this sheet *do not* bother to put your name, etc. on the top of each of the separate answer sheets. Just be sure that you have filled out this sheet completely.

Campus Address ____________________ Phone No. ______
Home Address ______________________ Phone No. ______
City _______________ State ______________ Zip Code ____

FOLLOW-UP TEST
PERSONAL DATA SHEET

Name ______________________ Age ________ Sex M F

Current Academic Standing (in terms of the number of terms you have attended college): Freshman Sophomore Junior Senior

Other than your weekly groups, have you had any other counseling or therapy since the beginning of this term: YES NO

If yes, briefly explain: ______________________

____

____

Approximately how many sessions did you have? ________

Have you *ever* had counseling or therapy for personal or vocational problems prior to the beginning of this semester: YES NO

If yes, briefly explain: ______________________

____

____

Approximately how many sessions did you have? ________

If you have filled out your name and age on this sheet *do not* bother to put your name, etc. on the top of each of the separate answer sheets. Just be sure that you have filled out this sheet completely.

Campus Address ____________________ Phone No. ______

Home Address ______________________ Phone No. ______

City ______________ State __________ Zip Code ______

*Appendix C • Interpersonal Anxiety Scales (Forms A and B)**

FORM A: INTERPERSONAL ANXIETY SCALES

DIRECTIONS

This inventory consists of a series of numbered statements. Read each statement *carefully* and decide whether it is *true as applied to you* or *false as applied to you.*

You are to mark your answer true or false on the answer sheet provided with this booklet. Look at the example below.

1. T === F === 2. T === F === 3. T === F ===

If a numbered statement is *True* or *Mostly True,* as applied to you, then blacken in between the lines in the column headed T (see 1 above). If a numbered statement is *False* or *Not Usually True,* as applied to you, blacken in between the lines in the column headed F (see 2 above). If you have never done what the question asks or been involved in the situation which the statement describes, then answer it according to how you think you would act if you actually were in that situation.

It is important to keep in mind that there are no right or wrong answers to the questions in this booklet. They are simply true as applied to you or false as applied to you.

Important: Remember, *do not* answer these questions with the intention of portraying yourself in the most favorable light possible or in terms of the person you would like to be. Please answer all questions in terms of how you *actually behave* in the various situations described. We assure you that all information will be treated with the strictest of confidence, so please be truthful.

Do not leave any blank spaces. In marking your answers on the answer sheet, check periodically to be sure that the number of the statement you are working on agrees with the number on the answer sheet. Please do not mark in this booklet.

NOW OPEN THE BOOKLET AND BEGIN

*Half of the items in Form A and in Form B are keyed "true" (T), and half are keyed "false" (F). Unlike the questionnaires administered, the forms as they are presented here indicate the keyed answers.

1. You hardly ever feel a pain or tenseness in the muscles in the back of your neck. (F)
2. You find if difficult overcoming the feeling that you are inferior to others in many respects. (T)
3. You get angry or disgusted with yourself when you are unable to speak up in a group or voice your opinion. (T)
4. It is not hard for you to ask for help from your friends, even though you cannot return the favor. (F)
5. You feel timid and unsure of yourself in the presence of other people you regard as your superiors. (T)
6. You go out of your way to avoid meeting someone you dislike. (T)
7. It is easy for you to act naturally wherever you are. (F)
8. You are comfortable and at ease while being introduced to a person for the first time. (F)
9. You feel equally at ease when both men and women are present. (F)
10. When people become bossy or domineering with you, you tend to "slow down" or do the opposite of everything they tell you to do. (T)
11. You have little difficulty telling nosy people to mind their own business. (F)
12. You enjoy applying for a job in person. (F)
13. You are not likely to give up your plans even when there is a good deal of opposition by your peers. (F)
14. You feel at ease in all the groups you attend. (F)
15. You give the real reason when you do not want to do something or go somewhere rather than think up a good sounding excuse. (F)
16. The thought of making a speech to a group does not frighten you. (F)
17. When a parent, teacher, *or* boss treats you unfairly, you are likely to directly confront them with their unfairness. (F)
18. Because you find it difficult to say "no," people take advantage of you. (T)
19. It is difficult for you to calmly search your mind for the right words to express your thoughts when someone in a group asks you a question unexpectedly. (T)
20. You have little or no stomach trouble (indigestion, gas pains, upset stomach, etc.). (F)
21. You usually say what you feel like saying at the moment. (F)

22. You find it hard to sit still in a small group of unfamiliar people. (T)
23. *You* feel that is it important to be liked by all your friends. (T)
24. You are relaxed and at ease when you have to introduce people to each other. (F)
25. It is easy for you to take the lead in enlivening a dull social affair. (F)
26. When you get anxious in a social situation, the skin on your neck, chest, or arms is likely to break out into a rash or spots of red. (T)
27. If you don't get what you want you fight for it. (F)
28. You become anxious and uneasy if it looks like you are going to be late for an appointment. (T)
29. There are only a few friends with whom you can relax and have a good time. (T)
30. You do not feel self-conscious in the presence of important people. (F)
31. When you resent the actions of another person, you promptly tell him so. (F)
32. A person should be fair to a disagreeable or obnoxious person in the presence of others. (T)
33. You talk easily with people as soon as you meet them. (F)
34. If someone you know has been spreading untrue or bad stories about you, you see them immediately and have a talk with them about it. (F)
35. You do not perspire easily even when anxious or upset. (F)
36. If you hold an opinion that is radically different from that expressed by an instructor, you are likely to tell him about it either during or after the class. (F)
37. In a group, you usually think about what you're going to say over and over before you finally say it. (T)
38. You attempt new games at social affairs even when you haven't played them before. (F)
39. In a group or at a social gathering your mouth, tongue, or lips are likely to get dry if you become anxious. (T)
40. You are willing to take a chance alone in a situation where the outcome is doubtful. (F)
41. You feel relaxed and comfortable while speaking before a group. (F)

42. You would feel uneasy or self-conscious if you had to volunteer an idea to start a discussion among a group of people. (T)
43. You would like to tell certain of your friends a thing or two but probably won't. (T)
44. You are no more nervous than most others. (F)
45. It is not right to humiliate a person publicly, even if they deserve it. (T)
46. When you are attracted to a person whom you have not met, you make an active attempt to get acquainted. (F)
47. You like to entertain guests. (F)
48. Before speaking, you get a lump in your throat that may interfere with your speech. (T)
49. You avoid arguing over a price with a clerk or salesman. (T)
50. You do not have difficulty making new friends. (F)
51. When someone is not "playing fair," you surely let him know about it. (F)
52. You are able to put a disagreeable person "in his place" by direct rather than devious or roundabout means. (F)
53. It is easy for you to stand up for your rights when you are in the minority. (F)
54. You look forward to an opportunity to speak in a group. (F)
55. You avoid social contacts for fear of doing or saying the wrong thing and hurting another's feelings. (T)
56. You are troubled by nausea and/or vomiting when you know it's your turn to get up before a class and give a talk. (T)
57. You find it uncomfortable and anxiety producing to meet new people and make new acquaintances. (T)
58. You are always loyal to your friends. (T)
59. After being introduced to someone for the first time, you usually stick to conventional topics of discussion (school, weather, job, etc.). (T)
60. Sometimes your interpersonal relations are so tense and anxiety producing that your sleep is disturbed *that* evening. (T)
61. You would have no difficulty saying "no" to a salesman who was trying to sell you something you did not really want. (F)
62. When things go wrong for you, you feel you are more to blame than anyone else. (T)
63. When a clerk in a store waits on others who should come after you, you call his attention to the fact. (F)

64. You are able to tell a roommate that he has done something that upsets you, right there and then when it happens. (F)
65. Your mood is easily influenced by the people around you. (T)
66. You frequently have to fight against showing that you are bashful. (T)
67. You feel tense and uneasy when you first enter a social gathering. (T)
68. You are restless and uneasy in the presence of unfamiliar people. (T)
69. You are able to do things without regard for what others might think or say. (F)
70. You seem to be about as capable and smart as most others around you. (F)
71. When you are in a group, you accept the leadership of someone else in deciding what the group is going to do. (T)
72. You do not become tense and anxious when you have to voice a dissenting opinion. (F)
73. You feel that it is your friends' duty to sympathize with you and to cheer you up when you are depressed. (T)
74. You have stayed away from another person because you feared losing your temper and doing or saying something that you might regret afterwards. (T)
75. Even though you can conceal it, you feel anxious in new social situations. (T)
76. Your hands tremble when you try to handle food, refreshments, etc., at a social gathering. (T)
77. It is important to *you* to be liked by those around you. (T)
78. You find yourself upset rather than helped by personal criticism. (T)
79. You would feel uneasy telling a superior that he had done a bad job on something. (T)
80. When in a group of people you rarely have trouble thinking of the right thing to talk about. (F)
81. You find it very hard to "get tough" with people who are rude and annoying. (T)
82. You feel socially secure. (F)
83. Your thoughts often race ahead faster than you can speak them. (T)
84. Your muscles (neck, legs, arms, etc.) get strained and tense when you are in a group of people you have just met. (T)

85. It is not unusual for you to express strong approval or disapproval of the actions of others. (F)
86. You feel your friends should encourage, not criticize, you. (T)
87. You are very open about revealing your "true self" to friends and acquaintances. (F)
88. Life is a strain for you much of the time. (T)
89. You do not try to cover up your poor opinion of a person, so that he won't know how you feel about him. (F)
90. You wish you could be as at ease in social situations as others seem to be. (T)
91. Your stomach gets tight, fluttery, upset, etc., when you are in a group of people you don't know very well. (T)
92. You do not worry too long over unpleasant or humiliating personal experiences. (F)
93. You usually "lay your cards on the table" rather than "beat around the bush" when you disagree with someone. (F)
94. You are likely to stutter or otherwise indicate your anxiety in your voice when you get upset, anxious, or excited in the presence of others. (T)
95. You do not feel self-conscious because of your personal appearance. (F)
96. You speak out in a group to oppose those who you feel sure are wrong. (F)
97. It is not very difficult for you to express strong feelings of love or affection toward another. (F)
98. You doubt whether people you talk to are really interested in what you say. (T)
99. When riding on a train, bus, etc., you engage fellow travelers in conversation. (F)
100. Criticism usually upsets or disturbs you greatly. (T)

FORM B: INTERPERSONAL ANXIETY SCALES

DIRECTIONS

This inventory consists of a series of numbered statements. Read each statement *carefully* and decide whether it is *true as applied to you* or *false as applied to you.*

You are to make your answers true or false on the answer sheet provided with this booklet. Look at the example below.

1. T === F ===   2. T === F ===   3. T === F ===

If a numbered statement is *True* or *Mostly True,* as applied to you, then blacken in between the lines in the column headed T (see 1 above). If a numbered statement is *False* or *Not Usually True,* as applied to you, blacken in between the lines in the column headed F (see 2 above). If you have never done what the question asks or been involved in the situation which the statement describes, then answer it according to how you think you would act if you actually were in that situation.

It is important to keep in mind that there are no right or wrong answers to the questions in this booklet. They are simply true as applied to you or false as applied to you.

Important: Remember, do not answer these questions with the intention of portraying yourself in the most favorable light possible or in terms of the person you would like to be. Please answer all questions in terms of how you *actually behave* in the various situations described. We assure you that all information will be treated with the strictest of confidence, so please be truthful.

Do not leave any blank spaces. In marking your answers on the answer sheet, check periodically to be sure that the number of the statement you are working on agrees with the number on the answer sheet. Please do not mark in this booklet.

NOW OPEN THE BOOKLET AND GO AHEAD

1. When you think you recognize someone you see in a public place, you ask him whether you have met him before. (F)
2. You take the lead in putting life into a dull party. (F)
3. You seek to avoid trouble with people whenever possible. (T)
4. You feel like telling nosey people to mind their own business, but you seldom do. (T)
5. You can express yourself more easily in speech than in writing. (F)
6. You have little or no trouble with your muscles twitching or jumping. (F)
7. It does not make you feel uneasy walking into a group of people late or when you know that everyone's eyes will be upon you. (F)
8. It is not difficult for you to turn down unreasonable requests made by a close friend. (F)
9. You feel uneasy or uncomfortable when you are alone with important people. (T)
10. You prefer to pass by school friends, or people you know but have not seen for a long time, unless they speak to you first. (T)
11. It is not difficult for you to raise your hand in class and disagree with what another person has said. (F)
12. When you are bossed around or unfairly treated by others, you are more likely to do the opposite of what they request rather than tell them to their face how you feel. (T)
13. It is not difficult for you to openly express strong feelings of affection toward another. (F)
14. You are a self-confident person. (F)
15. When you meet people for the first time or begin to speak in an unfamiliar group, your heart starts pounding faster and faster and your breathing may be uneven. (T)
16. You have many ways of hiding your anxiety and uneasiness in social situations, even though they may not always be as effective as you would like. (T)
17. Your thoughts become confused and jumbled when you have to speak up unexpectedly in a group. (T)
18. You expect your friends to always treat you kindly. (T)
19. You are able to say what you really feel and believe in a group. (F)
20. You feel relaxed and at ease while getting acquainted with people. (F)

21. When upset, embarrassed, or anxious, you break out in a sweat that annoys you greatly. (T)
22. When a rude or unpleasant person hurts your feelings, you let him know how he makes you feel inside. (F)
23. You rarely cross the street in order not to meet someone you see. (F)
24. When you have a real grievance with a close friend, you are able to handle it directly with him. (F)
25. Although you talk fluently with a friend, you are at a loss for words in a group. (T)
26. You find if difficult to ask a friend to return something (book, money, etc.) he has borrowed and forgotten about, even though it may make you angry. (T)
27. You do not become tense and anxious at the prospect of approaching an employer in seeking a raise. (F)
28. You feel at ease and have little difficulty helping others have a good time at social gatherings. (F)
29. You like to be a host or hostess for parties at a club. (F)
30. You may be able to hide your anxiety from others, but you can usually feel it yourself. (T)
31. Although it may anger you, you find it difficult to fight for what you believe is right. (T)
32. It is necessary to be friendly to those you meet for the first time. (T)
33. You would not go out of your way to avoid speaking in a group, if this were possible. (F)
34. When the actions of a friend or roommate irritate you, you are likely to confront them with it right then and there. (F)
35. You are likely to talk back to a policeman or other person in authority over you if you feel unjustly treated by him. (F)
36. You find it easy to start a conversation with a stranger. (F)
37. There is a lack of real affection *or* closeness in your interpersonal relations. (T)
38. Your feelings are easily hurt. (T)
39. When you have to meet new people or speak in groups, the muscles in the back of your neck tighten up. (T)
40. You do not feel obligated to do things for your close friends. (F)
41. You are able to show some temper in order to get what is coming to you. (F)

42. You are fearful and tense all the while you are speaking before a group of people. (T)
43. You avoid arguing over a grade with an instructor. (T)
44. You limit your friendships mostly to members of your own sex. (T)
45. In your interpersonal relations you function under a great deal of tension. (T)
46. You like to say what you think about things. (F)
47. If someone steps ahead of you in line, he is likely to hear from you about it. (F)
48. You are able to "talk back" to people who often irritate you. (F)
49. The thought of speaking up in a group of people does not upset you or make you anxious. (F)
50. You like to form new friendships. (F)
51. When you find that something you have bought is defective, you complain or demand an exchange or refund. (F)
52. If you were thrown together by chance with a stranger, you would be relaxed and at ease. (F)
53. You are not bothered by acid stomach. (F)
54. You are likely not to speak to people until they speak to you. (T)
55. You certainly feel useless a good deal of the time. (T)
56. You feel disgusted with yourself after trying to address a group of people. (T)
57. Usually, you simply forgive your friends when they hurt your feelings rather than mention it and create even more difficulty. (T)
58. When you are served stale or inferior food in a restaurant, you immediately complain about it to someone in charge. (F)
59. After being introduced to someone for the first time, you just can't seem to think of things to say or make good conversation. (T)
60. You are no more nervous than most others. (F)
61. You feel depressed by your inability to handle various situations. (T)
62. What others think of you does not bother you. (F)
63. You stand up for your rights in a group when you are in the minority. (F)
64. You like your friends to show a great deal of affection toward you. (T)

65. When a person does not "play fair," you hesitate to say anything about it to him. (T)
66. You would rather apply for a job by going through a personal interview than by writing a letter. (F)
67. You often think about the anxiety you feel inside when you have to meet new people. (T)
68. You seldom express your anger directly toward the person who has upset you. (T)
69. You have no fears about going into a room by yourself where other people have already gathered and are talking. (F)
70. You are relaxed and at ease when you have to discuss or defend your ideas or opinions with others in a group. (F)
71. Friends should always encourage you when you have met with failure. (T)
72. It is not difficult for you to criticize people who are in a position of authority. (F)
73. Meeting people makes you anxious. (T)
74. When someone says silly or ignorant things about something that you know about, you try to set him straight. (F)
75. Few of your friends know the "real you." (T)
76. It is easier for you to annoy or otherwise create minor problems for an unreasonable boss than to confront him with his unreasonableness. (T)
77. You worry about the image you present socially. (T)
78. You rarely find it necessary to cough or clear your throat before speaking. (F)
79. Criticism of scolding does not hurt your feelings very much. (F)
80. It does not make you nervous or uneasy to have to wait for others. (F)
81. You seldom tell your friends what you really think of them. (T)
82. You feel uncomfortable meeting people at social affairs. (T)
83. You feel inclined to tremble when you are afraid. (T)
84. You are certainly lacking in self-confidence. (T)
85. You like to let people know where you stand on things. (F)
86. You have no fear of facing an audience. (F)
87. You find it awfully difficult to stand up for what you think is right. (T)
88. You have difficulty thinking clearly when you get worried or excited. (T)

89. When you are in an unfamiliar group, your posture feels strained or unnatural. (T)
90. You are hesitant to shake hands with people you first meet because your palms are moist and clammy. (T)
91. You strongly defend your own opinions as a rule. (F)
92. You feel that you can say what you believe even when you know it may hurt another's feelings. (F)
93. You are not overly sensitive to the comments of others. (F)
94. You are not a nervous person. (F)
95. People often disappoint you. (T)
96. You find yourself worrying a good deal about your social relations. (T)
97. If you were a guest at an important dinner, you would do without something rather than ask to have it passed to you. (T)
98. If you came late to a meeting you would rather stand or leave than take a front seat. (T)
99. In school, it is not difficult for you to give an oral report before a class. (F)
100. You take disappointments so keenly that you can't seem to put them out of your mind. (T)

Appendix D • Index of Interpersonal Activity

Indicate in the boxes below the number of "dates" you have had in the last week, that is, since your last group meeting. Use the following criteria as a definition of the term "date."

1. It may be with a member of either sex.
2. *Do not* include regular or routine activities such as those involving parents, relatives, roommates, or members of your weekly group.
3. *You* must be the one to have asked *them* for the "date." Do not include activities where someone asked you to do something or go somewhere.
4. The destination of this "date" must be to a place or activity outside of your dorm (Union, McDonald's, show, shopping, etc.) and other than to the library for a "study date," *only.*
5. You may include situations in which all of the above criteria were met, but the other person refused or was unable to attend.

Keep track of the number of times *each day* your activities conform to the above criteria and record them in the boxes below. It is important that you record these activities on a daily, not a weekly, basis.

MON.	TUES.	WED.	THURS.	FRI.	SAT.	SUN.

Please hang this form where it will be easily noticed each day—for example, on your bulletin board or near your telephone.

Appendix E • *Therapist Rating Sheet*

THERAPIST RATINGS OF CLIENT'S ANXIETY

Please rate *S*s on degree of behavioral and intra-psychic anxiety, (fidgeting, tenseness, stammering, shaking, etc.).

Therapist:________________ Groups: SD 1 SD 2 CC 1 CC 2 RT 1 RT 2

Date ________

Subjects:	(1) Anxiety-Level	(2) Anxiety-Level	(3) Anxiety-Level	(4) Anxiety-Level	(5) Anxiety-Level
1.________	1 2 3 4 5	1 2 3 4 5	1 2 3 4 5	1 2 3 4 5	1 2 3 4 5
2.________	1 2 3 4 5	1 2 3 4 5	1 2 3 4 5	1 2 3 4 5	1 2 3 4 5
3.________	1 2 3 4 5	1 2 3 4 5	1 2 3 4 5	1 2 3 4 5	1 2 3 4 5
4.________	1 2 3 4 5	1 2 3 4 5	1 2 3 4 5	1 2 3 4 5	1 2 3 4 5
5.________	1 2 3 4 5	1 2 3 4 5	1 2 3 4 5	1 2 3 4 5	1 2 3 4 5

Date ________

	(6) Anxiety-Level	(7) Anxiety-Level	(8) Anxiety-Level	(9) Anxiety-Level	(10) Anxiety-Level
1.________	1 2 3 4 5	1 2 3 4 5	1 2 3 4 5	1 2 3 4 5	1 2 3 4 5
2.________	1 2 3 4 5	1 2 3 4 5	1 2 3 4 5	1 2 3 4 5	1 2 3 4 5
3.________	1 2 3 4 5	1 2 3 4 5	1 2 3 4 5	1 2 3 4 5	1 2 3 4 5
4.________	1 2 3 4 5	1 2 3 4 5	1 2 3 4 5	1 2 3 4 5	1 2 3 4 5
5.________	1 2 3 4 5	1 2 3 4 5	1 2 3 4 5	1 2 3 4 5	1 2 3 4 5

Appendix F • Therapist Personal Data Sheet and Therapist Orientation Sheet

THERAPIST ORIENTATION SHEET

Gordan L. Paul
University of Illinois

The following pages contain a number of areas in which psychotherapists have been found to differ. Please indicate your position with regard to each area by placing a checkmark on the scale accompanying each area.

For example: 1. Activity-frequency:

If you feel that with *most* clients you are usually active (talkative), or *usually* passive, you would place the checkmark as follows:

Active X : ___ : ___ : ___ : ___ Passive/Active ___ : ___ : ___ : ___ : X Passive

If you feel you are *more often* active than passive, or *more often* passive than active, you would check as follows:

Active ___ : X : ___ : ___ : ___ Passive/Active ___ : ___ : ___ : X : ___ Passive

If you feel you are *about equally* active and passive with most clients, or active with as many clients as passive, you would check the middle space:

Active ___ : ___ : X : ___ : ___ Passive

1. Activity-frequency:
   Active ___ : ___ : ___ : ___ : ___ Passive
   (talkative) (non-talkative)
2. Activity-type:
   Directive ___ : ___ : ___ : ___ : ___ Non-directive
3. Activity-structure:
   Informal ___ : ___ : ___ : ___ : ___ Formal
4. Relationship-tenor:
   Personal ___ : ___ : ___ : ___ : ___ Impersonal
   (involved) (detached)
5. Relationship-structure:
   Unstructures ___ : ___ : ___ : ___ : ___ Structures
6. Relationship-atmosphere:
   Permissive ___ : ___ : ___ : ___ : ___ Non-permissive
7. Relationship-therapist actions:
   Planned ___ : ___ : ___ : ___ : ___ Spontaneous
8. Relationship-client dynamics:
   Non-conceptualized ___ : ___ : ___ : ___ : ___ Conceptualized
9. Goals-source:
   Therapist ___ : ___ : ___ : ___ : ___ Client
10. Goals-formalization
    Planned ___ : ___ : ___ : ___ : ___ Unplanned
    (formalized) (unformalized)
11. Therapist Comfort and Security:
    Always Secure ___ : ___ : ___ : ___ : ___ Never Secure
    (comfortable) (uncomfortable)
12. Client Comfort and Security:
    Never Secure ___ : ___ : ___ : ___ : ___ Always Secure
    (uncomfortable) (comfortable)
13. Client Personal Growth:
    Non-inherent ___ : ___ : ___ : ___ : ___ Inherent
14. Therapeutic Gains–self-understanding (cognitive insight)
    Important ___ : ___ : ___ : ___ : ___ Unimportant
15. Therapeutic Gains–emotional-understanding (affective awareness)
    Unimportant ___ : ___ : ___ : ___ : ___ Important
16. Therapeutic Gains-"symptom" reduction:
    Important ___ : ___ : ___ : ___ : ___ Unimportant
17. Therapeutic Gains–self-disclosure:
    Unimportant ___ : ___ : ___ : ___ : ___ Important
18. Therapeutic Gains-social adjustment:
    Important ___ : ___ : ___ : ___ : ___ Unimportant

19. Therapeutic Gains-confidence in effecting change:
Confident ___ : ___ : ___ : ___ : ___ Unconfident
20. Learning Process in Therapy:
Verbal-conceptual ___ : ___ : ___ : ___ : ___ Non-verbal-affective
21. Therapeutically Significant Topics:
Historical ___ : ___ : ___ : ___ : ___ Current
22. Therapeutically Significant Topics:
Client-centered ___ : ___ : ___ : ___ : ___ Theory-centered
23. Therapeutically Significant Topics:
Ego functions ___ : ___ : ___ : ___ : ___ Super-ego, Id
24. Theory of Motivation:
Unconscious ___ : ___ : ___ : ___ : ___ Conscious
25. Curative Aspects of Therapist:
Personality ___ : ___ : ___ : ___ : ___ Training
26. Curative Aspects of Therapist:
Relationship ___ : ___ : ___ : ___ : ___ Techniques

The following items refer to the use of *specific techniques* in psychotherapy. Please check to indicate whether you use each technique: Almost always, Usually, About half the time, Only occasionally, Never.

	Use of Techniques
	Almost Always 50/50 Never
27. Reflection and Clarification of Feelings:	___ : ___ : ___ : ___ : ___
28. Reflection and Clarification of Thinking:	___ : ___ : ___ : ___ : ___
29. Reflection and Clarification of Content:	___ : ___ : ___ : ___ : ___
30. Reflection and Clarification of Behavior:	___ : ___ : ___ : ___ : ___
31. Questioning of Feelings:	___ : ___ : ___ : ___ : ___
32. Questioning of Thinking:	___ : ___ : ___ : ___ : ___
33. Questioning of Content:	___ : ___ : ___ : ___ : ___
34. Questioning of Behavior:	___ : ___ : ___ : ___ : ___
35. Interpretation of Feelings:	___ : ___ : ___ : ___ : ___
36. Interpretation of Thinking:	___ : ___ : ___ : ___ : ___
37. Interpretation of Content:	___ : ___ : ___ : ___ : ___
38. Interpretation of Behavior:	___ : ___ : ___ : ___ : ___
39. Direct Confrontation of Feelings:	___ : ___ : ___ : ___ : ___

40. Direct Confrontation of Thinking: ___ : ___ : ___ : ___ : ___
41. Direct Confrontation of Content: ___ : ___ : ___ : ___ : ___
42. Direct Confrontation of Behavior: ___ : ___ : ___ : ___ : ___
43. Suggestion (not hypnosis): ___ : ___ : ___ : ___ : ___
44. Reassurance: ___ : ___ : ___ : ___ : ___
45. Information and Advice Giving: ___ : ___ : ___ : ___ : ___
46. Redirecting Questions Back to Client or Group: ___ : ___ : ___ : ___ : ___
47. Attentive Listening: ___ : ___ : ___ : ___ : ___
48. Self-disclosure: ___ : ___ : ___ : ___ : ___
49. Modeling Techniques: ___ : ___ : ___ : ___ : ___
50. Positive Attitude-confidence: ___ : ___ : ___ : ___ : ___
51. Warmth and Understanding: ___ : ___ : ___ : ___ : ___
52. Reinforcement (Approval-Disapproval): ___ : ___ : ___ : ___ : ___
53. Conditioning, Counter-conditioning: ___ : ___ : ___ : ___ : ___
54. Free Association: ___ : ___ : ___ : ___ : ___
55. Homework Assignments: ___ : ___ : ___ : ___ : ___
56. Other (please specify): ___ : ___ : ___ : ___ : ___

THERAPIST PERSONAL DATA SHEET

A. Indicate, in order of preference, the three or four authors who have been most influential in shaping your *present* approach to psychotherapy.
   1. ______________________________
   2. ______________________________
   3. ______________________________

B. Indicate the "school" or "schools" of psychotherapy with which you feel most identified and related in terms of your therapy approach.
   1. ______________________________
   2. ______________________________

C. Indicate the number of years of therapy experience you have gained to the present time.

   ____

D. Indicate the number of years of experience with the "techniques" of the school(s) identified in question B above: ________________

E. Have you obtained personal analysis and/or psychotherapy?
____

(If yes):

1. Number of sessions: ________________
2. Type (individual, group, both). Indicate the number of sessions for each if your answer is both: ________________
____
3. Type of therapy (psychoanalysis, client-centered, Rational-Emotive, Behavioral, etc.) ________________
____

Appendix G • Explanation of Interpersonal Anxiety and Rationale of Treatment Approaches Given to the Treatment Groups

Included here are the treatment rationale and an explanation of interpersonal anxiety, as well as a brief outline of the procedures followed by each of the CC, RT, and SD therapists. The explanations of interpersonal anxiety and the treatment rationales were not read directly to the *S*s. It was felt that this would detract from the personal quality of the treatment. Instead, each counselor familiarized himself with the following material and attempted to present the same ideas in his own words, using his own examples whenever possible. However, since the explanations and rationales that follow were prepared in conjunction with the individual therapists, their presentations followed very closely the descriptions included in the following pages.

SYSTEMATIC DESENSITIZATION TREATMENT

Explanation of interpersonal anxiety

Each of you is here today because you have indicated that you have a common problem—interpersonal anxiety. This emotional reaction that you experience and call anxiety is the result of your previous experiences with people. In other words, you learn to react to people with anxiousness; and, too often, this reaction easily can become habitual so that, before long, you always begin to feel anxious and tense when in the presence of others. However, the fact that interpersonal anxiety is *learned* means that it can be *unlearned*.

There are a number of ways you can learn to associate tension and anxiety with people or situations involving other people. One of the most frequent ways this happens is by being disappointed or hurt by others. Frequently, this involves doing something and then being "shocked," so to speak, by another person's reaction to you. This may happen many times in the course of your lifetime; and, before long, you begin to fear others and what they might say or do to you. Since it's impossible to completely avoid people or to be sure of their reaction to you, you are left with no alternative except fear, tension, and anxiety. Each of you probably can think of a number of instances where this has happened.

Through the repetition of such experiences, you begin to associate this fear and tension with *other* people and situations involving *other* people. One of the things known about anxiety is that it tends to spread and generalize, so that while initially you may fear only certain people and certain situations, this fear spreads to people in general and social situations in general. This is why you frequently can't understand the interpersonal anxiety you experience *now;* it may be inappropriate to the present situation and people.

Before long you may even try to anticipate this fear and anxiety long before it ever happens and begin to avoid people and activities involving people. When this happens, your anxiety only gets worse. It's a lot like the person who falls off a horse. The longer he waits to get back on, the harder it is for him. Similarly, the more you avoid people and interpersonal situations, the more anxious you get.

The key to overcoming this anxiety, as you will see in a minute, is to gradually and indirectly introduce yourself back into social situations in a controlled fashion. However, before this discussion proceeds to an explanation of the treatment or the *unlearning* process, are there any questions on how interpersonal anxiety is *learned?*

Treatment rationale

As long as you can recall or visualize how you've felt in anxious situations, it is possible to work with your reactions of tension and anxiety right here in this room. You need only to imagine as vividly as possible how you reacted in these actual situations.

The specific technique of treatment you will receive is one called desensitization. This technique utilizes two main procedures to reduce your anxiety—relaxation and counter-conditioning. The relaxation procedure is based upon years of work which Dr. Jacobsen started in the 1930's. He developed a method of inducing relaxation. This method can be learned very quickly and will allow you to become more deeply relaxed than ever before. The real advantage of relaxation is that the muscle systems in your body cannot be both tense and relaxed at the same time. Therefore, once you have learned the relaxation technique, it can be used to counter anxiety, tenseness, and feelings such as those you experience in interpersonal situations.

Relaxation *alone* can be used to reduce anxiety and tension. Often, however, relaxation is inconvenient to use and really by itself, does not permanently overcome anxiety. Therefore, the relaxation technique is often combined with the psychological principal of counter-conditioning to *desensitize* you to interpersonal situations, so that the anxiety no longer occurs.

The way in which this technique functions is to determine first the situations in which you become progressively more anxious and then to build a hierarchy from least to most anxious situations with regard to interpersonal relationships, that is, relationships involving other people. Next, you learn the technique of progressive relaxation. You will see very shortly how this operates, when actual training begins. After you are more relaxed than ever before, the counter-conditioning will begin. This will be done by having you repeatedly imagine, while under relaxation, specific interpersonal situations from the anxiety hierarchy. By having you visualize, very briefly and while you are deeply relaxed, the interpersonal situations that normally arouse anxiety, those situations gradually become desensitized, so that they no longer make you anxious. The treatment will start with those interpersonal situations that bother you the least and gradually work up to those that bother you the most. Since each visualization will lower your anxiety to the next item, a full-fledged anxiety reaction never occurs.

These procedures have been used, with excellent results on many different types of problems and persons, including students with interpersonal anxiety. Most of these procedures will become clearer after treatment begins. Do you have any questions about the treatment approach before the discussion continues?

Procedure

This approach consists of a slightly modified and formalized version of the SD treatment advanced by Lazarus & Rachman (1957), Wolpe (1958), and Wolpe & Lazarus (1966) and adapted for group use by Lazarus (1961) and Paul (1966a). While the five fundamental aspects involved in the application of SD were maintained (Paul, 1966), two major innovations were introduced. First, since *S*s were desensitized in groups of five, a hierarchy common to all five group members was employed. Second, in an attempt to further standardize the administration of the SD treatment across counselors, a tape recording of the relaxation portion of the SD treatment was employed. The tape is identical to the one utilized by Weinstein (1968).

Prior to meeting with any *S*s, both SD counselors were given a list consisting of each test item from the various self-report questionnaires of interpersonal anxiety which *all* five group members endorsed in the direction of "high anxiousness." A separate listing was prepared for each group. In this manner the item pool from which the ultimate hierarchies were finally constructed contained *only* situations common to all group members.

During the first hour approximately ten minutes were spent exploring the history and current status of the *S*s' problem. The next ten minutes were spent explaining how interpersonal anxiety is learned and presenting the rationale underlying the SD treatment. The next ten minutes of the first hour and the first thirty minutes of the second treatment session were spent constructing a thematic hierarchy made up of situations related to interpersonal anxiety. Separate hierarchies were constructed for each group.

As indicated above, each group member, including the therapist, received a copy of each test item from the various self-report questionnaires that all five group members endorsed in the direction of "high anxiousness." Working together, each *S* and counselor further embellished and added items until all of them were satisfied as to the completeness of the list. Each group member was then instructed to arrange the various situations described by each item in order of their anxiety eliciting potential, beginning with those that arouse very slight, controllable amounts of anxiety and working up to those that cause extreme anxiety. In this manner, a thematic anxiety hierarchy, ranging along the stimulus generalization gradient of interpersonal situations, was formed.

The following are the actual hierarchies employed in the present study:

A. Hierarchy for Counselor B's Introverts

Imagine that:

1. You are greeting someone you know slightly, and he doesn't acknowledge you.
2. You are greeting someone by mistake.
3. You are ordering food in a restaurant.
4. You are talking with someone who knows more about the subject than you do.

5. You are bumping into someone, and he doesn't forgive you.
6. You are asking a friend to return something he has forgotten about.
7. You are late for a *small* class and are coming in the front door.
8. You are late for a *large* class and are coming in the front door.
9. You are asking a question in a *small* class.
10. You are asking a question in a *medium-sized* class.
11. You are asking a question in a *large* class.
12. You are being asked a specific question in a *small* class.
13. You are being asked a specific question in a *medium-sized* class.
14. You are being asked a specific question in a *large* class.
15. You are asking for a refund on bad merchandise.
16. You are asking someone for a date to a *football* game.
17. You are asking someone for a date to a *concert*.
18. You are asking someone for a date to a *movie*.
19. You are asking a classmate to have a coke with you after class.
20. You are asking for a dance at a mixer.
21. You are bringing your girlfriend or boyfriend home to meet your parents.
22. Your girlfriend or boyfriend is taking you home to meet his parents for the first time.
23. You are dropping a tray full of food at dinner in the cafeteria and everyone looks.
24. You are tripping and falling as you walk into your introductory psychology class.

B. Hierarchy for Counselor B's Introverts

Imagine that:

1. You are at a large party.
2. You are giving a speech before a group of people.
3. You are interviewing for an important job.
4. You are asking a friend to return something he has forgotten about.
5. Someone nosy is prying into your affairs.
6. You are talking with someone whose name you can't remember.

7. While talking loudly about someone you notice him standing nearby.
8. You are waiting for someone to keep an appointment with you.
9. You are late for an appointment.

*1. You are getting out your books to begin studying.
2. You are trying to study before a test and see you can't cover everything.
3. You are trying to figure out a problem and can't.
4. You have *six* hours left to study before a test.
5. You have *five* hours left to study before a test.
6. You have *two* hours left to study before a test.
7. You have *one* hour left to study before a test.
8. You are walking into the test room and sitting down.
9. You are glancing through the test and don't recognize some of the material.

10. You are meeting your girlfriend's or boyfriend's parents for the first time.
11. You are trying to be nice to an obnoxious person in the presence of others.
12. You are meeting someone you are trying to avoid for fear of losing your temper.
13. A close friend is asking you to do something unreasonable, and you are turning him down.
14. You are being criticized.

C. Hierarchy for Counselor b's Introverts

Imagine that:

1. You are sitting in a doctor's waiting room before a physical examination.
2. You are walking into a psychology experiment with three other subjects.
3. You have an appointment to meet a professor for lunch.
4. You are discussing low grades with your parents.

*Due to excessive anxiety over pending mid-term examinations, both *S*s and counselor decided to work on a test anxiety hierarchy for two sessions (nine items).

5. You are expecting an argument between your roommate and you.
6. You are asking your parents for later hours.
7. You are going to talk to your professor about the test he has given.
8. You are telling your roommates about their irritating habits.
9. You are going to be late for an important appointment.
10. You are the host at a party.
11. You are going into an interview for an important position in a company.
12. You are going to meet a new date.
13. You are going to meet someone who has insulted you before your friends.
14. You are asking a professor a question in class about something you do not understand.
15. You are getting up to give a speech before a large group.
16. You are trying to carry on a conversation with a total stranger.
17. You are going to be meeting your steady's parents for the first time in a few minutes.

D. Hierarchy for Counselor b's Extroverts

Imagine that:

1. You are walking into a psychology experiment with three other subjects.
2. You are at a party and notice that a large crowd has gathered.
3. You are asking your parents for later hours.
4. You are meeting someone for the first time.
5. You are discussing low grades with your parents.
6. You are going to be meeting your steady's parents for the first time in a few minutes.
7. You are meeting the movie star you admire most.
8. You are telling your roommates about their irritating habits.
9. You have an appointment to meet a professor for lunch.
10. You are asking a professor a question in class about something you do not understand.
11. You are the host at a party.
12. You are going to meet someone who has insulted you before your friends.

13. You are expecting an argument between your roommate and you.
14. As you walk into the cafeteria for dinner you drop your full tray.
15. You are going into an interview for an important position in a company.
16. You are going to be late for an important appointment.
17. You are getting up to give a speech before a large group.
18. You are about to tell your parents about your sudden marriage plans.

During the final thirty minutes of both the first and second sessions, each *S* received training in progressive relaxation by means of an audio tape recording (approximate length, 28 minutes). This procedure consisted of an accelerated form of Jacobsen's (1938) original routine and involved alternately tensing and relaxing gross-muscle groups, learning to focus attention on these muscles while moving progressively through the body extremities and trunk region until a state of deep muscle relaxation was achieved. The sequence in the tape recording followed very closely the one's outlined by Paul (1966).

During the two relaxation training periods each *S* was instructed to make a "mental note" of any one or two exercises (neck, legs, back, face, etc.) which were *particularly* relaxing and also note at which point, if any, relaxation training ceased to be beneficial, that is, relaxing. The former information was utilized during the desensitization proper to help get a *S* relaxed again after he had signaled anxiety associated with a hierarchy item. The latter information was used during the desensitization proper to progressively reduce the time spent in muscle relaxation. By noting at which point no further relaxation ensued, and by communicating this to the therapist by means of the familiar index-finger signal, the therapist could stop the relaxation training tape when all members signaled complete relaxation. In this manner, the time required to achieve deep levels of muscle relaxation was shorter with each treatment hour, leaving more time each session for the desensitization proper.

The third through ninth sessions were conducted as follows. The first five minutes were spent in either a general discussion or question and answer period. Since no verbal communication was allowed during the desensitization proper, it was felt that this brief time period was required for verbal interchanges among *S*s and between

*S*s and counselor. Thus, it was not limited exclusively to treatment related material and, on occasion, was dispensed with altogether when *S*s had nothing to discuss. Those portions of the seven treatment interviews concerned with the desensitization proper were conducted in the manner described by Paul (1966). During the last few minutes of each session, following the *successful completion* of an item, the *S*s were aroused and reactions to images, etc., were discussed. Each counselor was instructed to maintain a warm, interested, and helpful attitude as in any therapeutic relationship.

RATIONAL-EMOTIVE TREATMENT

Explanation of interpersonal anxiety

Each of you is here today because you have indicated that you have a common problem—interpersonal anxiety. This emotional reaction that you experience and call anxiety is the result of your previous experiences with other people. In other words, you *learn* to react to people with anxiousness; and, too often, this reaction can easily become habitual, so that before long you always begin to feel anxious and tense when in the presence of others. However, the fact that interpersonal anxiety is *learned* means that it can be *unlearned.*

The way you learn to experience emotions such as tension and anxiety around other people or in situations involving other people is fairly well understood, and part of the agenda for today is to explain this process to you.

There are many ways in which emotions can be classified. For example, you can classify them as positive or negative, depending on whether they make you feel good or bad. You can also classify emotions as transient or enduring, depending on how long they last. Your counselors are more interested here in *negative* emotions, since they are the ones that cause you trouble, that is, make you feel bad. In addition, they are further interested in *enduring* emotions, since they are the ones that make you feel bad over and over again, that is, they endure over time. Interpersonal anxiety is just such an enduring, negative emotion. It frequently makes you feel bad and occurs almost every time you have to deal with people or situations involving people. Thus, interpersonal anxiety, or anxiety that results from simple, routine interactions with other people, is particularly debilitating, since it can disrupt normal but required daily routines, make otherwise healthy individuals unhappy and dissatisfied with themselves, and generally create discomforts that are unfortunate and otherwise avoidable.

How are enduring negative emotions such as interpersonal anxiety learned? It may not be immediately apparent, but *all* enduring emotions are caused by our thinking. Any emotion that is not transient—that endures over time—is maintained by our thoughts. For example, if you are upset by a car accident, your upset, whatever it may be, will disappear soon after you leave, that is, when the external event, the accident, is gone. In short, it is transient. Enduring, negative emotions such as anger, depression, anxiety, etc., *do not* go away when the thing you are angry, depressed, or anxious about is gone. The reason they don't go away is because you continue to think about them, you continue to tell yourself something about it. For example, if a friend or roommate says something negative about you, you may be angry, depressed, or anxious for weeks. The anger doesn't go away when the situation is passed, because you continue to think about it over and over for weeks on end. You continue to tell yourself something, usually something silly or irrational, about the interchange between you and your friend that maintains your angry, depressed, or anxious state.

Let's look at this sequence more closely. (At this point, the diagram below was put on the blackboard.)

A. Your friend or roomate tells you something he dislikes about you.

B.

C. You get upset, that is, angry, depressed, or anxious.

Something happens to you at point A, and you get upset at point C. You erroneously believe that A causes C, when in fact B, or what you tell yourself about A, is what causes you to get upset at C. As long as you continue to believe B, you will get upset over and over and stay upset.

The kinds of things you tell yourself at B are, of course, learned. Usually, they are silly, irrational beliefs that you have learned in the process of growing up and have never challenged or unlearned. In this case, for example, you might be telling yourself something like (at this point, the following B statements were also put on the blackboard):

B. What others think and/or say about me is more important than what I think about myself.

B.′ I have no right to do what I want if it might hurt someone else's feelings.
B.″ He has no right to say that to me.
B.‴ I need people's approval for what I do.

Without these silly, irrational statements you tell yourself at B, the feelings you have at point C could not endure over time. This is the chief difference between the transient negative feelings everyone experiences, but which come and go, and the enduring feelings, such as interpersonal anxiety, which linger on and on for weeks, months, and sometimes years. Without these statements at B, your negative, upsetting feelings at C would last only a short time, at most.

The key to overcoming this upset at C is discovering what irrational statements you are telling yourself at B and gradually correcting or replacing them with more rational ones, so that your upset feelings at C will disappear. However, before going into an explanation of the treatment or the *unlearning* process, are there any questions on what causes interpersonal anxiety?

Treatment rationale

The goal of this group will be to help each other uncover, challenge, and correct as many as possible of the irrational statements at point B. Each of you will try to accomplish this in two different ways. First, you will have to take the responsibility of confronting both yourself and other group members. By this I mean that all of you must be willing to share your emotional reactions with the group and help each other *pinpoint clearly* the actual B sentences that keep these negative emotions alive. This is the only way you can ever hope to overcome these painful emotional states. Second, you will have regular homework assignments designed to elicit various feelings. Your reactions to these assignments will be discussed regularly in the hopes of discovering what statements you are telling yourself to maintain your upsetness.*

*While initial homework assignments were given at large, later assignments were tailored to each individual *S*. For example, the first assignment given to all *S*s was to go into a restaurant, order a cup of coffee, then when the waitress brings it tell her he changed his mind and now wants a coke. As an example of a tailored homework assignment, one girl, who was upset by her inability to tell busdrivers to stop when she saw someone running to catch the bus, was told to do just that, even if the bus was crowded.

To overcome the negative emotions that create troublesome interpersonal relationships you first must uncover the irrational statements or beliefs that cause your anxiety and second literally replace them with more functional or rational statements or beliefs. In order to uncover your irrational beliefs, you must be willing to examine the interpersonal situations in which you feel anxious and discuss them here in the group. Furthermore, you must make active attempts to engage in interpersonal situations, that is, do the homework assignments, and share these experiences with the group, so that every group member can help each other. Do you have any questions about the treatment approach before we continue?

Procedure

Following questions relative to the treatment rationale, the RT therapists asked each *S* if he was presently feeling anxious. Those *S*s who indicated the most anxiety and the greatest willingness to begin treatment were the focus of the therapists' initial therapeutic efforts. In addition, every effort was made before the end of the first session to get as many group members as possible involved, both directly and indirectly. The first session ended with the aforementioned homework assignment.

Each session began typically with a review of the successes and failures relative to the weekly homework assignments. Feelings elicited during attempts to conduct these assignments were elucidated and related to maladaptive and irrational philosophies of living and their derivatives. At each session, every effort was made to get *S*s to challenge each other and help other *S*s develop more adaptive, rational, and functional B statements. Each counselor was instructed to maintain a warm, interested, and helpful attitude, as in any therapeutic relationship.

CLIENT-CENTERED TREATMENT

Explanation of interpersonal anxiety

Each of you is here today because you have indicated that you have a common problem—interpersonal anxiety. This emotional reaction that you experience and call anxiety is the result of your previous experiences with other people. In other words, you *learn* to react to people with anxiousness; and, too often, this reaction can easily become habitual, so that before long you always begin to feel anxious and tense when in the presence of others. However, the fact that interpersonal anxiety is *learned* means that it can be *unlearned.*

The way you learn to experience emotions such as tension and anxiety around other people or in situations involving other people is fairly well understood, and part of what will be said here today is to explain this process to you.

In order to understand any type of anxiety, you have to have some working concepts about how people function. First, we can divide areas of human life into three spheres: thinking, feeling, and behaving. If we compare anxious with non-anxious people, we will soon see that in the former group these three areas operate independently of and often at odds with one another, whereas in the latter group these three areas seem to "flow together" more or less as a whole. In other words, a person who is anxious is one who may think one thing, feel another, and do, that is, behave, a third way. This is exactly why he is anxious. In many ways the anxious person is analogous to a machine in which all the parts do not fit together very well. As the machine runs, it builds up friction, and the friction in the machine is analogous to anxiety in humans; it results from all the parts not working *together.* In the non-anxious person thoughts, feelings, and behavior "flow together"; they form a unit, a whole. In this way, little friction or anxiety results.

Let's make this more specific. If a non-anxious person is bored by a peer's conversation (boredom being a feeling or emotion), he will probably start focusing his attention (thinking) on this boredom and try to figure out why he is bored. He might behave in a bored manner, that is, leave, tell his friend how boring *his* conversation is, or make the conversation more exciting—that is, behave differently. This is a rather simplified example of what is meant by functioning as a whole person or as a unit. The anxious person, in this same situation, may *feel* bored but continue on with the discussion *as if he were interested* (behavior) and simply *think* to himself how he wished he could leave, or about how wrong it is for him to be bored, etc. In any case, the important point is that he is not functioning as a whole unit. At the feeling level he is bored, behaviorally he acts interested, and in terms of thinking he is either wishing the conversation were over or condemning himself or the other person. This disjointed mode of functioning is what causes friction or anxiety.

The key to understanding the difference between the wholely functioning, non-anxious person and the disjointedly functioning, anxious person lies in the ability to *listen uncritically,* be *honest,* and be *accepting.* In the example above, uncritical listening allows the non-anxious person to accept his boredom. He doesn't have to feel guilty and thus pretend he is interested or blame himself or his friend for *making him bored.* He simply uncritically accepts his feeling of boredom. He is being honest with both himself and his friend by conveying his boredom to his friend, not with the intent of blaming but with the idea of, "Let's make this unboring!"

Thus, the key to reducing or getting rid of interpersonal anxiety is to get all the parts—behavior, thinking, and feeling—functioning as a unit or a whole. The way to do this is to listen uncritically to the feelings others elicit in you, accept them as valid *for you,* communicate your feelings honestly and with the desire of wanting to work together to do something about these feelings. If you are unable to listen uncritically, accept your feelings, and/or communicate them honestly, you are simply going to "split" yourself apart, thinking one thing, feeling another, and doing something altogether different. Once you begin to do this, the only consequence is friction or anxiety.

Although I do not want to spend to much time discussing how people get "split apart," I do want to say that you *learn* this, probably as a child growing up. You learn to feel guilty when bored and to blame yourself or others. You learn to pretend you are interested when you are not. But you can *unlearn* it by learning to be a noncritical listener, accepting and honest in interpersonal relationships.

As indicated above, the key to overcoming this anxiety is to listen uncritically, to be accepting of your feelings, and to communicate them honestly. This is not easy to do, but it is what this group will spend the next nine weeks trying to do. However, before going into an explanation of the treatment or *unlearning* process, are there any questions on what causes interpersonal anxiety?

Treatment rationale

The goal of this group will be first to develop uncritical listening skills and second to try to create an atmosphere that lends itself to acceptance of feelings and honest communication among the members of this group. The atmosphere of honesty and acceptance is of such importance that it cannot be stressed too much. Each person here should feel that he can say whatever he is feeling, and if he "makes mistakes," as he inevitably will, that he can maintain enough of a willingness and openness to go back and look at things and try and sort out what happened in that "mistake."

The way we can begin is to try to respond to each other, not in terms of the content of what is said, but in terms of the feelings the speaker elicits in us. For example, if the counselor says something, and some feeling inside of you says, "No that's not right," tell the counselor about it. Try to describe that feeling. That feeling tells the counselor how you experience him, and that's the way he can learn and change. He can say, "Yes, that's right. I didn't really mean that. Now why did I say that? Did I just want to impress you? Was that my way of saying I like you, or what?"

This may seem relatively simple to you, but as you will see when you try it, it is not. People have been taught for so long to pay attention to content or, more importantly, to disregard feelings, that many times they may have trouble even deciding what feelings a person elicits in them. But this is how you learn to listen uncritically; you focus on what, *in fact,* is coming across to you, not on classifying it as good or bad, right or wrong, etc. This holds even for feelings of anger. If they are there, then trying to decide if they are important, bad, etc., makes no sense. They're just there.

Learning to communicate, honestly of course, goes hand in hand with sensitive listening. In fact, the more I think about it, the more I think one flows from the other. If you can listen uncritically, with the intent of trying to figure out what feelings people elicit in you, you're going to be less blaming and less condemning of yourself and others. If you are less blaming and less condemning, people are going to feel freer and easier in communicating with you about their feelings.

Where does that leave us? What we have to do to start with is to watch ourselves so that we pay attention to the feelings we have when others talk, and communicate these feelings so that others know how we experience them. Do you have any questions about the treatment approach before we continue?

Procedure

Following questions relative to the treatment rationale, the CC counselors asked each *S* if he was presently feeling anxious. Those *S*s who indicated the most anxiety and the greatest willingness to begin treatment were the focus of the therapists' initial therapeutic efforts. In addition, every effort was made before the end of the first session to get as many group members as possible involved, both directly and indirectly.

Little or no structure was imposed on the content of each group interview. *S*s brought up and dealt with material that was current and pressing. Feelings about group members were stressed, while reactions to friends, relatives, etc., though not excluded, were given secondary consideration. Each therapist was instructed to maintain a warm, interested, and helpful attitude, as in any therapeutic relationship.

Appendix H • *Profiles of Therapists' Scores on the* Edwards Personal Preference Schedule, Myer-Briggs Type Indicator, *and* Interpersonal Checklist

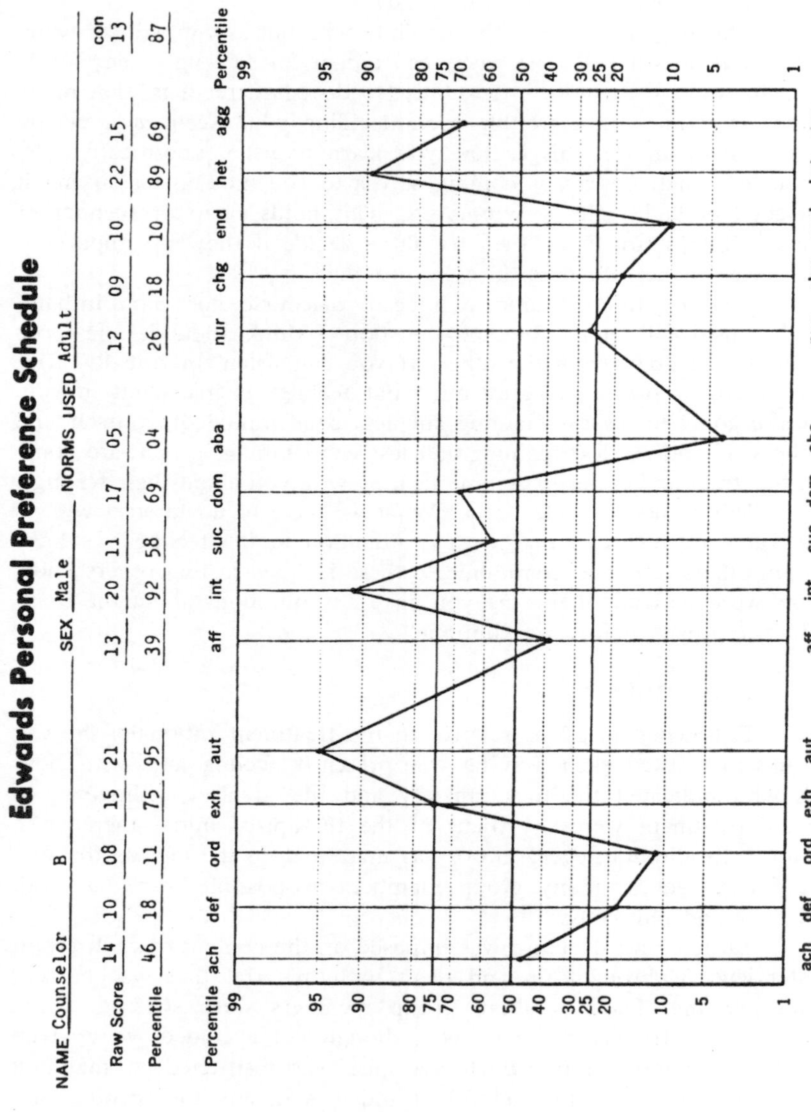

Edwards Personal Preference Schedule

NAME Counselor b SEX Male NORMS USED Adult

	ach	def	ord	exh	aut	aff	int	suc	dom	aba	nur	chg	end	het	agg	con
Raw Score	13	07	10	17	19	15	26	09	15	08	12	15	09	21	16	12
Percentile	37	04	20	87	88	58	99	42	57	12	26	62	07	87	76	70

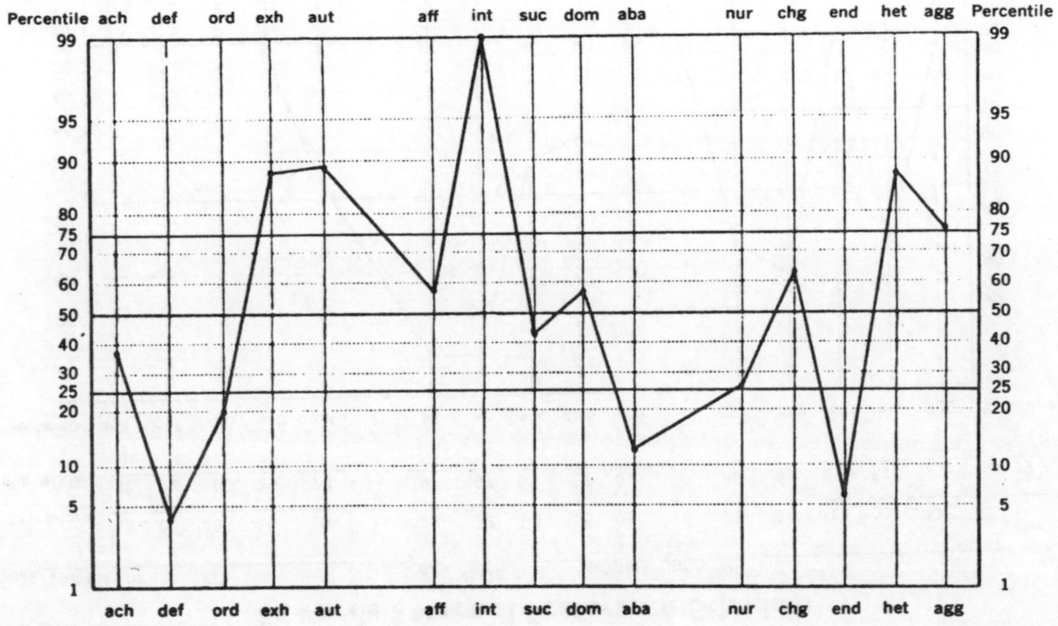

Appendix H.1

Edwards Personal Preference Schedule

NAME Counselor C SEX Male NORMS USED Adult

	ach	def	ord	exh	aut	aff	int	suc	dom	aba	nur	chg	end	het	agg	con
Raw Score	13	06	03	10	16	22	22	12	15	03	21	20	13	21	10	15
Percentile	37	02	00	29	70	97	97	65	57	01	86	91	23	87	29	93

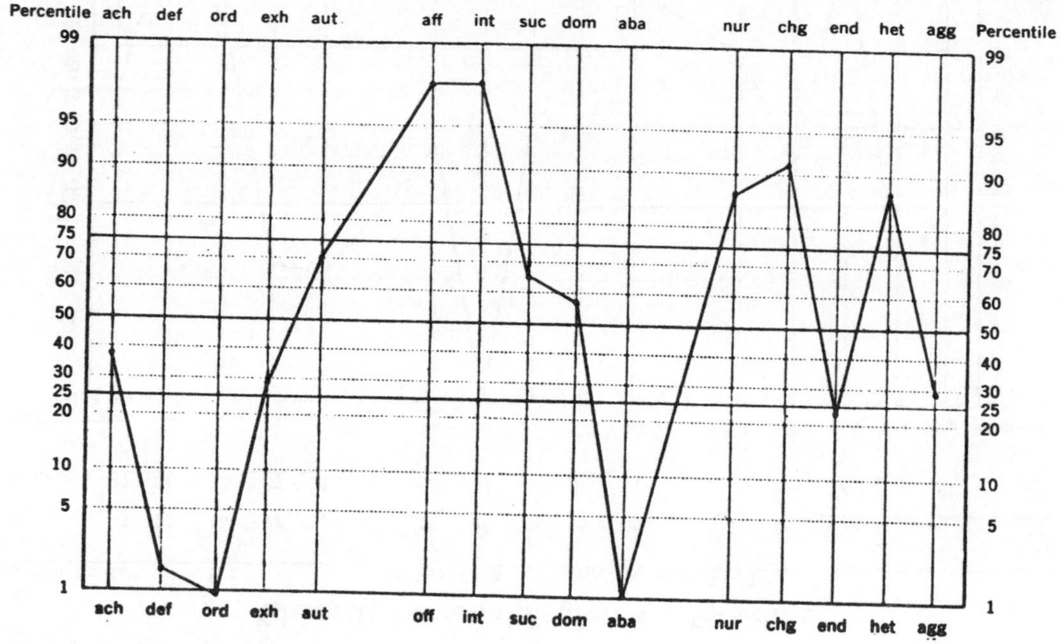

Appendix H.1 · *Continued*

Edwards Personal Preference Schedule

NAME Counselor c SEX Male NORMS USED Adult

	ach	def	ord	exh	aut	aff	int	suc	dom	aba	nur	chg	end	het	agg	con
Raw Score	14	10	02	12	18	21	24	13	13	07	21	22	09	17	12	12
Percentile	46	18	00	47	84	94	99	71	44	09	86	96	07	76	46	70

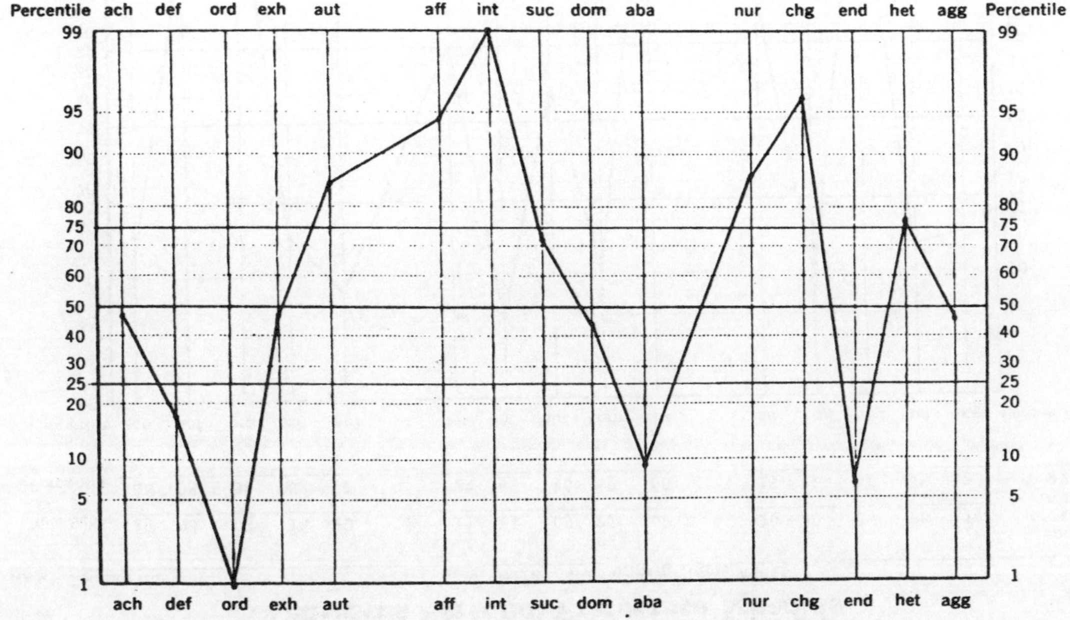

Appendix H.1 • Continued

Edwards Personal Preference Schedule

NAME Counselor R SEX Male NORMS USED Adult

	ach	def	ord	exh	aut	aff	int	suc	dom	aba	nur	chg	end	het	agg	con
Raw Score	19	08	03	16	20	11	21	09	21	02	10	20	05	20	17	14
Percentile	86	05	00	82	92	24	95	40	89	00	15	91	01	85	82	97

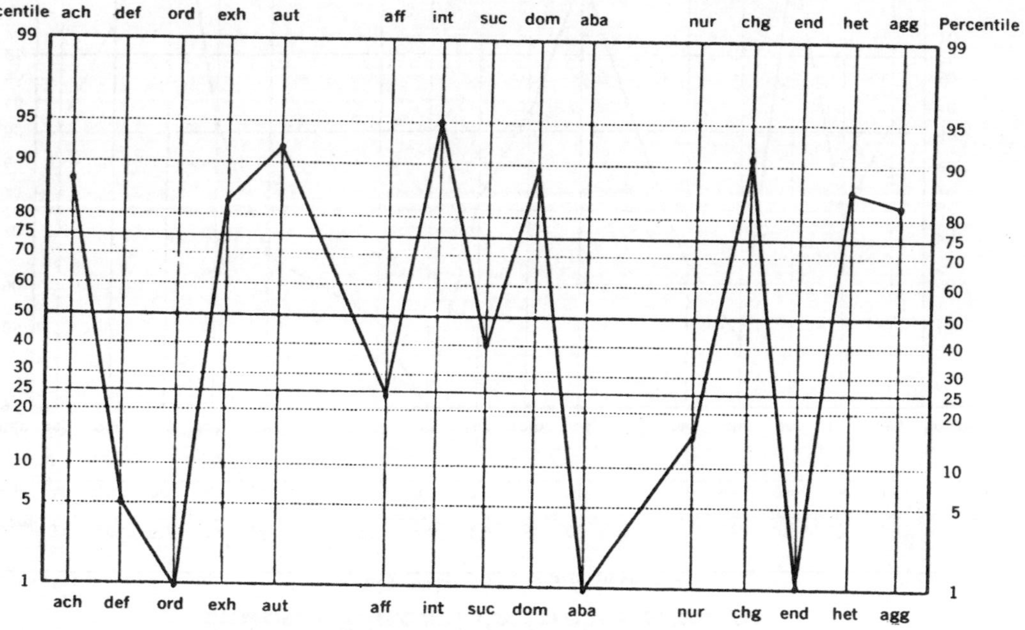

Appendix H.1 • *Continued*

Edwards Personal Preference Schedule

NAME Counselor r SEX Male NORMS USED Adult

	ach	def	ord	exh	aut	aff	int	suc	dom	aba	nur	chg	end	het	agg	con
Raw Score	23	06	04	20	23	10	20	08	19	03	08	20	07	21	18	14
Percentile	98	02	01	97	98	18	92	33	80	01	07	91	03	87	87	97

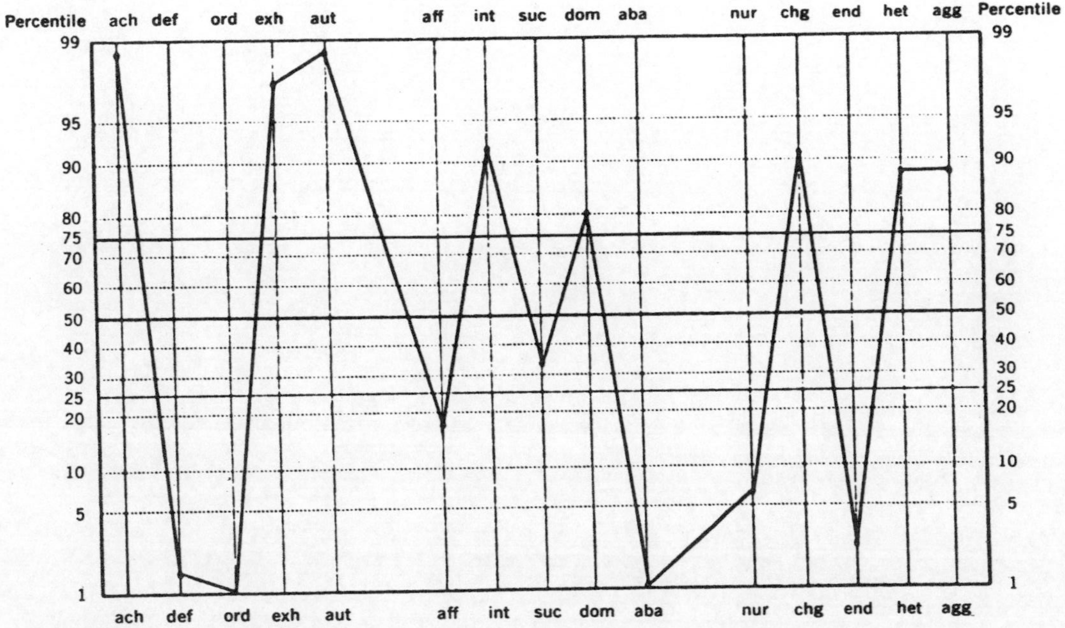

Appendix H.1 • Continued

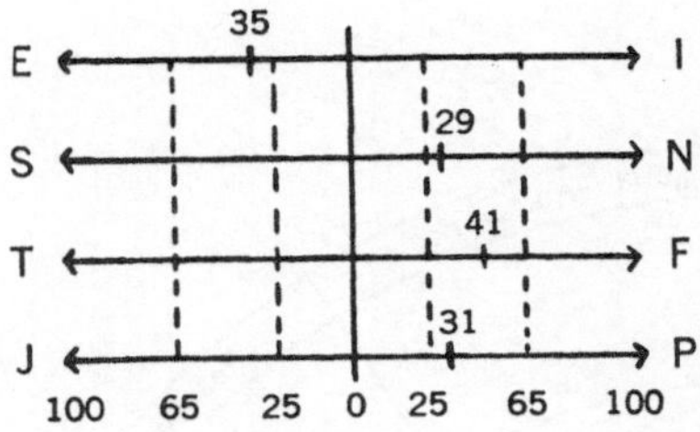

Counselor C

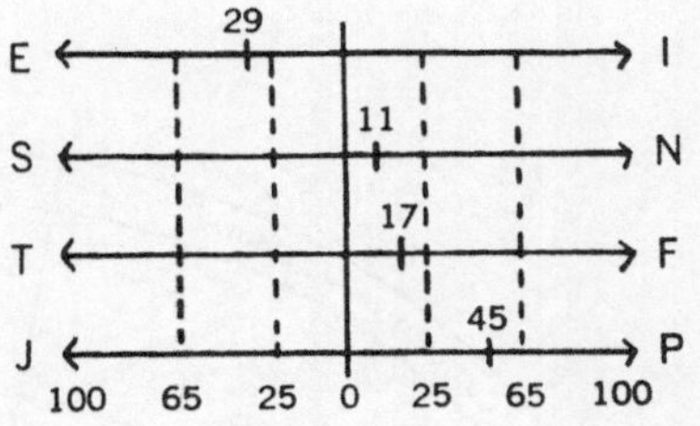

Counselor c

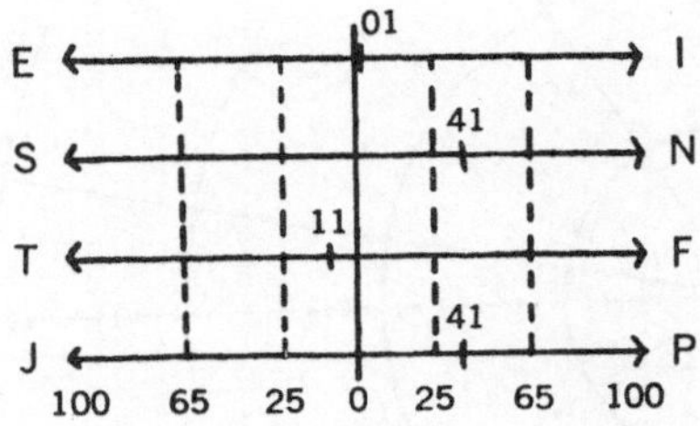

Counselor B

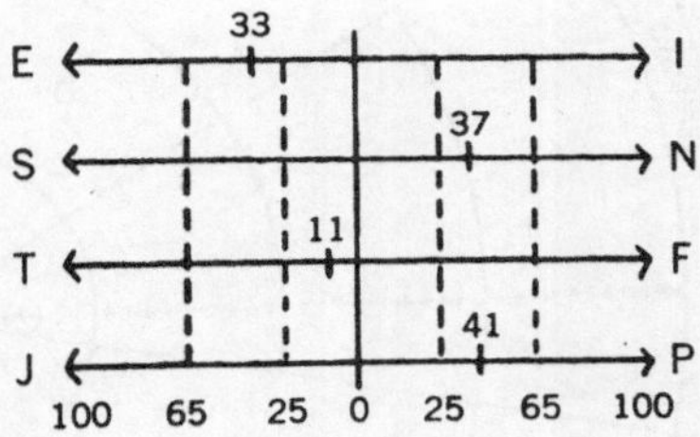

Counselor b

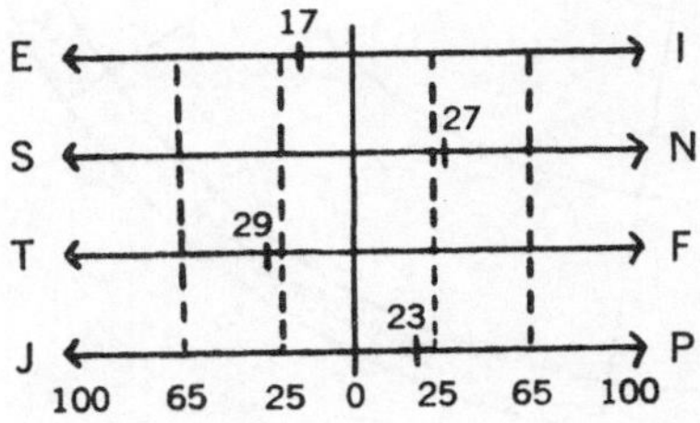

Counselor R

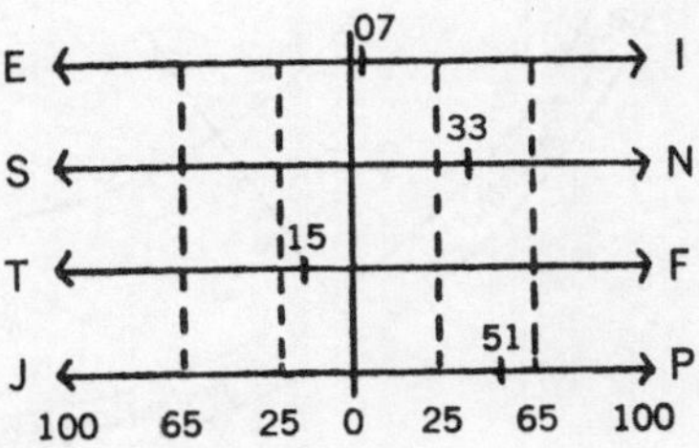

Counselor r

Appendix H.2 · *Graphic Representation of Therapist Self-Ratings on the* Myers-Briggs Type Indicator

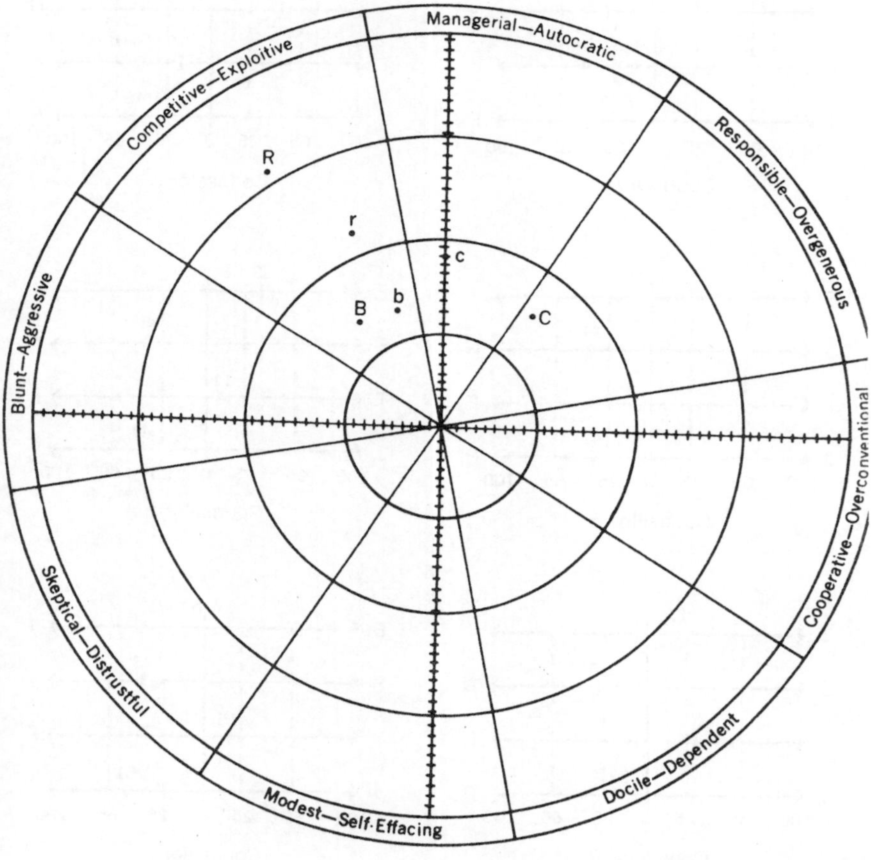

Appendix H.3 · Graphic Representation of Therapist Self-Ratings on the Interpersonal Checklist

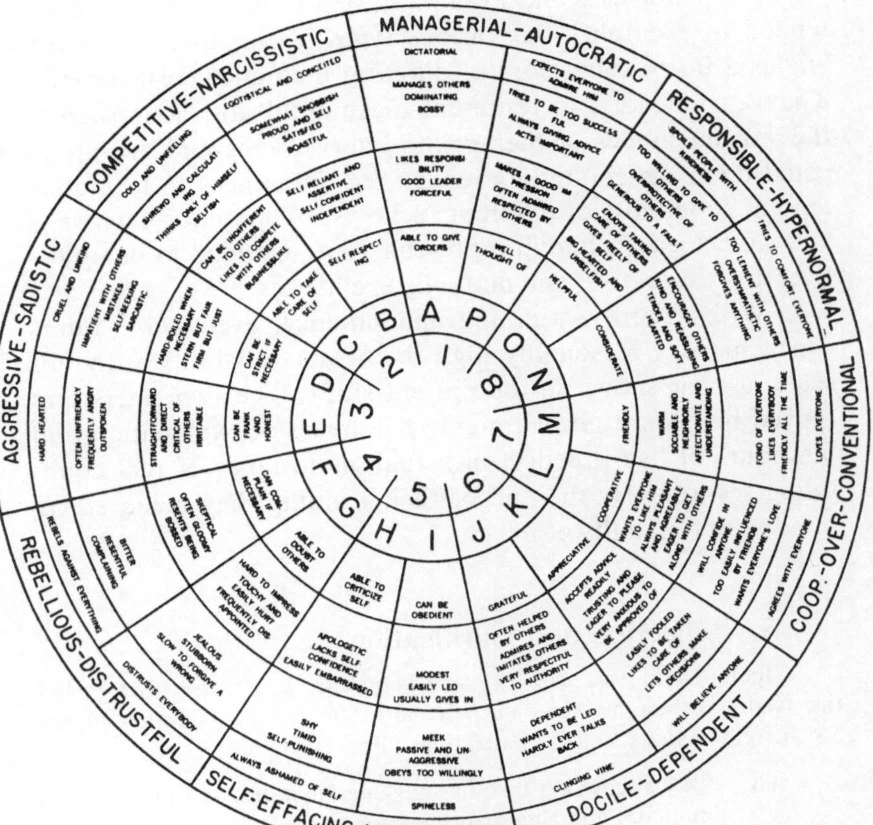

Appendix H.4 · Interpersonal Checklist *Illustrating the Classification of Interpersonal Behaviors into 16 Variable Categories*

Appendix I • *Manual for Classifying Therapist's Behavior*

The categories and examples listed in this manual are intended to exemplify the various types of therapeutic activity engaged in by counselors of differing theoretical orientations. They are intended to represent meaningful abstractions from the various modes of therapeutic interventions and are predicated upon the commonly recognized differences in technique among counselors of different "schools." The major categories and subcategories herein represented are intended to be objective, non-evaluative, and mutually exclusive.

With *extensive* training and practice, even naïve raters can achieve a reasonably high inter-rater reliability with this scale, as was shown in the present study. The two raters employed here were given roughly five hours of explanation and ten hours of live practice on actual audio tapes of real counseling sessions. By the end of their training they achieved an inter-rater reliability of .831.

1. Reflection and clarification

Included in this category are counselor statements that reflect the feelings, thoughts, and/or behaviors "behind" or implied in the *S*'s current actions and verbalizations. For example:

Cl: "I just couldn't take her nagging anymore, so I just grabbed my coat and slammed the door as I left."
Th: "You must have felt terribly angry at her."
Cl: "I could have killed the bitch."
Th: "She must have hurt you very deeply."

Both of these therapist statements would be classified as "reflection of feelings." In both cases the counselor is clearly referring to the *S*'s feelings, that is, anger and hurt. In particular, he is referring to those feelings that he believes lurk behind or are implied in the *S*'s verbally related behavior.

In many instances the tape samples you will be rating will not be as clearly recognizable as the above sequence. For example, the therapist, in this same instance, may have said, "I'll bet you were feeling pretty angry," or "I wonder if you were feeling hurt again?" Although this may at first seem like a question that would be classified under heading 2 below, it seems obvious that the counselor believes the feeling he is reflecting is or was present, and he is simply asking a rhetorical question in order to make the *S* aware of its presence.

The following is another example of reflection. In this case the counselor is reflecting the *S*'s thoughts rather than his feelings.

> Cl: "I just sat there feeling more and more depressed as the evening went on."
>
> Th: "I can't help but wonder if you weren't just sitting there thinking about what you thought *would* happen if you would have gotten up and began moving around more socially."

Here, again, the therapist is reflecting, that is, stating what he feels is "behind" or implied in the *S*'s statement; but his focus, in this case, is the *S*'s thought processes. Statements of this nature would be classified as "reflection of thinking."

In addition, the counselor may use reflection in relation to the *S*'s *behavior* rather than in relation to his thoughts or feelings as above. For example:

> Cl: "It seemed like the only alternative I had was to tell him to shut up. Well . . . , I could have left . . . , I guess?"
>
> Th: "It does seem like those are the only ways you have, right now at least, of stopping arguments from getting out of hand."

Counselor statements of this type are classified as "reflection of behavior."

Thus, the basic criteria for the inclusion of counselor statements under the heading of "reflection" are: (a) a minimum of interpretation; (b) reflection of what the therapist feels is "behind" or implied in the *S*s statement. Notice that, unlike interpretation, the therapist here accepts the *S*'s formulation without introducing a new frame of reference and simply reflects what he feels is "behind" it. Even if the counselor's reflections are simply a preamble to a more focused question or interpretation, if they meet the above criteria they will be classified as reflection.

Clarification is taken to mean a restatement of the content of the *S*s verbalizations, including simple repetition of words or phrases, for purposes of clarification. Summaries that are essentially non-interpretative will also be classified as clarification. "Reflection of content" and "clarification of content" will be considered identical for the purposes of this study. As with reflection, clarification may include questions when they are essentially rhetorical in nature, that is, for purposes of clarification as opposed to information seeking or gathering, as well as clarifications that serve as a precursor to other kinds of statements. The following are examples of clarification.

Cl: "I can't do that, I just can't!"
Th: "Can't?"

Cl: "I get upset when he does that."
Th: "You mean when your boyfriend sits down and tries to tell you how he feels, *that* upsets you?"

Cl: "Uh (sigh). Everytime I think about that it turns me off."
Th: "Then just *thinking* about not being a good sex partner turns you off, as you say."

As with reflection, clarification may refer to either thoughts, feelings (motives), or behavior. The three samples above are examples of clarification of behavior, feelings, and thoughts, respectively.

2. Questioning

Here we are interested in counselor statements that are essentially exploratory in nature. Questions that are information seeking or geared at information gathering are classified here. For example:

Cl: "I put everything I have into every class I take."
Th: "What happens if, or when, you begin noticing that you're not doing as well in a class as you would like to?"

It seems clear in this example that the counselor is seeking information. Thus, this response would be classified as "questioning." Since the therapist is referring more to the *S*'s behavior than his thoughts or feelings, this response is further classified as "questioning of behavior."

Cl: "I just get upset when I'm around him."
Th: "What do you mean, upset? Do you get angry, depressed, disgusted, or what?"

The example above is also considered a question. However, the content of the counselor's statement classifies this response as "questioning of feelings."

In addition to exploratory probings such as these, counselor statements that requisition examples, elaborations, case history information, etc., from the client are also classified as "questioning." For example:

Cl: "I don't ever get mad. Outwardly mad."
Th: "Can you think of a specific instance when you were angry and kept it inside?"

Cl: "We had more fun before we got to know each other."
Th: "Can you tell me more about that?"

Cl: "I feel bad when I buy things for myself."
Th: "How did your father react when you brought something new home?"

Each of the above samples reflects the requisitioning of examples, elaborations, and case history material, respectively. Furthermore, while the second example represents "questioning of behavior," the first and third example represent "questioning of feelings."

Thus, the basic criteria for inclusion in this category is information gathering. This may be done by direct probing ("Why?" "What do you do on the weekends?" "Why did you do that?" "How would you *like* to be able to handle that?") or by asking for examples, elaborations, and so forth. Even if these questions serve only as a groundwork for an interpretation, they will be classified here if they meet the above criteria. Questions that are obviously rhetorical in nature are classified under heading 1.

Finally, "questioning of content" will be reserved for those therapist responses that meet all of the above criteria but do not *clearly* refer to either the *S*'s thoughts, feelings, or behaviors.

3. Interpretation

Here we are concerned with counselor statements that are essentially analytic in nature. Such statements include defining the *S*s problem, establishing connections, analyzing defenses, etc. It differs from "reflection and clarification" in that, with interpretation, the therapist goes beyond the *S*'s formulations and introduces a new frame of reference for analyzing defenses, establishing connections, etc. For an example of establishing connections:

Cl: "It does seem like the men I pick out are more helpless and dependent."

Th: "It seems like this is the same kind of relationship you had with your father, also. He was always the helpless and dependent one and you were also the one who rescued him."

In many, but not all, interpretations there is great emphasis placed on time periods other than the present in the *S*'s life, for example, childhood, adolescence, etc. The example above, since it refers to the *S*'s *activity,* is classified as "interpretation of behavior." Below is another example of "interpretation of behavior," but in this case the counselor is analyzing the *S*'s defenses.

Cl: "I always feel terrible when I meet people for the first time. It's like I'm going to get shot down or rejected."

Th: "And your way of preventing this from happening is either running away from the relationship or continually doing things for people over and over so they won't reject you."

Again, statements in the form of a (rhetorical) question may be disguised interpretations.

Cl: "I just feel like there's nothing I can do to please her."

Th: "You've had that feeling before, haven't you? Remember what you said about your parents?"

Once again, it seems clear that the counselor is not seeking information but imparting it, albeit somewhat indirectly. In this case the statement is classified as an "interpretation of feeling."

By "interpretation of content" is meant an interpretation on either the thinking, feeling, or activity level that is based solely on what the *S* has just said. No attempt is made to pull together past and present knowledge. For example:

Cl: "Boy, I sure don't like getting up this early in the morning to come here."

Th: "You mean you're mad at me for making you come this early to group."

This example is classified as "interpretation of content" (feeling), since a new frame of reference is offered. Feeling is the focus of the therapist statement, and the entire statement is contemporary, that is, based solely on the *S*'s last verbalization.

The important questions to ask in classifying interpretations are: (a) do they impose a new frame of reference on the *S;* (b) are they analytic, (c) do they *usually* involve reference to elements in the *S*'s past? In addition they can refer to either thinking, feeling, or behaving, and should be classified as such.

4. Direct confrontation

Here are classified counselor statements that challenge, oppose, or otherwise forcefully point out to the *S* the inconsistencies in his thinking, feeling, and/or behavior. For example:

Cl: "I'm upset because I know he doesn't even care for me."
Th: "No you're not, you're upset because you believe his not caring for you is important to your existence."

Here the therapist is opposing the *S*'s point of view and pointing out what he believes to be the cause of her problem. Although he does present a new frame of reference, as in "interpretation," the forcefulness of his presentation, as well as his exclusive reliance on contemporary and mostly intra-psychic events distinguishes "confrontation" from "interpretation." Confrontation involves very active, emotive encounters. Since the therapist in the above example is confronting the *S* with her beliefs, this would be classified as "direct confrontation with thinking."

Cl: "That really hurt my feelings."
Th: "How can he hurt your feelings? What you mean is that you took what he said and hurt your own feelings with it."

Here the counselor is showing the *S* how she blames others but in effect is the one who is ultimately hurting herself. Direct, personalized explanations of this nature are classified as "confrontation with feeling."

Cl: "Whenever I do what I want they just start yelling and screaming at me."
Th: "What you're doing now is the same as the blaming you were doing before. You want to do what you want but not be responsible for your actions."

In the above case the therapist is pointing out inconsistencies in the *S*'s behavior. Thus, this sample would be classified as "confrontation with behavior" as would the examples below.

Cl: (*S* speaking and acting like a "little girl.")
Th: "I'm sure that half the reason why people don't want to be around you is because you act like a damn nine-year-old spoiled brat."

Cl: "He's just as unreliable as he is reliable."
Th: "Yeah, and that's just the way you want it so you can blame *all* your anxieties on *his* unreliability."

Thus, much of the technique of direct confrontation involves a forced re-orientation or re-evaluation by the therapist. He accomplishes this by challenging, opposing, or otherwise pointing out to the *S* his loosely organized explanations and forcefully offering alternative explanations of the *S*'s problem.

By "confrontation with content" is meant a challenge or pointing-out of inconsistencies or discrepancies in the *S*'s prior comment, with no reference to other people, times, or places. For example:

Cl: "I don't . . . no, that doesn't bother me."
Th: "Oh, bullshit! You're shaking and all upset and can't even talk straight, now why is it so hard for you to admit that?"

5. Suggestion

By suggestion is meant counselor behaviors that either seek *indirectly* to get the *S* to think, feel, or behave in a given way or try to present a number of alternatives from which the *S* must choose. The *S* is always left the final say in matters of suggestion. For example:

Cl: "I'm not really sure how he feels about me."
Th: "Well, you could always try asking him."

Cl: "She's beautiful!"
Th: "Why don't you try asking her for a date."

Cl: "I don't really know what to do. I do need the money."
Th: "Well, if it were I, I probably wouldn't take it, because I think you're right. There are too many strings attached."

While all three of the above are examples of indirect suggestion, only the first two would be so classified. The last example, although suggestive in nature, would be classified under heading 8 (self-disclosure), since the counselor is explicitly using himself as a reference. The following are examples of suggesting alternatives.

Cl: "I'd like to visit them, but I don't know what to do about school."

Th: "Well, it seems like you have at least three alternatives. You can take an incomplete and make up the exam later, just forget about it and hope your other test scores will carry you through, or talk to the instructor and see if he can help you."

Cl: "I enjoy sex, but I want more than that."

Th: "Couldn't you discuss this with him to see if this relationship has more to offer or start dating other guys who can offer you more than just sex."

While "suggestion" is usually easy to discern, it can be confused with "self-disclosure" or "questioning." In the former case, the therapist uses himself, not just his opinion, as a frame of reference. In the latter case, the therapist is seeking information quite directly, not trying to impart it indirectly.

6. Information and advice giving

Counselor statements that involve structuring the therapeutic situation (describing the functions and tasks of therapy), discussions about theory, etc., are all classified under this heading, as well as *direct* suggestions for activity within and outside of treatment. Statements of this nature imply "the therapist as expert." He gives information and advice, states opinions, and answers direct questions. These communications are primarily objective. When they are *used* to convey reassurance (warmth) or rejection (disapproval), they will be classified under heading 10 (reinforcement). For example:

Cl: "My boyfriend doesn't like that."

Th: "I don't want to hear about what he wants. What do you want?"

The following is also an example of counselor statements that structure the counseling relationship and thus are classified as "information and advice giving."

Cl: "I don't think it helps much to talk about them."

Th: "No, neither do I."

Counselor statements that are intended to explain an idea, concept, or theory are also classified here. For example:

Cl: "I fight it with everything I have but can't seem to get anywhere."

Th: "I believe that, because, well I just don't think people change by trying to disect-out those parts of themselves they dislike. You have to accept what you despise about yourself, not try to cut it out like the bad part of an apple."

These statements are usually relatively easy to identify since they typically make reference to people in general. For example:

Cl: "I can't believe that people are that selfish."
Th: "It seems to me that most or perhaps—yes, all people do things for selfish reasons, I think. But I do feel that if you know yourself well, then when you act in accord with this true self your selfishness is also benevolent.

Although many references such as "you" and "your" are made, they seem to refer to people in general, that is, not to this *S* exclusively, and are thus classified as conceptual explanations.

Finally, the most direct form of information and advice giving is exemplified below.

Cl: "Do you think I should drop out of school?"
Th: "No!"

Here the therapist simply responds *directly* (not with suggestion or by redirecting the question back to the individual or group) to a question by the *S*.

7. Redirecting questions

Here the therapist avoids a committed response by redirecting questions back to their source, that is, either the individual or the group.

Cl: "Do you think I should have sexual relations with him?"
Th: "I think you already know the answer to that question."

Cl: "I wonder if I should even try to explain my feelings to her?"
Th: "Only you can decide that for yourself, Bob."

Cl: "Should I even tell my parents?"
Th: "What do you think?"

Cl: "I wonder if I shouldn't just drop out and transfer to a junior college?"
Th: "Let's see what the rest of the group thinks about that."

Cl: "I would like to try it. (pause) What do you think?"
Th: "I wonder, how does the rest of the group feel about that?"

These examples cover nearly all variations of "redirecting questions." Remember, the counselor simply puts the responsibility for a specific answer either back on the individual or the group.

8. Self-disclosure

Counselor statements classified here involve the therapist revealing his feelings either about the *S* or his feelings about a person, place, or thing to which the *S* is presently reacting. The following are examples of the latter.

Cl: "We just don't communicate. He *never* seems to understand me."
Th: "I know what you mean. Whenever I don't feel heard or understood by someone, I can't help but feel very isolated and alone."

Cl: "Many times I never really understand my anger."
Th: "Something I recently learned may be of help to you. I find that when I'm angry the only way I ever understand it is by blowing up. Then later, when I look at it, somehow I just *know* whether it was appropriate or justified or whatever. I know what I contributed to it and what's not mine."

Cl: "They just can't seem to understand that church and I are just incompatible. I can't explain it, but that's the way it is."
Th: "I know exactly what you mean. I always feel kind of out of place in church, like I walked into the ladies' restroom or something."

Self-disclosure may serve to reveal the therapist's feelings or reactions to the client per se, as well. For example:

Cl: "He says he doesn't trust me."
Th: "I wouldn't either. I think what you do is so far removed from your inner feelings that I just wouldn't trust you with what I think are the important parts of me."

Cl: "Yes, but . . ."
Th: "Now just shut up, God damn it, and *listen* to me for a change . . . , o.k."

Cl: (*S* acting and speaking like a "little girl.")

Th: "Boy that irritates the hell out of me when you act like a little girl. I can't help but feel others must react to you in the same way also."

9. Free association

Here one classifies those counselor statements that require the *S* to verbalize the first thing that comes to mind upon the presentation of a cue by the therapist.

Th: "I'm going to say a word and, when I do, I want you to tell me the first thing that comes to mind. Don't hold anything back. Just say what pops into your mind."

Th: "What does that make you think of when you say that word? What's the first thing that comes into your mind?"

10. Reinforcement

Here we are interested in counselor statements that convey approval or disapproval, warmth or rejection, etc. If the reinforcing aspects of a counselor's statements are incidental to the communication itself, then they should be classified under the appropriate heading above. However, if the therapist seems to be trying to encourage or discourage certain thoughts, feelings, or behaviors, then the response will be classified as "reinforcement." For example:

Cl: "I think about what you say; I don't accept it blindly on faith, it's not like . . ."

Th: "Beautiful."

Cl: " . . . not . . . "

Th: "That's great, I don't want you to."

Cl: "I do seem to understand things much better when I focus on what's going on inside of me rather than on what other people are doing to me."

Th: "Ah, that's great. Wow, do you know that some people never learn that all their lives. Beautiful!"

Cl: "I know that most of the time it's as much a problem in my communicating as it is in their listening. It's like . . . (long pause)."

Th: "Oh, Christ, don't stop now. Go ahead, go ahead."

Cl: "Well, it's like if I were really clear about what I wanted to say, then I could probably get by her barriers as well as mine."

Cl: "It *is* his fault. He started it."
Th: "No, no, no, shit no!"
Cl: "What do you mean, no?"
Th: "It's not even important whose fault it was. Until you stop blaming him and see your role in it, you're never going to get anywhere."

While the first therapist statement is classified as "reinforce ment" (disapproval), his second statement would be classified as "direct confrontation with behavior," since he is actively challenging and pointing out to the *S* what he believes is important. It is not classified as "information and advice giving," even though direct suggestion and structuring are involved, because of the active, emotive nature of the encounter. The following are also examples of "reinforcement" via disapproval.

Cl: "I really think I could do better at another university."
Th: "I think you're like a bar of Ivory soap. 99 and 44/100 percent gas and hot air."

Cl: "Sometimes I wonder why that always happens to me."
Th: "Uh (sigh)."
Cl: "Ha!"
Th: "Uh, just uh. That's a bado, a no-no, you know?"

The examples above should help clarify some of the difficulties inherent in classifying a statement as "reinforcement." The central criteria should rest on whether or not you think the therapist's intent is *solely* to encourage or discourage. If this is the case, then the response will be classified here.

11. Unclassifiable

Here one classifies activities not clearly relevant to the task of therapy, for example, greetings, small talk, endings, etc. Other than such occasions, this category will not be used, unless therapist statements absolutely cannot be otherwise classified.

Index